A HISTORY OF
RACE RELATIONS
RESEARCH

OTHER RECENT VOLUMES IN THE
SAGE FOCUS EDITIONS

A HISTORY OF RACE RELATIONS RESEARCH

First-Generation Recollections

John H. Stanfield II
editor

SAGE PUBLICATIONS
International Educational and Professional Publisher
Newbury Park   London   New Delhi

For information address:

 SAGE Publications, Inc.
2455 Teller Road
Newbury Park, California 91320

SAGE Publications Ltd.
6 Bonhill Street
London EC2A 4PU
United Kingdom

SAGE Publications India Pvt. Ltd.
M-32 Market
Greater Kailash I
New Delhi 110 048 India

Printed in the United States of America

Library of Congress Cataloging-in-Publication Data

A history of race relations research : First-generation recollections /
edited by John H. Stanfield II.
    p. cm.—(Sage focus editions : 159)
    Includes bibliographical references.
    ISBN 0-8039-5004-7.—ISBN 0-8039-5005-5 (pbk.)
    1. Race relations—Study and teaching (Higher)—United States.
2. Minorities—Study and teaching (Higher)—United States.
3. Sociology—United States—Historiography. 4. Sociologists—
United States—Historiography. I. Stanfield, John H.
HT1506.H52 1993
305.8'00973—dc20   93-17609
                                                                 CIP

93 94 95 96 97 10 9 8 7 6 5 4 3 2 1

Sage Production Editor: Judith L. Hunter

Contents

Contributors to This Volume

Bob Blauner is Professor of Sociology at the University of California, Berkeley.

Daniel R. Fusfeld is Professor Emeritus of Economics at the University of Michigan, Ann Arbor.

Milton M. Gordon is Professor Emeritus of Sociology at the University of Massachusetts, Amherst.

Lewis M. Killian is Professor Emeritus of Sociology at the University of Massachusetts, Amherst, and a faculty associate at the University of West Florida, Pensacola.

Harry H. L. Kitano is Professor of Social Welfare and Sociology at the University of California, Los Angeles.

Hylan Lewis is Professor, Ph.D. Program in Sociology, Graduate Center, City University of New York, and Professor Emeritus, Brooklyn College, CUNY.

Stanley Lieberson is the Abbott Lawrence Lowell Professor of Sociology at Harvard University.

Thomas F. Pettigrew is Professor of Social Psychology at the University of California, Santa Cruz.

Richard Robbins is Professor Emeritus of Sociology and American Studies, University of Massachusetts, Boston, and Visiting Professor of Sociology, Stonehill College, North Easton, Massachusetts.

Peter I. Rose is Sophia Smith Professor of Sociology and Anthropology and Director of the American Studies Diploma Program at Smith College, and a member of the Graduate Faculty of the University of Massachusetts, Amherst.

Pierre L. van den Berghe is Professor of Sociology and Anthropology at the University of Washington in Seattle.

Frank R. Westie retired in 1983 from his position as Professor of Sociology at Indiana University, and is now Adjunct Professor at Arizona State University, Tempe.

Introduction

JOHN H. STANFIELD II

A *sociological generation* is made up of people born into sequential birth cohorts who gain a sense of collective identity by going through the same dramatic historical events. The Depression sociological generation comprises birth cohorts of Americans born between 1911 and 1938; these individuals' collective identity was shaped by the Great Depression, World War II, the Korean War, McCarthyism, and the emergence of the civil rights movement and the Vietnam War as center-stage societal issues. Those in this sociological generation were educated during the 1930s at the earliest and in the mid-1950s at the latest. Their most significant intellectual contributions were usually made between the early 1950s and the mid-1970s.

During the late 1980s and the 1990s, we are witnessing the fading away of the sociological generation of social scientists who laid the foundations of their post-World War II disciplines principally in the 1950s and 1960s. Those fortunate enough still to be living have witnessed the critique and demise of many of their foundational ideas in a new conservative era dominated by emerging baby boomer intellectual leadership. Such is to be expected; generations come and go, along with the relevance of many, if not most, of their ideas.

My dissertation research was on the cohort of social scientists who laid the foundations of race relations studies in the social sciences in the period between World Wars I and II (see Stanfield, 1977). My application of Ryder's (1971) fascinating concepts of cohort and sociological generation to these scholars and to their generational predecessors could not help but make me wonder about their generational successors. This is why I decided to organize this project on Depression sociological generation sociologists and other social scientists who by the 1970s had laid important paradigmatic foundations for post-World War II race and ethnicity social science research. It turned out to be an opportune time to contact these prominent scholars; most were retired or semi-retired and thus were in reflective moods about their careers and about their probable places in history (as an amusing commentary on the retrospective navel-gazing comparisons in which sociologists tend to enjoy indulging, Frank Westie gave me permission to publish his gracious response to my invitation letter to him as an appendix to this volume). Since most of this sociological generation did their most influential scholarship from the 1950s through the mid-1970s, it has been possible for them not only to step back and analyze the impact of their work with some degree of objectivity, but to report on how their views have changed since the 1970s in the context of post-1970s societal conditions.

As much as scientists may claim to embrace objective, value-free logics of inquiry, the production of their knowledge and the creation and reproduction of their social organizational forms and links to the real society are very much social constructions of realities. Thus autobiographical analysis and other biographical techniques are fascinating methods through which we can get a glimpse of the origins and transformations of disciplines and their subfields.

To the extent to which historians and sociologists have embraced that contention, they have tended to focus on subjects in the physical and biological sciences (see, e.g., Holton, 1974; Rhodes, 1986). That is, particularly in the post-1970s era, comprehensive biographical analyses have been published on Darwin, Einstein, Newton, and other renowned physical and biological scientists in attempts to understand the broad institutional and historical contexts of their disciplines' origins and transformations. This is not the case when it comes to the social sciences. Rarely does one find historians of the social sciences and sociologists using biographical materials to weave the stories of disciplines and their relationships to the larger society and to the global community. Social scientists have not been as forthcoming as physical and biological scientists about how their lives shaped their disciplines and, as noted, historians of such fields have been reluctant to use such materials. Thus the usual histories of social science disciplines continue to be impersonal accounts of trends or, if they are biographical assessments, such examinations tend to reify subjects from societal contexts and political economic considerations (e.g., Matthews, 1977; Park, 1973). There are some major exceptions to this silence in the history and sociology of the social sciences, such as the fascinating biographical work done on Freud, Keynes, Marx, Durkheim, and Weber. It is noteworthy that these exceptions have concentrated on European rather than American scholars.

The reluctance on the part of social scientists and the chroniclers of their disciplines to bare the souls of the disciplines has much to do with the insecurity of the social sciences as sciences. Anthropologists and sociologists, in particular, because they work in disciplines with serious legitimation problems, experience grave difficulties in acknowledging the value basis of their vocations. They have tried their best to embrace methodologies and even professional jargon that creates the aura of "value freeness." Once in a while, in the form of well-publicized scandals or ethical controversies, such as southern congressmen's attacks on sociology in the aftermath of Myrdal's (1944) *An American Dilemma* project (which almost eliminated sociology from the planned National Science Foundation), Project Camelot, *Tearoom Trade,* and Margaret Mead's early work, social scientists are reminded of how fragile their crafted value-free images actually are.

Human beings do not always stay in their places the way atoms do, and sometimes they have advocates, watchdogs, and, adversaries, so it is no wonder the social sciences in an American culture of science dominated by logical positivistic epistemology have had profound difficulty in being taken seriously. In the post-World War II years, sociologists and anthropologists were bashed in the 1950s through the 1970s, and now in the more conservative 1980s and 1990s, economists and psychologists are finding their legitimacy as scientists being questioned as these "softer" sciences are experiencing a deepening credibility crisis.

The legitimacy of American social science knowledge becomes especially suspect when the focus is on sensitive social, moral, and political issues. Sociologists and other social scientists who dare to write on issues such as race and ethnicity, gender, deviance, dying and death, and capitalism often find their work questioned beyond the norms of skepticism set by their professional communities. It is not uncommon to find social scientists in this country who study sensitive social and political issues to find not only their work being critiqued but also their persons. This has resulted, in many cases, in social scientists' shying away from and actually stigmatizing subfields that could be ideologically explosive. Areas such as race and ethnic relations, gender stratification, dying and death, and deviance are not viewed as prime areas for establishing a career in sociology.

Further, social researchers who do study controversial social issues have been reluctant to come forward with autobiographical statements lest they be accused of promoting their own ideologies. Some feminists have been somewhat open in this area, explaining how their experiences as women have shaped their work, but as yet there have been no needed discussions by white feminists of how their class and ethnic origins have influenced their scholarship (nor have any such influences been addressed in the growing feminist critique by women of color in the social sciences).

In the subfield of race and ethnic studies, social scientists have been hesitant to reflect on how their personal lives have contributed to the creation, institutionalization, and transformation of disciplinary paradigms, institutions, and invisible colleges. Although there has been much discussion about the ways in which the pre-1940s Chicago school attempted to develop university faculty and a network of students doing value-free qualitative and quantitative scholarship on race and ethnic issues, the chief personalities involved left at most sketchy autobiographical evidence about their lives and contributions (e.g., Park, 1973). Additionally, even in their personal papers, Robert E. Park, Ernest Burgess, Louis Wirth, E. Franklin Frazier, Charles S. Johnson, and Ellsworth Faris did not leave much comprehensive autobiographical evidence about the professionalization of race and ethnic sociology that their invisible college engineered. If we put aside the conventional celebratory assessments of those Chicago years, we are still very much in the dark regarding the development of racial and ethnic sociology at Chicago as the northern school of a new professionalized subfield. The same can be said about the movement to professionalize race relations sociology in the South in the 1920s and 1930s by Howard W. Odum and his Chapel Hill school (e.g., Guy B. Johnson, Arthur R. Raper, Thomas Woofter, Jr.). They produced great archives and celebration pieces, but no comprehensive autobiographical evidence of what really went on from the standpoint of personal experiences.

The point of this lengthy discussion is to explain why I decided to organize this project. I wanted to find out why, given the conditions of the 1950s and 1960s, some social scientists, mostly sociologists, decided to make careers as racial and ethnic studies specialists. The fact that the most of these prominent scholars were white men of southern and/or Jewish heritage made me even more fascinated by the Depression sociological generation.

When one thinks about the societal and political conditions of the period in which these (mostly) men were in graduate school and building professional careers, their personal accounts of how they went about doing their work become even more fascinating. It was after the war, when McCarthyism and the Cold War were beginning to crystallize, that these scholars embarked on a career line that was politically suspect— the study of race and ethnic relations. Although the policy implications of the U.S. Supreme Court's *Brown* decision and the civil rights movement would establish the professional credentials of many of these race and ethnicity experts, it would also put them in a position contradictory to a growing militant Black presence, in society in general and especially on college campuses. By the early 1970s, it was tough being a white (male or female) race relations specialist. Many who started out in the 1940s and 1950s if not a bit later would retire in the 1970s and 1980s, embittered over being rejected by the very people of color for whom they had long served as advocates.

I remember attending a session at a national sociology meeting in the early 1970s where one prominent member of this generation tearfully complained about his rejection and the establishment of Black studies as, in his words, "a second-class academic field." Such wailing and gnashing of teeth among members of this generation were quite common in those years. So was the conversion to conservatism and neoliberalism on the part of white experts who found the transition from advocating the theory of equality and assimilation they embraced to the practice of accepting Black colleagues and superiors too difficult to swallow.

Needless to say, most of the wailers and gnashers of teeth, and those who have moved to the right, declined to participate in this project. Confronting old wounds and remembering rejection are two emotions most people would rather avoid. Usually, when an invitee was honest enough to send me a "dear John" letter explaining in vague terms the hurt feelings, I would try to persuade a bit more and then back off, trying to understand how it must feel to build a career and then be shoved aside. On the other hand, to be blunt, I am not naive enough to think that all the kicks in the teeth or the rear end that many of these "old boys" eventually received from scholars, students, and community activists of color were altogether undeserved. Some did take liberties, abusing and exploiting their nonwhite graduate students and colleagues for professional gain (see the essays in Ladner, 1973). It is no wonder that the greatest abusers and exploiters refused to give personal accounts of their careers; many would face the possibility of being confronted by former research assistants and junior colleagues who are now well placed enough to counter their claims publicly and to tell what really happened. All we can do is anxiously await the day when their archives are opened to public investigation and their abused and exploited students and colleagues feel comfortable telling their stories in print. With that said, I will not do what I planned to do in the beginning of this project, and that is to publish the list of those who rejected or ignored the invitation to participate. That may do injury to the innocent and not too innocent. It would be far from my goal to encourage readers to guess why so-and-so said no or did not even bother to respond.

So, unfortunately, the reader will have to take my word when I say, scout's honor, every major sociologist and most major social scientists in general who were in graduate school in the 1940s and 1950s and who did major race and ethnicity work in the 1940s through the very early 1970s were contacted at least twice. By *major work,* I mean work that had an especially significant impact on the development of thought in post-World War II race and ethnic studies, work that was disseminated through influential articles in flagship professional journals and through influential books. I was also concerned with the generation who set the pace for the race and ethnic studies generation that emerged in the 1970s, made up of such persons as Edna Bonacich, James Blackwell, Charles V. Willie, William J. Wilson, Robert Staples, Joyce Ladner, and James Pitts (and, as the old saying goes in Black church circles, I'd better stop there before I miss somebody and really get in trouble).

One notices in the partial list of the 1970s generation a predominance of Black male sociologists. This was the direct result of the penetration of the civil rights movement into American professional social science associations and doctoral programs in the 1970s, which created opportunity structures for Afro-Americans, especially males, to become credentialed and to gain access to publishers and funding agencies. It was also the time when several elite sociology and other social science and humanities departments began to look for a Black to anoint. As the prominent white sponsor of the only Black in his prestigious department boasted to me as I sat in his living room sipping something or other several years ago, "So-and-so is the greatest Black [fill in the blank—one of the humanities or social sciences] in the world and I discovered him"—a great empirical example of Allport's pet theory, if I may say so myself. Lest the reader should embark on the hazardous course of trying to guess with whom I was sipping whatever it was, and who the lucky anointed Black was and still is, keep in mind that the search for Black pets became an extensive elite pastime in academia during the 1970s as a form of Veblenian conspicuous consumption. The practice continued into the 1980s and is still with us in the 1990s.

The question is, What happened to Afro-American sociologists and other social scientists between the 1940s and 1970s? Why was the post-World War II race and ethnic studies subfield a white male intellectual enclave? During the 1940s and 1950s the most senior productive Afro-American social scientists who made their names earlier were beginning to rotate out of research roles, at least in the United States. In the late 1940s, Charles S. Johnson became the president of Fisk University; in the 1950s, E. Franklin Frazier became involved in UNESCO and Ralph Bunche also became active in the United Nations. Some social scientists, such as Kenneth Clark and economist Robert Weaver, became involved in the nonprofit sector or started independent research firms. Horace Cayton and Zora Neale Hurston eventually died in obscurity, never completing their doctoral degrees. By the time the 1960s rolled around, the only three Afro-American social scientists with senior professorships in major white universities were Hylan Lewis at the City University of New York Graduate School, Allison Davis in the Department of Education in the University of Chicago, and St. Clair Drake at Roosevelt University and eventually Stanford University.

This pattern certainly indicates that Afro-Americans and other social scientists of color experienced grave difficulties in making careers in academia. Many gave up, going into nonacademic careers or merely sticking to teaching in underfunded Black colleges, realizing there were no other opportunities. Others, such as Holland of Hampton Institute, went into Black college administration.

Because the Black academic institutions to which Du Bois, Frazier, and Johnson were confined during the pre-World War II years and afterward had no doctoral programs, and no power to place their students in dominant institutions of higher learning even if they did, there was no way for them to develop well-institutionalized, expansive schools of thought. They had no way of getting credit for credentialed students who could contribute to if not actually shape academic approaches to race and ethnic relations in the 1950s and 1960s.

Meanwhile, predominantly white, elite social science departments were not making any concerted effort to turn out a significant number of Afro-American Ph.D. holders during the 1940s and 1950s. Those who did make it through tended to go into administrative positions in government and in the Black college circuit. A precious few became teachers in junior colleges. Washington State University was the exception to this rule. During the 1950s, through the mentorship of Mississippi-born and -reared sociologist and academic administrator Donald Kennedy, Washington State became the most significant producer of Black doctorates in sociology. In fact, most of the visible members of the Black 1970s cohort received their degrees from Washington State in the 1950s and early 1960s (William J. Wilson is the most distinguished member of the Washington State cohort).

The absence of a critical mass of productive Afro-American social scientists in Black and white institutions during the 1950s and 1960s created a vacuum that would be filled quickly by white social scientists who were well positioned to make careers out of the opportunities generated from the Myrdal project and the policy implementation demands of the *Brown* decision and civil rights legislation. When the federal and foundation dollars began to flow to organize the first big 1960s projects to formulate race public policy, most of the funding went to white scholars in prominent white institutions. Some of these projects that made names for their white principal investigators were also data sources for dissertations produced by Afro-American and other students of color who are now senior 1970s scholars. Lee Rainwater's (1970) St. Louis housing project study and Joyce Ladner's dissertation work from its data base are cases in point. An interesting instance of role reversal, incidentally, is the NIMH grant program Hylan Lewis ran, which would be the funding source for Elliot Liebow's *Tally's Corner* (1967).

Characteristics of the Contributors

I do not pretend that the contributors to this volume are representative of the first post-World War II sociological generation of race and ethnic studies social scientists. These authors represent far from a random sample, and certainly this group is too overloaded with sociologists to say very much about social scientists in general. Rather than trying to make anything universal out of this collection of distinguished scholars, I will simply point out some of their most striking characteristics, particularly those they have in common. Thus my goals in this section and in this whole anthology are actually quite modest.

Only one contributor (Kitano) was born and reared in the far western United States, and only one was born and reared in a foreign country (van den Berghe). All the others were born and reared in the Midwest (Blauner, Westie), the Northeast/New England (Gordon, Lieberson, Robbins, Rose), and the South/border areas (Killian, Lewis, Pettigrew).

The accounts the contributors give as to why they became involved in race and ethnicity research focus on their personal experiences, during childhood, adolescence, or early adulthood. For most of those of Jewish heritage, studying race relations, especially the experiences of Afro-Americans, became a channel through which they tried to understand their own minority status. For others, work experiences with Afro-Americans in early adulthood stimulated their interest in race relations. Radical political party participation was a source of interaction with Afro-Americans for some (Blauner, Robbins), and this sparked interest. None of the contributors became interested in race relations out of vacuous academic consideration. Even those who went on to embrace theories and methods far removed from firsthand experience have personal stories to tell about how their own experiences lured them into the race and ethnicity subfield.

The van den Berghe essay is important because it highlights a pattern that, frankly, I did not expect to find, but when it became evident I quickly recognized its relevance. In his chapter, van den Berghe discusses how growing up in Zaire and spending research time in South Africa had profound influences on what he saw and sees in American race relations. Several of the other contributors discuss how going abroad during their early adult years before or after graduate school had a lasting influence on how they approached race and ethnic relations in the United States. Anyone even mildly interested in American race relations cannot help but return from a lengthy trip abroad in another race-centered society and be astounded by what he or she sees. It is no wonder that the comparison between racism in America and racism abroad became a personal experience that many of the contributors have never quite gotten over. The comparative sense of racism they developed as a life-history component became, I would imagine, a rich source of creative and in some cases bold theorizing and activism in American racial affairs. It is not surprising that as American academics and policymakers turned their attention away from race relations issues in the 1970s, several of the contributors resumed their international travels and stays abroad, and have since become more comparative in their work in the post-1980s years.[1]

In regard to race relations research, the 1950s and 1960s were a heady time for those in the position to become authorities in the subfield. It was a period in which there was a flood of federal and private foundation dollars for doing policy-related research and consulting on school desegregation, ghetto problems, and community conflict resolution. The demand for fast answers to pressing social problems left little time for lofty theorizing. It is little wonder that no comprehensive theoretical work on American racial issues came out of this period. The closest thing was the Kerner Commission report, which was more of a political document than a scholarly work.

To the extent to which lasting theoretical work came out of the 1950s and 1960s, it was social psychological in orientation, influenced by classics such as Adorno, Frenkel-Brunswick, Levinson, and Sanford's *The Authoritarian Personality* (1950) and Gordon Allport's *The Nature of Prejudice* (1954). More macro approaches in race and ethnic studies would not begin to appear in the literature until the mid-1970s and 1980s, though micro approaches are still preferred.

The contributors and other members of their generation also embraced or critiqued three other theoretical traditions. The first was Gunnar Myrdal's American creed thesis articulated in *An American Dilemma* (1944). Members of this generation were—at least in print—true believers in the concept that racism is a moral wrong in an otherwise democratic society. It is no coincidence, then, that more than a few members of this cohort became disturbed by the emergence of the Black power movement and other movements that called into question moral definitions of racism and that offered critiques of the very fabric of American society. They would become equally upset in the 1980s, a time when the right wing would take center stage in the national political culture, condoning explicit racist norms and attitudes in the process.

A second theoretical perspective this cohort invented, defended, critiqued, and transformed was that of the culture of poverty. Books and government reports by Oscar Lewis, Michael Harrington, Patrick Moynihan, Joyce Ladner, Kenneth Clark, Edward Banfield, and Elliot Liebow from the 1950s through the early 1970s symbolized an era in which American middle and upper classes were becoming more cognizant of poor people. As a target for federal intervention in the 1960s, the Black ghetto became the ecological archetype of American poverty problems. The label *culture of poverty* was attached to the ghetto and its residents as a way of explaining the alleged pathologies and social deficiencies that were preventing Blacks from blending into "the mainstream." The culture of poverty concept was employed also to explain why Blacks were not keeping pace with whites in education and economic attainment. It also became the liberal rationale for Blacks' lagging behind whites in standardized test performance.

The culture of poverty explanation, in other words, was the liberal response to biological and genetic rationales regarding Black achievement and mobility problems. Because it dealt with attitudes and beliefs rather than with structure, the culture of poverty became a well-accepted conceptual framework of the sociological generation in question. Although some would serve as critics of this concept, as seen in the Rainwater and Yancey (1967) anthology responding to the Moynihan Report, the culture of poverty would remain as a central paradigmatic notion in spirit if not in letter, even when it became unfashionable in the 1970s to use the term (consider the culture of poverty premises of the Coleman Report as a case in point). Ironically, in the post-1980s world, the culture of poverty concept has been conservatized by the New Right and given new ideological rubric, such as "the absence of family values."

Park's race cycle model was the third and final conceptual framework this generation grappled with in significant ways. This generation was interested not only in the problem of racism as a moral contradiction in American society but also (as seen in their invention of the culture of poverty idea) in the cultural assimilation and social integration of people of color into mainstream America. This resulted in concerted efforts to develop modified cycle models designed to fit the experiences of people of color in a desegregating society. The best example of this effort is Milton Gordon's classic work on cultural and social assimilation in the early 1960s and his editorship of an influential Prentice-Hall race and ethnic studies series, in which the volume authors attempted to apply his model to specific culturally distinct and racially oppressed populations. Another example is the social pluralism concept van den Berghe developed in his classic work *Race and Racism* (1967), according to which socially defined racial populations share the same culture but segregate in parallel communities and institutions. Using Blacks as the archetype of racial minorities, van den Berghe claimed that the United States was a socially pluralistic society, which fits quite well into the assumptions his generation made about the Americanism of Blacks and their subsequent lack of indigenous culture (very much a Parkian assumption).

Substantive focus is very much a generational phenomenon in scientific disciplines and other intellectual enterprises. This generation focused largely on Black experiences, given the nature of the times. Kitano represents the very few researchers who did research on other people of color. The focus on Blacks developed a number of questions about ethnicity and race relations that would be applied to other populations by younger scholars in the post-1970s years with uneven success. As many issues related to Black experiences do not fit those of other people of color, increasingly social scientists interested in people of color other than Blacks have had to start from scratch in developing research questions adequate for their lines of inquiry. For instance, although the Depression sociological generation could easily dismiss the validity of African-descent culture in Afro-American life because of long-standing professional traditions and ideologies, the presence and persistence of ethnic cultures among newly arrived nonwhite immigrants and refugees and aboriginal populations cannot be so easily denied. Their political and economic power is just too great in this day and time, in contrast to 30 years ago and earlier. Post-1970s social scientists of race and ethnicity who wish to develop powerful theoretical explanations must take ethnic cultural variables into account.

The Depression sociological generation was the last significant generation of race and ethnicity social scientists in the twentieth century. This is because in the 1970s and 1980s ethnic and especially race relations research declined in popularity as the United States and the global community shifted gears and moved into a new era. The big bucks were no longer flowing from federal agencies and from foundations for large-scale race relations studies. The Reagan administration dismantled most of the funding apparatus through which federal funding of race relations work was administered. The growing conservatism of the federal judicial and executive branches and of state and local governments destroyed the lucrative race relations industry that Lewis Killian describes. With the loss of opportunities to build careers, influential researchers who had become great grantsmen and -women stopped doing race relations research and did not train anyone to pick up the ball from the 1960s.

The emergence of a new generation of academics, along with Depression generation cohorts resentful of affirmative action and hostile to having Black colleagues "put on them," made the study of race relations unpopular as well. The controversial emergence of ethnic studies programs in the 1970s and the multicultural curriculum movement of the 1980s added fuel to the negative fire. The crystallizing configuration of professional social science association meetings shows clearly how disinterested white baby boomers in emerging leadership roles are in race and ethnic research. Although the new white leaders in the social sciences allow people of color to go off in a corner someplace to discuss racial and ethnic issues, they for the most part keep their mainstream sessions "pure," avoiding such "tainted" issues.

The rise, and entrenchment, of the right wing within and outside the hallowed halls of academia has created a cultural taste for race relations work touted more for its conservative ideological stands than for any theoretical and methodological adequacy. This, incidentally, has created and institutionalized a new form of insidious academic racism in which Afro-Americans and other people of color working on race questions are rewarded professionally more for their conservative or at least accommodative neoliberal stands than for the quality of their productivity. (Of course, one can argue that is the case for American academics in general, especially those in the social and behavioral sciences. American academia is, after all, a very conservative business.)

The "bad taste in the mouth" reputation of race relations has also persuaded many social scientists of color not to go into the ethnicity and race subfield lest they be labeled and ghettoized. Many go to great lengths to cleanse the word *race* from their specialty descriptions.

Bob Blauner's sobering account in this volume serves as an example of what happened to many liberal and radical race relations scholars of the 1950s and 1960s who found their work ignored or misinterpreted in the 1970s. They experienced difficulty in gaining the respect of their more mainstream colleagues and of students and colleagues of color, who began to arrive on their campuses in unprecedented numbers. Some began to avoid offering race relations classes all together. The bitter experience of being rejected and marginalized and of feeling ineffectual is the reason at least two persons gave in refusing the invitation to contribute to this volume.

Meanwhile, most of the serious race and ethnicity theorizing that has been and is being done in the post-1970s years has come from Europe and from the Third World. American social scientists have done very little new critical work in the past 20 years, and what they have done has been ignored or discredited when it has offered sobering accounts of the primacy of American racism. This is why, although this has always been the case, and is so in this era more than ever before, the most accurate accounts of contemporary racial inequality in the United States are being published by journalists rather than social scientists.

The nebulous state of race and ethnicity social science as a field of study in the United States is symbolized by the controversial National

Academy of Science report on the status of Black Americans in the early and mid-1980s, which was published as *Common Destiny* (Jaynes & Williams, 1989). This foundation sector project, which had a price tag of almost $2 million, was predicted to be a post-1970s version of Myrdal's *An American Dilemma* project in structure and public influence. Instead, it became the focus of a storm that would seriously damage the influence of *Common Destiny* before it rolled off the presses. The fact that the prominent scholars of the Depression sociological generation and the National Academy of Science staff could not foresee how their plans and actions would be perceived and criticized draws attention to the Achilles' heel of the traditional liberalism of that generation: the arrogant assumption that Afro-Americans can be told what to do and will fall in line, passively following the lead of white authority, with at most marginal input in decision-making processes.

This is certainly what happened in the Myrdal project. Given the tenor of the Jim Crow race relations of the times, it was viewed as a fact of life even by the otherwise radical E. Franklin Frazier and the diplomatic Charles S. Johnson that it was appropriate for them to participate in a project designed and led by whites. Without fear of damaging public outcry, Myrdal could subcontract both white and Afro-American social scientists to write manuscripts that would actually become chapter drafts for which he would get credit. He could also exclude critical-minded scholars such as Horace Cayton, William E. B. Du Bois, and Carter G. Woodson, who would not tolerate their work's being siphoned off by Myrdal and who had more radical perspectives than the moralistic points of view of the included scholars. After the Myrdal project was over, a few of the white social scientists who were involved, such as Arnold Rose, did receive significant career rewards. But the Afro-Americans returned to their underfunded segregated institutions, and it has yet to be recognized how deeply indebted Myrdal was to them for their "research notes."

Forgetting that the 1980s were not the 1940s, foundation executives and National Academy of Science staff assumed they could operate much as the Carnegie Corporation and Myrdal did in developing a definitive research report on Afro-Americans with only marginal Afro-American participation in decision making. The plan was to appoint a governing committee chaired by a prominent member of the Depression sociological generation with impeccable progressive credentials. The committee would be composed of prominent white and Afro-American liberal and neoliberal scholars and influential public figures. Initially, at least until a prominent Afro-American social scientist made a strong informal objection to foundation officers, there were plans on the part of the person in charge of the project at the National Academy of Science to appoint a white executive director. When this person was pressured into selecting an Afro-American, the scholar selected was not an Afro-American with distinguished credentials in social research on contemporary Afro-American experiences, but a rather obscure scholar who was apparently chosen more because of his ideological views than for his scholarly credentials. At least that was the criticism advanced by both Afro-American and white scholars once the name of the director was announced at an annual National Research Council meeting of postdoctoral fellows of color.[2] Furthermore, it became more than apparent to critics that scholars selected for subcontract work were of the liberal and neoliberal bent. Prominent race relations specialists with more radical and critical orientations were absent.

The published report, which was predicted to create a great political splash and to make its principal investigators famous, fell on its face, so to speak. A few scholars were able to make names, or bigger names, for themselves, but the published report had nothing earth-shattering to say. It was grounded in assumptions that had been around for a long time and that to some seemed passé. The liberal/neoliberal premises of *Common Destiny* produced a work that symbolized the decline of a sociological generation rather than offering a refreshing theoretical perspective on a new era in American history (Stanfield, 1993). As in the case of the "declining significance of race" ideology, the 1992 Los Angeles riots demonstrated the serious limitations of *Common Destiny* as what should have been a significant piece of research. The study was also a sad commentary on the unsuccessful effort to pass the mantle to a younger generation of like-minded social scientists who, as is the case with their sponsoring elders, either are out of touch with contemporaneous empirical realities or lack the paradigmatic tools to understand them. The 1980s mortally wounded the liberal approach to race relations, not only because of the well-organized right wing in political culture and in academia but also because it is a paradigmatic perspective that does not explain well at all the nature of the post-1970s United States as a race-centered society.

It is no wonder, with all this said, that when Los Angeles blew up in the spring of 1992 there were few well-placed older or younger sociologists or other social scientists of race relations around with adequate ideas to explain why the tragedy occurred. All most self-appointed experts and conservative and accommodating academics could do, and all they are doing, is to dust off books published in the 1960s and otherwise sputter. The absence of intellectual giants among academic baby boomers to offer adequate and sobering explanations is not only disturbing but quite embarrassing. The most we can do is babble in postmodern lingo, lost in the vines of ivy.

I realize how difficult it is to bare one's soul to the public, and I want to give all the contributors to this volume a big thank you for their courage in doing so. Working with them on this project has been a wonderful experience. I also want to thank those who wanted to contribute but whose schedules or ill health (such as Elliot Liebow) prevented them. A special tribute is in order for the late Herbert Blalock, who passed away before having the opportunity to respond to the invitation.

As might be expected in any highly personal project, there is some unevenness in the essays that follow. Once again, however, I want to express my deepest thanks to the contributors for their willingness to go public when it is much easier and vastly more comfortable not to say anything at all about one's personal views in print. Special thanks to my editors, Mitch Allen and Judy Hunter, and to my research assistant, Crystal Lyles.

Notes

1. I can relate to the influence of international travel on professional careers and personal lives quite well after spending 18 months abroad recently, 10 months in Sierra Leone and 8 months in Great Britain. I spent a total of five weeks during that time traveling through West Africa, the Canary Islands, and Continental Europe. It was my first extended trip abroad, and when I returned to the United States, I was and still am amazed about what I now see, understand, and wonder about regarding American racial issues. That unforgettable experience is reshaping my scholarly interests and perspectives in ways I had no way of anticipating before leaving the country. Going abroad and coming back cannot help but change your mind about the United States in profound ways. I now understand, I think, what provoked E. Franklin Frazier to write during his residence in France and why Malcolm X changed his philosophy of life after returning from Mecca.

2. My comments on this National Academy of Science project do not come only from my reading of published commentaries. The project was formulated and critiqued in a Yale network during my last years in New Haven. I had the good and sometimes disturbing fortune to meet and discuss the project with some of the project's staunch informal critics and supporters many months before the dog mess hit the fan.

References

Adorno, T. W., Frenkel-Brunswick, E., Levinson, D. J., & Sanford, R. N. (1950). *The authoritarian personality.* New York: Harper Brothers.

Allport, G. W. (1954). *The nature of prejudice.* Reading, MA: Addison-Wesley.

Holton, G. (1974). *Thematic origins of scientific thought: Kepler to Einstein.* Cambridge, MA: Harvard University Press.

Jaynes, G., & Williams, R. (1989). *Common destiny: Black and American society.* Washington, DC: National Academy Press.

Ladner, J. (Ed.). (1973). *The death of white sociology.* New York: Random House.

Liebow, E. (1967). *Tally's corner: A study of Negro street corner men.* Boston: Little, Brown.

Matthews, F. (1977). *Quest for an American sociology: Robert E. Park and the Chicago school.* Montreal: McGill-Queen's University Press.

Myrdal, G., with Sterner, R., & Rose, A. (1944). *An American dilemma: The Negro problem and modern democracy.* New York: Harper & Row.

Park, R. E. (1973). Life history. *American Journal of Sociology, 79,* 251-260.

Rainwater, L. (1970). *Behind ghetto walls: Black families in a ghetto slum.* Chicago: Aldine.

Rainwater, L., & Yancey, C. (Eds.). (1967). *The Moynihan report and the politics of controversy.* New Brunswick, NJ: Transaction.

Rhodes, R. (1986). *The making of the atomic bomb.* New York: Simon & Schuster.

Ryder, N. B. (1971). *Reproduction in the United States, 1965.* Princeton, NJ: Princeton University Press.

Stanfield, J. H., II. (1977). *Race rationalization as a cohort experience, 1928-1948.* Unpublished doctoral dissertation, Northwestern University.

Stanfield, J. H., II. (1993). The nebulous state of American race relations theories: Paradigmatic erosion and decline. In *Annual on Race and Ethnic Relations, 7.*

van den Berghe, P. L. (1967) *Race and racism: A comparative perspective.* New York: John Wiley.

"But Things Are Much Worse for the Negro People"

Race and Radicalism in My Life and Work

BOB BLAUNER

> Somewhere among my feelings must have been the hope that if Black people could become free, of the immense political and social burdens they were forced to bear, I too could become free, of all the ghosts and shadows of my childhood, named and unnamed.
>
> Adrienne Rich, "Split at the Root," 1985

"But things are much worse for the Negro people," I would always chime in when my high school friends and I were hanging around talking about how hard it was to be Jewish. Today I can't even recall those talks that remain so vivid in my old friends' memories or, more important, how I even would have known anything back then about Blacks and the state of race relations. I grew up without any real contact with people of color. Rogers Park on Chicago's far North Side then was

AUTHOR'S NOTE: For their reactions to an earlier version of this essay, I would like to thank my friends Bob Ehrlich, David Matza, and Barbara Christian, and for their encouragement and ideas that helped shape this final product, I thank my editor, John Stanfield, and my wife, Karina Epperlein.

pretty evenly divided among Jews, Irish Catholics, and white Protestants. True, there was Selma Hahn, one very assimilated Korean American in my class, and one of our "maids," before the hard times of the 1930s made them all unaffordable, was African American, but she wasn't the one who profoundly influenced me. That was Molly, an Irish immigrant.

So for years I've wrestled intellectually with the whys of my lifelong interest in racial justice and affinity for Black people and their culture. Certainly it must go back to the times I grew up in, my peculiar family, the fact that they were Jewish—or, better, the way we suppressed that reality. This produced a vacuum in my inner self that demanded filling, the need for a tribe, some sense of identity, a set of loyalties outside the immediate family. My Jewishness could not serve here because my parents were not like the parents of those high school friends who held fast to their ethnicity and their religion. My mother and father almost totally played down their Jewishness, bringing up my sister and me as 100% Americans, celebrating Christmas rather than Channukah—or indeed any Jewish holiday. Within my earshot anyway, Esther Blauner never spoke the Yiddish she grew up with, even though she did maintain some ties to parts of her family that remained traditional. And neither did my father, despite the fact that he spent the first eight years of his life in Polish Galicia. America must have totally transformed his character and certainly his dreams. His heroes were the great poets of the English language—and baseball players.

My father was a shadowy figure within the family, quiet, withdrawn, brooding. He was very subservient to my mother, who did not always hide her contempt for him, particularly after he lost status in her eyes during the Depression. So without brothers or other strong male figures in the family, I would have had some problems with my maleness even if I had not been the shortest kid in my class, a physical coward, and a "brain" to boot. I compensated for all this by becoming competent in sports and obsessed with major league baseball. By the age of 7 I found in the Chicago Cubs that tribe I was looking for. Sports provided my heroes also: I can remember identifying with Joe Louis as early as the 1937 Tommy Farr fight. Two years earlier, when I was 6, I began listening to his fights on the radio and knew that he had come back from an earlier defeat to knock out Max Schmeling, the champion of Hitler's Reich. To this day the name Bernie Jefferson thrills me as I recall the radio announcer's excitement describing the "18-year-old colored boy" returning a kickoff 98 yards for Northwestern (Jefferson was an obscure running back in the late 1930s). I don't think I even noticed that all baseball players were white then. But on some unconscious level Bernie Jefferson and Joe Louis filled more of those vacuums in my selfhood, representing models of masculine strength as well as a persecuted race, not unlike my own.

We didn't talk about anti-Semitism in my family, but it was all around us. Hitler was sweeping across Europe, and as I charted the growth of the Nazi empire with pins on the map, anti-Jewish sentiment was growing in America. So there was fear as well as shame, and perhaps a certain pragmatism behind my parents' denial. Irish Catholics we saw— perhaps unjustly—as most likely to be Jew haters. We were a little afraid of these proletarians in our otherwise lower-middle-class midst: They were the janitors, the tavern keepers, the factory workers. Irish kids were strong and tough, or so I thought, walking a little faster past St. Ignatius school yard on my way to take the El downtown. But unlike most of my Jewish friends, I played ball, traded baseball cards, and listened to Cubs games with many of these Irish kids.

My parents were liberal Democrats who worshiped FDR. They encouraged me to view all people as equals, but I don't remember any specific teachings about minority groups. But coming of age during World War II and its aftermath, we all felt engaged in a battle against the forces of evil. For many years the glow of idealism and social consciousness remained. And when it waned in the late 1940s, this was another vacuum in my inner core waiting to be filled. This was a need for meaning, intensified by the spiritual emptiness of American capitalism, and for me even more so by my family's rejection of religion and ethnicity. But I think here I was also carrying something common in the Jewish immigration experience, an experience that has been romanticized by social commentators and even sociologists who stress our remarkable economic success and supposedly strong families. But there was also pain and loss and a spiritual desolation involved in the process of Americanization. One way to mask this was to adopt the causes of other victims: in the thirties, workers; in the fifties and sixties, African Americans. So race and the Black experience gave me a cause that could channel my strong sense of social justice and give direction to my life, providing models of manhood outside the realm of my flawed family and even a group to identify with as I distanced myself from my own ethnic background.

The year I moved from high school to college was the same year Jackie Robinson broke the color barrier in white baseball. Each day I would check the sports pages to see how many hits he had made, how many bases he had stolen. That year, and the following, when he was called up to the Dodgers from Montreal, my loyalties were unwittingly changing: from the Chicago Cubs to Robinson—and in time to the rest of the new Black players. Thus Jackie to me was more than just another sports hero. He helped usher in my shift of tribal identification from baseball to Black America.

As the Illinois Central carried me past the South Side tenements on my way to the University of Chicago, I saw large numbers of African Americans for the first time. I studied the faces and bearing of the Black people boarding the train, noticed the variety of colors and human types, and wondered about their lives. I looked for answers in books, especially Myrdal's *An American Dilemma* (1944), which we read in my freshman social science course. I was now so interested in reading about race relations and "the Negro people" that I devoured every page, including all the appendices, footnotes, and tables, of that 1,483 page tome. Myrdal's great work, soon to be unfairly attacked by Herbert Aptheker and other critics as "idealist," was only two years old then. It provided a first historical and sociological framework for my developing interest in Black-white relations. It distresses me that Myrdal's work, like too many other sociological classics, is so little read today.

In letters to my high school friends who had moved from Chicago I urged them to read Richard Wright's *Black Boy* and told them of the other Black writers and poets I was discovering. I got to know Black students, discussed race relations with them and with whites, joined the NAACP. The NAACP organized a mobilization in the nation's capital to pass an antilynching law, and I went. Passing through Virginia and Maryland I saw southern-style segregation and noted the contrast between official Washington and its impoverished ghettos. For a 20-year-old liberal who was already beginning to feel a need to be liked and accepted by Black people, it was heady stuff to stay in a Black neighborhood and share a room with an African American activist. I congratulated myself on my presumed lack of racial prejudice.

I don't want to give the impression that race and Black people were becoming an obsession with me. I went out only with white women, one of whom I married, and I was discovering music, art, radical politics, and even the beginnings of a positive ethnic identity, as I learned that Marx, Freud, Einstein, and many other intellectual giants were Jewish. Still I had this passion to know more about Negroes. Race relations was one of the main reasons I chose sociology for further study after completing the two-year B.A. of the Hutchins era. So I selected an all-Black census tract to immerse myself in, anthropologistlike, in Everett Hughes's field methods course. It was still a time when an innocent white boy could walk around in no apparent danger, making "friends," attending church services, and being invited into people's homes to ask them their opinions about Paul Robeson, who was at the time under attack for his radical politics.

Becoming a Communist and a Worker

Robeson had become an idol for me. With my left-leaning friends, I went to his concerts and listened to his records. The depth of feelings expressed in his singing awakened my own suppressed emotionality, and the range of his songs representing the people of every continent appealed to my yearning for international harmony. But it was his speeches that most stirred me. They were probably the prime influence working on my political consciousness, assuaging my hesitation in fully embracing a radical position. Before each of his concerts, Robeson would speak at great length about the struggle of the American Negro against racism, and he would connect these struggles with those of Asians and Africans against colonialism and of workers throughout the world against exploitation. With the recent Robeson renaissance, recordings of many of his concerts are now available, but not the speeches. I need to listen to them again to verify if he really was the powerful orator I remember, impressive in his own way as Martin Luther King and Malcolm X.

Of course, much of Robeson's magic must have come from a young man's psychological hunger for a larger-than-life hero. More than most young men, I needed a model of manhood, particularly someone who was fighting back against the world's injustices, unlike my father, who submitted to his fate passively and would not even stand up to my mother. But as I look back now I see that I was not simply substituting a strong father figure for a weak one. On a deeper level I was merging the two men, so as to give strength and weight to my dad as well as to me. In my unconscious mind my father had come to represent the symbol of "the Negro," a victim who was oppressed and beaten down. But unlike him, the succession of Black heroes I would adopt—from Joe Louis in my childhood to Robinson and Malcolm X—all were fighters.

Though far from a typical man, Samuel Blauner was an exaggerated example of the prototypical American father in his emotional (and physical) absence from my life, particularly during my adolescence. In his last years he felt much remorse about this, blaming himself for my youthful radicalism, believing that if he had been a strong father I would not have needed to join an authoritarian social movement. He was even convinced that I would not get tenure at Berkeley because of my Communist past.

But despite my own penchant for psychoanalytic theorizing, the reasons for my radicalization were much simpler and more sociological, what deviance theorists call *differential association.* My three best friends from high school were all becoming Communists, and after they joined me at the university, I followed in their footsteps—not without much ambivalence, however. Part of it was political: During my UC days I went back and forth in my assessment of Stalin's Russia. And the other part was fear. Helping to protect a Party bookstore, I never knew when more rocks would be thrown, and as I passed out left-wing leaflets at factory gates, my body tensed at the workers' hostility. It took a year in Paris in 1951, identifying with the French Left and the world Communist movement, to overcome these anxieties and fully commit myself to a radical life: We had gone abroad in the first place to escape an impending American fascism.

Today it is hard to believe that people in the forties and fifties might have become Communists out of patriotic reasons. But it was not until the 1960s that I began to question my basic love and respect for the United States and its institutions. As a youth I was still influenced by the myths of Washington, Lincoln, the Revolution, and the Civil War. Emerson's "Concord Bridge," Whitman's *Leaves of Grass,* and Benet's "American Names" all inspired an identification with my country's greatness. And Communists during the Popular Front period carried on this nationalist tradition. The Left seemed to be the only political tendency trying to bring America back from the Cold War to its true ideals, through a return to the social reforms of Roosevelt's New Deal and the internationalism of the wartime alliance that included the Soviet Union.

The number-one obstacle to the fulfillment of America's otherwise fathomless possibilities seemed to be the treatment of Black citizens. And in the late forties the only organizations that placed racial equality at the center of their programs were the NAACP and the Communist party. So it was really the issue of race that made me a Communist, just as a few years earlier it had brought me into sociology. The worlds of the Communists I knew in Chicago in the late forties and in California in the early fifties were remarkably integrated. I have never seen since as many interracial marriages, even in today's more open climate.

Race and racism were leading subjects for consciousness-raising. We regularly searched our souls and our practice for "white chauvinism." I remember leading an "educational" on Mexican Americans soon after reading Carey McWilliams's *North From Mexico*. And in our political action we campaigned against lynchings in Mississippi as well as "legal lynchings" in the North and West. Of course, Harold Cruse and other critics are right about the dogmatism of Communist ideology on racial questions, as well as the Party's paternalism and other ways it used its Black members and fellow travelers. But it is still true that no other predominantly white organization of that era was as serious (or as successful) in recruiting Blacks, in preparing them for leadership positions, and in protesting racial injustice.

There was also the Old Left's tendency to romanticize African Americans as noble and virtuous. In Europe in 1951 I met a young Communist from Brooklyn who told me how much he wished he had been born Black. I was already sophisticated enough to know that this was patronization at its worst, but without a sure sense of my own ethnic roots and personal identity, I probably felt the same way on a deeper level. And we had to like Negroes just because they were Black and oppressed. When I left the Party in 1956 following Kruschev's denunciation of the crimes of Stalin and the repression of popular revolt in Hungary and Poland, what a liberation it was to realize that my dislike for a Black man I worked with was a perfectly legitimate feeling!

During the 1950s the Communist youth movement was encouraging middle-class students to leave the universities (where no serious political action could be expected!) and join the working class in order to raise the consciousness of the only group with any real revolutionary potential. I can't say that my five years as a proletarian made any detectable (or for that matter undetectable) dent on working-class consciousness. However, my own life and outlook were significantly altered. I became much more realistic about the possibilities for radical change, given the values of my fellow workers. Socialism no longer seemed like an imminent possibility. My factory experiences also sensitized me to the views of ordinary Americans; in later years this awareness served as a counterbalance to the insularity and elitism of academic life.

The factory was my first exposure to the deep-seated racial bigotry that Myrdal had so well dissected. But there was also a paradoxical on-the-job egalitarianism. I have never forgotten a young man from Arkansas who exemplified this contradiction. As we rode to work together, he would spout off about how "the niggers should be sent back to Africa" because they were moving into the neighborhood near the plant; an hour later he would be working in great friendliness and harmony with his young Black partner on the assembly line. I myself tried to set a nonracist example by speaking up when someone said something blatantly prejudiced—how to do this without alienating people so that they would no longer take me seriously was always tricky—and by my friendships with Mexicans and Blacks, who were actually the people with whom I felt most comfortable. The plan was to recruit such minority "contacts" into Party-led "mass organizations," but the best I could do was to persuade one or two friends to attend an occasional meeting of our very conservative local union. These two ways of questioning not-to-be-questioned racial beliefs were enough to get me labeled as a "Jew-Communist college student," which of course I was. But this wasn't just bigotry. In the factory, ethnicity was the very heart of a person's identity. You simply had to be known as a Mexican or a "Portugee" or an "Arkie" or "Okie"—or by some other ethnic label—to be placed at all.

Without political motive to remain a worker after 1956, I was also tiring of the job, wanting more intellectual challenge, and even feeling renewed stirrings of ambition. So I returned to graduate school, having rejected as impractical such alternatives as journalism or full-time political organizing. I was grateful for another chance to make it in the system, amazed that the society was open enough to be forgiving. After all, I could have been locked up for years as a political prisoner.

I used graduate studies at Berkeley, then the world center for political sociology, to read about socialism, capitalism, working-class life, social movements, and bureaucracy. Michels, Mannheim, Bakunin, and others helped answer the questions that were rising in me and helped integrate the experiences of the recent past. But even though I eventually specialized in industrial sociology, writing a thesis on blue-collar work, I also wrote term papers on racial issues and followed closely the rapidly unfolding developments in civil rights. I would think of the men in the factory eating their lunch as they listened to John K. Chappell on the 12 o'clock news. Were my Black friends now able to speak out a little more? Were they walking the plant with an extra added bounce?

I was certainly much more confident myself than when I had left graduate school six years earlier. My factory and political experiences filled some of that earlier emptiness, made me feel more worldly, less of a kid. My factory days were a kind of initiation into manhood, the camaraderie of the workers and the satisfaction of exhausting physical work relieving some of my inner male insecurities. Today, 40 years later, I can recall quite vividly the names and faces of most of my fellow workers, while the memories of my political comrades with whom I spent endless hours in meetings have faded into near oblivion.

Reradicalizing in the 1960s

Wanting desperately to settle down, to be respectable, I began to temper my politics. But the sixties changed all that.

After completing my dissertation in 1962, I taught for a year at the University of Chicago. The atmosphere had changed from the days when I had walked the streets of the South Side so nonchalantly. With civil rights consciousness now strong, tensions between Blacks and whites, even between passersby on the sidewalk, were palpable. Living in a privileged community surrounded on three sides by Black ghettos was disquieting. I knew it was time to leave one spring evening when I caught myself feeling reassured by the sight of police cars circling our block in their never-ending patrol. I am convinced that had I stayed in Chicago, with its more conservative climate, I would have developed a very different career.

When the free speech movement broke out in the fall of 1964, I was already in my second year at Berkeley, happily teaching a course on social movements! I was immediately taken with the movement's energy and spontaneity—and that of the entire New Left—which contrasted so much with the bureaucratic deadness and theoretical dogmatism I had known in the Party. I participated in the faculty committee that supported the students and of course analyzed the conflict in my lectures. And it was the free speech movement that made me decide to work in race relations.

In Chicago I had taught a course in the field, but my research was on the sociology of death. In my personal life I was exploring my own mortality and other existential questions. (Or so I thought. On a subconscious level I was probably preparing for the death of my father.) But the free speech movement, along with the growing urgency of civil rights protest during the early 1960s, changed all that. The voices of the students in Berkeley's Sproul Plaza, as well as those from the urban ghettos where riots had broken out in the summer of 1964, seemed to be saying that it was the problems of the living and not of the dead or dying that needed attention. In the socially conscious 1960s, it seemed self-indulgent to express such personal preoccupations so patently in my work. So the death book became an article, and in 1965 I began teaching race relations on a regular basis.

Two essays I wrote in 1965 suggest how rapidly my views were changing. The difference between the unpublished "The Unique Americans," written in July just before the Watts riots, and "Whitewash Over Watts," my critique of the McCone Commission written in December, is as stark as night and day. In "The Unique Americans" I used an ethnic group model in which "the Negro" was the problem, not American society. I was so much a "culturalist" then that I even criticized Hauser, Handlin, and Pettigrew for overemphasizing objective conditions. Like Glazer and Moynihan, whom I cited favorably, I believed the success or failure of African Americans hinged on assimilation into the mainstream, though I differed with them on the methods that would be necessary for Blacks to succeed.

Although I had the foresight to highlight the issue of manhood and the special problems of Black men, I relied uncritically on Stanley Elkins's ideas to argue that slavery had completely destroyed African culture and emasculated African American males. I set forward one stereotype after another (e.g., "the Negro as an imitator"), uncritically praised the machismo of Mexican American men, and consistently downplayed the role of racism in the special oppression of Black men. There were flashes of insight also, ideas that appeared in later articles framed in a more satisfactory context. When I reread the piece in preparation for writing this chapter, I found it actually embarrassing. Written before more nuanced scholarship on slavery and Black history had appeared, it showed that I was still caught up in mechanical and reductionist thinking.

Nathan Glazer suggested that I send "The Unique Americans" to his friend D. P. Moynihan, then an assistant secretary of labor in Lyndon Johnson's administration. Moynihan must have been struck by the parallels between my ideas and his soon-to-be-published report on the Negro family. He sent a note calling my article brilliant and added, "You must be Jewish." Two years later I would send him an early draft of my essay on Black culture, in which I said that critics were wrong to call him and his report "racist" because his position reflected instead an attitude better called "neoracist"! Moynihan, not surprisingly, responded with anger, saying that my new term was quite dangerous and that the whole article should not be published because it would further polarize race relations.

Until recently, I had thought that the radicalization of my thinking had been relatively gradual, developing over the three years between "The Unique Americans" and "Internal Colonialism and Ghetto Revolt." So rereading "Whitewash Over Watts" also surprised me. With a much angrier tone, in that paper I emphasized the racism of institutions and the insensitivities of the power structure rather than the problem of "the Negro." Within a nascent model of internal colonialism, I interpreted manhood as fighting back against police brutality and other forms of oppression.

So what happened during the summer and fall of 1965? The rebellion in South Central Los Angeles must have convinced me that the integration of Black people into American society was much more problematic than I had imagined, that even radical tinkering with middle-class mobility models would not suffice. Identifying now with the frustrated and deprived ghetto masses, I hoped—like so many others at that time—that their violent acts would at least dramatize the seriousness of the situation and lead to some badly needed changes in racial and economic policies.

But this hope was shattered by my experience as a consultant to the research staff of the commission that was appointed by Governor Pat Brown to investigate the causes of those "riots." I found that the blue-ribbon McCone Commission was talking only to "important people," so I suggested a grass-roots survey of the citizens of Watts, in addition to the interviews with Negro leaders and the demographic analysis of the arrestees already in the works. The commission agreed to my proposal, and we began training "indigenous" interviewers. We got as far as the interview schedule. Perhaps the concept was threatening to the law-and-order-oriented commission—in any case, roadblocks began to be put in our way; the commission refused to finance or arrange this or that. It became clear that commission members did not want the survey carried out.

The commission's report, when it appeared, was even worse than I had feared. The hypocrisy of its carefully modulated concern angered me. My first experience with official power must have chipped away the faith that I still had that established institutions might respond creatively to the racial crisis.

So in the second half of the sixties I was more than ready to support the rapidly growing militancy of the Black movement. The expulsion of white members from SNCC and other civil rights organizations made sense to me. Not having worked in the South myself, the personal pain involved seemed abstract. And I welcomed the call to Black power when Stokely Carmichael first articulated it in the summer of 1966. Reading his rationale in the *New York Review of Books* or hearing him in the Greek Theater at Berkeley was even more convincing. I was angered by the media's distortion of his message, equating it with violence and domination rather than self-determination and the building of community and culture.

My father died of a heart attack during that same summer. In one of his last letters, he wrote in a somewhat pained tone how he felt that the young Blacks he observed daily from his pensioner's bench were hurting their group's just cause by acting so hostilely toward white people—especially white people like himself, who were prepared to support that cause. But in my writing and public action over the next few years, I increasingly championed the cause of such angry Blacks, including the Black power advocates, perhaps displacing some of my own anger at the loss of my father and at his unrealized life. As I had unconsciously identified my father as a "nigger"—a victim too beaten down to fight back against the world and demand the rewards and recognition due him—I may have seen the Black militants I was defending to be the carriers of his cause also.

The deep depression phase of my mourning lasted only one year. By the summer of 1967 I was writing again, this time an article on Black culture. That spring I had gained tenure, which to me came as no surprise. I had been confident, even cocky, since my return to Berkeley in 1963. I knew that *Alienation and Freedom,* published in 1964, was on the "cutting edge" of the field and, I took my social integration into the informal life of the department, especially the fact that I was invited to be a regular at a Friday-night poker game, as a Calvin-like sign of predestination. Yet the security of tenured employment may also have released certain inhibitions against more extreme radical political action and writing, even if those fears were subconscious at the time.

Being asked to chair the graduate admissions committee was a small price to pay for the prize of tenure. I quickly saw that I could do something meaningful with it. As only three or four Blacks had gone through our Ph.D. program during the 1950s and 1960s, I devised a plan to recruit minority students. With the solid support of the faculty, Charles Glock (then the chair) and I raised money for special fellowships. During the winter and spring I traveled inside and outside California to interview, recruiting nine Blacks and two Chicanos for the next fall's class. This is the model of affirmative action that has always appealed to me: one based on a case-by-case assessment of individual potential and one that takes into account the value of life experience. Unfortunately, this is very expensive to carry out on a large scale.

Martin Luther King, Jr., was assassinated the day before I flew South to interview prospective graduate students. I was at Tougaloo College in Mississippi during the time of his funeral. African Americans watched the televised ceremonies in the central auditorium; the few white students, faculty, and myself watched in Professor Ernst Borinski's study—it was not the most comfortable time to be a white man at a Black institution. King's assassination was a "defining moment," the radicalizing event for many people who would later appear in *Black Lives, White Lives*. For me it was the *coup de grace* confirming the desperateness of America's racial crisis and the need for extreme measures, in theory as well as practice. The assassination was the backdrop for my essay "Internal Colonialism and Ghetto Revolt," which I wrote in May and June of 1968. When I presented the paper at a UCLA conference on violence that June, the response was extremely positive, even admiring, suggesting how deeply the radical mood had penetrated the academy. But my ideas infuriated Bruno Bettelheim, who as a panel discussant claimed I was justifying violence and opening the door to fascism. Margaret Mead, much kinder and gentler, pulled me aside in the corridor and questioned whether race relations in America were really parallel to the colonialism she had witnessed in North Africa and Asia.

A month later I would appear as an expert witness for the defense in the Oakland murder trial of Black Panther leader Huey Newton. Putting forward a definition of white racism so broad that no Caucasian could be truly free of it, I was trying to help attorney Charles Garry establish an argument in support of his motion that Newton be tried by an all-Black jury made up of his ghetto peers. During the cross-examination, district attorney Lowell Jensen, later to be the number-two man in Reagan's Justice Department, at first was condescending to me. He virtually impugned the manhood of such an unworldly and impractical academic type as myself. But, a man of considerable intellectual power, he also began to relish our exchange of ideas. His strategy was to dilute my testimony by pointing out that according to my own logic I must be a white racist too. I cheerfully assented, adding that the important thing was to become aware of racist tendencies and then commit oneself to change. Testifying in court, especially holding my own in the cross with

Jensen, was a real high. Garry was impressed enough to ask me to help the defense team select the jury. Thus I was able to spend the whole summer attending the trial and discussing strategy with the lawyers. Newton, who I interviewed in his jail cell, gave me some of the best critical feedback I received on my Black culture article.

I was going to write a Norman Mailer-like nonfiction novel on the experience, as the trial and the whole police-Black Panther conflict seemed to epitomize the larger racial struggles of the time. But I could not pull it off, settling for an article on jury selection. I think my block must have had to do with unresolved conflicts about guilt and innocence, authority figures and their murder, as well as unconscious meanings of violence and Black masculinity. However, the summer-long involvement did seem to resolve not just my characterological doubts, but my basic dilemma: How could I justify my own success and privilege at a time when the nation's most oppressed people were fighting for their basic rights? By the end of the experience I saw myself as a social scientist in the service of the Black revolution and routinely referred to the police as pigs.[1]

The excitement of the late sixties invaded the classroom. By 1970, enrollments in my courses had grown from 60 to 300, 400, 500, and included sizable numbers of Native American, Chicano, and Asian students as well as Blacks and whites. Students yelled and shouted at one another, but almost never at me, as somehow I managed to mediate the clashing perspectives. (At times we discussed issues reasonably, also.) And outside the classroom, demonstrations and student strikes added more excitement but also frustration, as they shut down the campus and shortened the teaching term.

Attitudes toward Black militancy divided Berkeley's sociology faculty. During my graduate student years and through the mid-sixties, there was a strong sense of community in the department based in large part on a shared politics. There was not a great deal of distance between the most conservative and most radical professors because of the underlying liberal-leftist consensus among social scientists during the late Eisenhower and Kennedy years. This consensus began to crack with the free speech movement, and in the late sixties the department divided inexorably. Vietnam was the first issue, then student power, academic reform, and finally Black power and Black studies. Friendships of 10 to 20 years' duration broke up. People stopped talking to one another, and bitter conflict, especially over personnel and curriculum, replaced what had been a benign internal politics. Several of the more moderate (and prestigious) faculty members resigned and found jobs elsewhere.

For a period we radicals were buoyed by a larger community, that of "the movement." But when social protest was stilled by the combined effects of the conservative reaction expressed in Nixon's repressive politics and the mistakes of the movement itself, professors like myself, radicalized by the sixties, became demoralized. We had expected basic change, both in the universities and in the larger society, but without conceding much more than relatively minor reforms, social institutions had withstood the onslaught. So we felt isolated and abandoned. White radical students were cutting their beards and getting "establishment" jobs. Black militants were trimming their Afros, downplaying the street talk, and getting accepted in law school now that affirmative action was in effect. But for middle-aged professors still committed to late-sixties perspectives no longer viable, it was difficult to shift gears.

In 1972 I published the articles on Watts, internal colonialism, and the Newton jury, as well as others on Black culture and institutional racism, in a book called *Racial Oppression in America.* It was well received by minority scholars and by students but not by mainstream sociologists, especially by my own colleagues, whose dismissal of its merit resulted in my being turned down twice for a full professor promotion.

A few years later in primal therapy I would realize that *Racial Oppression* was my "bad boy" book, written not only in response to the realities of social relations, but also out of a need to attack the system, the one that had welcomed me back after the publication of my dissertation. The latter had been my "good boy" book, where I had followed the conventions of sociological research and analysis, but in an innovative way. I suppose it was my typical masculine hangups—the need to appear invulnerable, rational, and in control—that kept me from acknowledging at the time how deeply hurt I was by the rejection of my book, and more particularly by the humiliation of not being promoted for seven additional years. A rising star my first few years at Berkeley, I was now almost *persona non grata*; I still hold the department record for remaining the longest as an associate professor. Of course, to a great extent I had marginalized myself. In a key article I had analyzed the racism of liberal white professors and in a reckless dash of left-wing macho I had dedicated the book "to the memory of two writers, my father who encouraged me to write in the essay form, and George

Jackson, who was to be the subject of an essay I could not write—may his death be avenged."[2]

I was also being hoist by my own petard. In my support for Black power and call for the "decolonization" of social research, how could I complain when the spotlight shifted to minority scholars and I no longer got job offers or invitations to conferences? Thus I was also suffering from not being in the spotlight, from the lack of that centrality that men in general and smart boys especially are used to. One incident stands out. In the early 1970s, I was placed on the committee to select the director for a new institute of race relations, which was being established in response to student demands dating back to the Third World strike of 1969. I was at a point in my career where I was looking for a vehicle to express some of my ideas. So, although secretly I wanted the directorship for myself, I could not challenge the assumption that the post should go to a person of color—a position with which I also agreed.[3]

Black Lives, White Lives: *The First Stage*

During the late sixties I had also begun an interviewing project, but I preferred writing the more theoretical and political essays that would make up *Racial Oppression* and undoubtedly spent less time than I should have "minding the store," leaving most of the day-to-day running of the research in the hands of David Wellman. Perhaps this was in part because I had never intended an empirical work in the first place, envisioning that I would do some kind of "armchair" theoretical synthesis, comparing American ethnic groups and their place in the class structure. Working in the sociology of death had gotten me interested in cultural ideals of manhood, and as I read into different ethnic traditions, I was struck by the variety of these ideals and excited at the prospect of applying such an analysis to Black Americans.

So it is possible that if the University's Budget Committee had accepted my department's recommendation that I be promoted to tenure in 1966, *Black Lives, White Lives* might never have been written. But committee members said that my plans for the new research were too vague and undeveloped. While signaling the likelihood of tenure the following year, they asked for a comprehensive statement about the empirical research that would inform my theorizing. I was a little annoyed, but I reasoned, If they want methodology, give them methodology. Little did I know that I was beginning a project that would last more than 20 years.

That statement for the Budget Committee did eventually secure my tenure, but more important, it was so thorough—and to me convincing—that I developed it into a grant proposal called "Minority Manhood Orientations and the American Race Problem." I proposed an interview study of Black men to test the hypothesis that African Americans, particularly in the lower class, had developed a unique sense of what it means to be a man, an ideal that, although enriching Black ethnicity and empowering individuals, might be having a negative impact on assimilation and upward mobility. With questions being raised at that time about the capacity of Black men to compete in the marketplace—the themes of the culture of poverty were much in vogue in the mid-sixties—and my ideas resonating with the zeitgeist, I was generously funded by the National Institutes of Mental Health in 1967.

But these ideas were soon challenged by my own staff, as well as by my growing radicalization. At weekly seminars, Hardy Frye and Wellman vigorously argued that we had to look at manhood in the overall context of a racist society. Thus we decided to broaden our focus, to interview whites as well as Blacks, women as well as men, and we renamed the project: "Racism, Manhood, and Culture." The widespread criticism of Moynihan's (1965) thesis that the matriarchal Black family underlay the problems of Black men also influenced us. I felt that the criticisms of Moynihan were generally valid, but I also felt the response was exaggerated and even hysterical at times. Moynihan's "mistakes" were not so much substantive as matters of context and emphasis. Had he placed his ideas about matriarchy more squarely in the framework of a racist society, and had he talked about one *tendency* within a variety of Black family organizations, rather than calling his essay *The Negro Family,* he would have been on firmer ground. I was even more upset with the Black power critics for their attacks on William Styron, who had dared to get inside the head of a slave revolt leader in his *The Confessions of Nat Turner* (1967), a novel I found both moving and good literature.

Did I let the Black power mood throw me off my intellectual course? Rereading "The Unique Americans" has assured me that the problems with my original conceptual scheme may have been insurmountable. But it is fortunate that we kept much of our original interest in Black men and gender relations in the empirical research. By the time *Black*

Lives, White Lives appeared in 1989, the special problems of African American males had become central to the national debate on race.

The members of our interviewing staff, well trained by project coordinator David Wellman, were given virtually free rein to carry out interviews as they saw fit. For the most part they did an incredible job, bringing in life histories of great richness. They had to juggle two hard-to-reconcile goals of the research: getting enough material about the various topics covered in our interview guides so that we would have standardized data for analytic purposes, and at the same time getting each person's unique story. Recall that I was originally planning a more analytic book about the role of race and racism in everyday life, connecting the shifts in racial consciousness during the 1960s to earlier experiences in the life histories. The fact that by and large we did a much better job of getting people's unique stories than of providing comparable standardized data was one factor—among many—that would tilt the scale toward a first-person "oral history" book.

I was also ambivalent about presuming to analyze the lives of the people we had interviewed, particularly the African Americans. Some of this might have been white radical guilt. Some of it was also philosophical, the beginnings of doubts about empirical analysis itself. But mostly the problem was the enormity of making sense of 10,000 pages of transcripts. Thus I was more than ready for what I thought then would be an easy solution, a first-person interview book, although I didn't see it as a real alternative until Studs Terkel published *Working* in 1974. From *Working* I learned the potential of narrative for illuminating not only personal lives, but the inner workings of society itself. By using Terkel as my model, I could let people speak for themselves, satisfying my basic populist impulses and neatly finessing the problem of presuming to write about Black people.

Interlude: The 1970s and Personal Life

Despite the centrality of social commitment in my life story, the political life has never really suited me. In my youth the Communist ideal filled some deep need for meaning, and the Party provided system and order in my life. But that experience also soured me on organizational politics. As I've grown older I have become more of an anarchist than a socialist, temperamentally as well as philosophically. And though the political ferment of the 1960s was exciting, the constant conflict was uncomfortable. I always felt that I should be doing more. So I was more than ready for the 1970s shift from political involvement to private life.

In 1969 and then again in 1971 my wife and I adopted our two children. Without any conscious decision based on politics or ideology, we fell into a division of labor in which each of us became a primary parent for one of them. So through most of the 1970s, being a father became more important than my work. Already in my 40s, parenting at first exhausted then finally rejuvenated me, as it put me in touch with the energy, openness, and wonder that children express—until society crushes so much of it out of them. I think I preferred to spend time with my children because the rewards felt more real, and certainly more immediate, than those coming from work. The response and recognition and love were daily blessings, in sharp contrast to the articles and books, which were not only frustrating to produce but took years to see the light of day.

The middle years of the 1970s were the years of my mid-life crisis, years of important work, none of which appears on my curriculum vita. But if I had not delved so deeply into my biography, if I had not faced so squarely the range of my emotions in therapy, I could not have portrayed the lives of the subjects in *Black Lives, White Lives* with as much authenticity and feeling.

For three years, primal therapy was my central interest. I taught my classes to draw my salary, but I did no writing, no research. I could not and I did not want to. Sociology, especially its theories and abstractions, became meaningless. I was discovering the inner life, the world of feelings, and probing into my early family dynamics. I read mostly novels in this period. I became more interested in my health, giving up coffee and cigars, eating better, running regularly. Playing tennis, I eschewed competition, preferring to rally for an hour without keeping score. The greatest gift was feeling more deeply the beauty of the natural world. I would walk, run, bike, or just rest in Tilden Park, a near-wilderness area close to the Berkeley campus.

I was the featured speaker at the sociology graduation in June 1974. Before the free speech movement, all graduates had received their diplomas en masse at the Greek Theater. But after, graduations were decentralized in an attempt to build community into the multiversity. I took note of this legacy of the movement, taking its upcoming tenth anniversary as my theme, and told the mostly parental audience of its history. I talked about how so many of our liberal-leftist faculty had been demoralized by the conservative retrenchment of the 1970s. Harry

Edwards, sitting in the audience, later told me he overheard a parent comment to his spouse: "With professors like that at Berkeley, it's no wonder Patty Hearst joined the SLA."

The Symbionese Liberation Army and Watergate were subjects we talked about in my American society class as I experimented with my teaching, trying to find subject matter closer to my life experience. I saw that I had been adopting the causes of and analyzing everyone but myself. So in 1975 I decided to teach a course on men and masculinity. I was, after all, a man. Though the existence of courses on women helped legitimate the idea for me, my own questioning of traditional manhood did not come primarily from feminism, but rather from those psychological changes that enabled me to begin integrating my "feminine side." I designed the course to counter the prevailing male mode of teaching. I minimized formal lecturing, threw off the mantle of expert, and narrowed the distance between me and my students. As I talked openly about my own life, students were more able to share their own experiences.

After three years of this "psychosocial moratorium" I was ready to get back to professional work. A men's group I joined in 1977 helped me sort out the ways in which I was colluding with my own victimization and using my sense of grievance at "the system" as a reason to hold back my creative power. The group still nourishes my personal growth and provides an important audience for my writing.

The transition back into work was a delicate one, because my mental and psychic life had been seriously shaken up. I was so into "right brain" thinking, my intellectual nerve endings so fragile, that I literally could not read anything with a grain of abstraction, unless the ideas were contained within a very personal voice. So I could not even consider returning to the theoretical book I had been writing on race-class relations in a colonial capitalist society, the book I had promised my readers in *Racial Oppression* and for which I had already accepted a generous advance from my prospective publisher.[4] Still not knowing what I was going to work on, I began reading the interviews that had been waiting patiently in my files for so many years. I was fascinated by the people's stories and how they made the late 1960s and its racial politics come alive.

I also had some principled objections to social theory, feeling that it often gets in the way of a fresh, creative look at reality. This skepticism was also connected to my growing doubts over the concept of internal colonialism, with which I had become identified—too identified, I felt, as I had never seen that perspective as the essence of my 1972 book. I was troubled by the fact that the logic of internal colonialism—unlike classic colonial situations, in which the colonizers can be driven out— does not suggest any real solutions to racial oppression in its unique American setting. I was still enough of a Marxist to believe that a correct theory must point the way to a workable political practice. I also wanted to disassociate myself from the faddish use of the idea, the many applications of the concept that seemed mechanical, even dogmatic. I was constantly struck by how identified other people were with that framework and how upset they became when I expressed my doubts, as I did at a colloquium in the late 1970s at Berkeley's Institute of Social Change. Of course, I had been burned professionally by my embrace of the colonial perspective—this was the "principled" reason my colleagues lacked enthusiasm for my work and I was not promoted. So I think a part of me felt that it would be safer to ground my future work in the concrete life experiences of real people, downplaying the bigger questions in a charged field such as race relations, where the lines between theoretical analysis and political advocacy easily get fuzzy.

My decision to do a "longitudinal" study was a historical accident. When I began editing the 1968 interviews in 1977 I envisioned a book that would tie the late 1960s transformations in consciousness to people's earlier racial experiences. But I had two quarters of sabbatical leave accumulated and I needed a grant to supplement my salary. Charles Glock thought that a foundation might be interested in the idea of a 10-year follow-up, and he was right.

The idea of meeting the people whose lives and words I had been poring over was very appealing. I felt I already knew them. I had all kinds of questions tailored to each individual, and of course I wanted to ask everyone how their lives had changed and what effects the sixties had had, both on their own lives and on America's race relations. Because the intense polarization of the late sixties had given way to a more relaxed mood, I gambled on the fact that I could interview Blacks as well as whites, unlike in the late 1960s, when we relied almost entirely on same-race interviews. But the thread of the contact with the original interviewer was indispensable: When I could say that I was the friend or teacher of Hardy Frye, Alex Papillon, or Sheila Gibson, people welcomed me. Although an African American researcher probably would have gotten deeper material on certain private issues of Black culture and family, only 2 of my 40 interviews (one Black, one white) were unusable because of lack of candor.

Finding people was difficult because we had not kept addresses or even full names. So from 1978 to 1982 I did considerable detective work, tracking people down with whatever clues were available, and in the case of "Gladys Hunt," whom I wanted very badly to locate, I even hired a private investigator, but to no avail. Some wonderful 1968 stories never got into the book because there were no follow-up interviews, particularly of hippies in the Haight-Ashbury, who used only first names and were the most footloose of the people we talked to. But I did find 40 of my original target of 50.

I did not prepare a carefully worked-out set schedule. On a 5 × 8 card I jotted down both specific questions and general topics. Because I had them memorized and a loose-flowing conversation better suits my interviewing style, I rarely consulted these notes. Yet I have wondered whether I might have gotten deeper and richer material had I asked as many sharply focused questions as we did in the late sixties. For a long time I felt somewhat inferior about my interviews, feeling that they did not match the power and eloquence of the original ones. But the 1960s were unique in the willingness they brought out in people to "let it all hang out" and, perhaps even more important, people tend to tell their best stories within a life-history format rather than in a 10-year follow-up.

I learned that good interviewing is a consciousness-raising experience. The interviewer as well as the subject becomes more self-reflective. Because I can be impatient, I learned how important it is to ask early the questions that most interested me. Most difficult was learning to listen intently and receptively to an informant and her story, resisting the temptation to interrupt with a follow-up, yet keeping that question alive in a corner of my mind so I could ask it when the time would be more ripe. Having a tendency to be abrupt and businesslike, I learned also to "hang out," both before turning on the tape recorder signaled the beginning of the formal interview and afterwards, when people often revealed their most intimate experiences. (Unfortunately, I only interviewed a few people more than once each round, but I am now a full believer in multiple interviewing, as trust and openness deepen with each succeeding encounter.)

I was often apprehensive or nervous about meeting people. I was awed by Howard Spence's grandeur, afraid that Florence Grier would reject me as a busybody white sociologist, and worried about the hostility of conservative white males. When a whole series of leads finally resulted—after three years—in a phone call from Larry Dillard, he was so angry I had found him out that I thought that I was going to be the white man he wanted to kill "just to put it on the books." He agreed only to meet with me to discuss the possibility of an interview. Appearing at the front door, he seemed almost menacing. What seemed to soften him was the beer I had bought. "That's my brand," he said of the Budweiser. The ice was further broken as we reminisced about a mutual acquaintance and traded stories about Huey Newton. He had intended to give me "a bad time," but he never got around to it because he was just enjoying too much talking about serious political ideas—it reminded him of the old days when he was in jail.

Dillard's changed attitude was a part of a general trend. The young Black men who had been the most militant and nationalistic in the late 1960s had given up most of their racial bitterness and, like Dillard, wanted to view "people as people" rather than in terms of Black and white. I found a similar "people are people" attitude among whites. Another surprise was how the white workers had become more sophisticated in their racial and other social-political discourses. And almost everyone seemed to have grown as human beings, with in many cases the sixties and its movements serving as the catalysts.

Being close to the lives and struggles of the people in the book filled some of my own needs for human contact and inspiration in a period when my emotional life was stagnant: the last two years of a marriage that had dried up. Thus my divorce in 1980 was a liberation, but because I am the kind of person for whom life often gets in the way of work, rather than the type who carries on come hell or high water, the excitement of new experience as well as the pain of change slowed down my progress for a period.

In the early 1980s I envisioned a series of case studies in which the 1979 interview would follow the 1968 interview of the same person, in that way underscoring transformations in consciousness and personal life. But this back-to-back arrangement posed almost insuperable difficulties in organizing the book as a whole. There seemed to be no natural way to cluster people into thematic chapters because the groups they formed in the late 1960s did not correspond well to those they fell into 10 years later. So even though my publishers had at first been enthusiastic, they pulled out just before issuing a contract, saying that my conception of the book was "too inchoate" and concerned also that my draft preface was too wishy-washy.

I wasted almost a year trying to find another commercial publisher, still guided by the fantasy that I had a best-seller on my hands. An editor at one leading house liked my material but told me that they already had one book about Blacks on their forthcoming list, and one was enough! Another publisher suggested that if only I had a book on Hispanics, then they might be interested. Most said that there was no longer enough interest in racial problems to risk publishing a book like mine.

I was very lucky that Jim Clark, director of the University of California Press, had long valued my work. An outside reviewer he recommended suggested that I reorganize the manuscript to emphasize the sociological rather than the personal. This dovetailed with my new plan of dividing the book by decades in order to highlight the larger social and political dynamics of racial change. It is interesting that many readers still prefer the earlier organization and bounce around the book from front to back, following the lives of the people who most interest them.

By the end of 1984 I had completed a good draft of the first (1968) half of the book. I bought a house and spent a month moving, painting, and doing repairs. Then I acquired a mysterious virus. The physical illness lasted months and led to a depression that virtually incapacitated me for all of 1985 and most of 1986. I kept teaching, but I was barely functional. I tried to keep writing, but I could not concentrate. Nothing helped, from meditation to medication. Desperate to finish, I hired a cowriter. It was helpful to talk with someone, but my sense of the book was too idiosyncratic, my writing too individuated, for easy collaboration.

Sick as I was in 1986, I could see that things were changing on the racial front. Reagan's policies were threatening the gains of the civil rights years as well as the economic situation of the poor. There seemed to be an upsurge of bigotry, the emergence of new protest (most notably the antiapartheid movement), and thus more public attention to racial issues. In 1979 I had titled a talk "What Happened to Race?" Now it seemed to be back in the news. Because we were in a different race relations situation, and because so much time had passed since I had last interviewed, I decided to talk to people for a third time.

It was good to see them again. They were becoming as familiar as a cast of characters must be to a novelist. Two refused to participate in the third round, and three additional people had died, including Florence Grier, whose help in the second round had meant so much to me. A month before I began interviewing, my mother died. At 87 she had had a long and largely good life, but I was not prepared for her death. It only deepened my despair. Thus I conducted the final interviews in a state of both depression and mourning. If this is not apparent to the reader, it is a testimony to the power of judicious editing. There were moments when it was agonizing to simulate interest, even to stay seated next to my tape recorder.

I remember thinking once I should give up on the book, but, being an optimist by nature, I never really doubted that I would someday finish. What made it possible was finding out that my depression was "biological." It responded rapidly to the specific medication required to repair the chemical breakdown in the neurotransmitter system of my brain. Thus by spring 1987 I had a complete final draft except for the last chapter, which required six different attempts before I found one that worked.

Finishing the book closed a number of chapters in my life. A project of more than 20 years was now completed, a burden lifted. Most important, I liked what I had. I felt none of the lingering dissatisfaction I had with my earlier books, the sense that I should have spent more time on them. I also knew that many of my colleagues had given up on me as a serious sociologist. They may have known that I was working on a long-term project, but after so many years few probably thought I would ever finish it. So completing *Black Lives, White Lives* was a kind of redemption—not so much in my own eyes, but of who I was in the eyes of others. It also covered up many of the holes in my vita, the long years of silence.

The 20-year gestation was actually a blessing in disguise. It made my research unique and gave the book more legitimacy. I had the time to get the writing and the organization right, so that the stories could move people and help educate a new generation about racism. Even more important, there was time to assess the direction of racial change. Had I published in 1980 I would have misread the situation, emphasizing too much the positive (and real) progress produced by the 1960s. At that time I was still too close to the sixties to fathom their complex legacy. The upsurge of racism during the 1980s made the "ambiguities of racial change" clearer, so that my eventual assessment would be more balanced and nuanced. That same upsurge of racism, in bringing race back into the news, created a more favorable climate for the book's appearance.

Except in the late sixties, I have never liked to take public positions. I am basically shy. Furthermore, since my mid-40s I have often been consumed with doubt about my beliefs. But promoting *Black Lives, White Lives* helped me to overcome this. Because I was representing the people in the book, I felt responsible to get their stories and the message of the book out to a wider audience. I made at least 50 appearances on radio and 12 on television, including *The Today Show,* and on two of these appearances I brought with me some of the "real authors" (Harold Sampson, Virginia Lawrence, and Larry Dillard). A typical interview began with the book but soon moved into a discussion of the current racial crisis. I would attribute the rise in racial violence first to the emergence of a new generation of whites too young to have experienced the sixties or early seventies, and therefore ignorant of the civil rights movement and the structures of traditional racism that gave rise to it. Then I would cite the policies of the Reagan administration. A third point was the more than 15 years of economic stagnation. I would speak of how Americans engage in racial, ethnic, and other diversionary scapegoating during times of economic crisis, rather than confronting the issue of class inequality, as has been customary in Europe or Latin America. But my talk of class struggle always got edited out.

Mostly I waited for the reaction of the people themselves. Several wrote appreciative letters, saying how much they had learned from the book. I sent Howard Spence a case of books to use the proceeds for his community-building projects in Mississippi. Visiting him in 1979 had been one of the high points of my career, even though, stressed out by jet lag, I didn't really interview him well. When he told me that the book validated the struggles of his life, it made my own feel worthwhile, for it was my affection for the people, even more than the issues per se, that had kept me going. Spence is special to me. As one ages, it gets harder to find people of the next older generation to look up to who combine involvement in good works with wisdom and compassion.

Millie Harding and Frank Casey attended a book party where eight of the people met for the first time and signed each others' copies. Harding talked of the people in her community who picked up the book, "whether in a bar, at church, on the street, or in the park [and] could not put it down because they saw themselves in it." Frank Casey expressed the hope that one day after he was gone his grandchildren would "pick up the book and know about their grandfather and what happened in the country three decades ago." But there were at least two people who felt misunderstood by my 1968 rendition of their lives, especially Len Davis, who thought I emphasized too much his despair and negativity.

The first review, by Jonathan Kirsch in the *Los Angeles Times,* was an author's fantasy. A few months later another positive one, by David Garrow, appeared in the *New York Times.* My colleagues in sociology also liked the book, and welcomed the recognition I was getting. Once again I felt a part of things, as I had in the middle sixties. The response of students in my classes was also enthusiastic. The only sour note was the university's personnel process. The Budget Committee cited the book's "shortcomings" as the reason for denying me a promotion to the step that indicates a professor has national and international stature. Committee members said the book's generalizability was limited because of the small California sample and because of its "relative lack of theorizing"; they suggested that it would have only popular appeal, rather than making "an impact on the sociology of race relations." At that time, reviews had not yet appeared in scholarly journals. Two years later, I sent committee members a file of seven glowing appreciations from journals, ranging from *Contemporary Sociology* to *Southern History* to *Black Economy* and *Oral History*. But in denying me again, they dismissed these reviews, saying that the book had already been fully credited. I am making public these confidential communications now because I am no longer able to collude silently in what has essentially become a form of harassment. Under the cloak of secrecy and non-accountability, university reviewing agencies too often use their control of purse strings and prestige to keep in line independent spirits such as myself who want to push the borders of acceptable academic work to encompass more creative and humanistic expressions.

Reassessing in the 1990s

Today, when I consider race relations sociology, I am more concerned than I was in the past with the social and political consequences of analytic frameworks and less with their abstract "theoretical correctness." It is in this spirit that I have been reassessing some of my earlier work.

"Colonized and Immigrant Minorities" is a 1971 essay that is still widely read (see Blauner, 1971/1987).[5] The argument turns on the contrast between the historical experiences of those white European ethnic groups who entered America voluntarily as immigrants, were able to move freely within the society, and worked as free laborers in industrial urban centers and those of the colonized minorities who became Americans against their will, lacked freedom of movement and access to the labor market, and were subjected to systematic racism rather than just ethnic prejudice.

Today I see the contrast as too sharply drawn. Because that essay was written at the peak of "Third World" unity movements, I searched for reasons to include Asians and Latinos within the colonial rubric, forcing them into a kind of theoretical Procrustean bed. Today I would no longer consider Asians and Hispanics colonized. Even though their historic entry into the United States shared some colonial aspects (especially for the conquered Mexicans), they are essentially immigrant groups. This is important because the American mentality remains that of a nation of immigrants. Newcomers to this country—for the most part— become the most motivated and identified of Americans.

It is no accident that the two groups that remain the most downtrodden, with significant numbers of their population cut off from structures of opportunity and even mainstream values, are those two minorities who did not come to America voluntarily: the Black Africans and the Red Indians. The "immigrant advantage" is not news to the African Americans in South Central Los Angeles. I suspect that when they targeted Korean stores they were protesting something larger than even the murder of a 15-year-old Black girl. Koreans, along with other immigrants, enter the country and in a relatively short period surpass the economic and social position of the Black poor, continuing a dynamic that has been taking place for 125 years.

Yet Koreans and other Asian immigrants—as well as Mexicans and Central Americans—are people of color who meet barriers of race and racism that did not exist for European newcomers. They may be advantaged as immigrants, but they are disadvantaged by their color and by the languages they speak. In the American racial hierarchy, the brown and yellow people occupy a middle ground between Black and white. So I would now suggest a three-way, rather than a two-way, classification.

And I would not draw such a total contrast between white ethnic groups and people of color. By highlighting so insistently their differences, my writing contributed to widening the gap between whites and nonwhites. The grandchildren of European immigrants who read this essay in their college classes often feel that the struggles of their forebears have been discounted, that they as their descendants lack moral standing. When one compares the histories of the Irish, the Italians, and the Jews in America with those of the Africans, the Mexicans, and the Native Americans, one can emphasize either the striking differences caused by racism and colonialism or the common experiences of being outsiders, undergoing poverty, facing prejudice and discrimination. Since the choice one makes is consequential, it is important to strike a careful balance between these two positions.

Though class has by no means replaced race in "significance," I find myself searching more often for a class perspective on American society these days.[6] Class analysis and class politics retain more potential for building coalitions than does strictly racial thinking. With all his flaws, Jesse Jackson remains a hero to me because his search for common ground has made him effective in mobilizing midwestern farmers and embattled union members on strike, as well as minorities and the urban poor. I was quite moved when he called the residents of the community of Howard Beach "victims of economic violence" after some of their working-class Italian youth murdered a Black New Yorker, rather than simply dismissing them as "racist."

We need to find some balance between today's emphasis on difference—racial and otherwise—that is our legacy from the sixties and seventies and the need to build coalitions across lines of color, ethnicity, and other dividing points. I support multiculturalism, diversity, curriculum reform, and other similar programs that are attacked as "politically correct," but only in an inclusive context, one that does not disparage or negate the claims of white people, including white males, to be equal partners in our muddled strivings toward a better society. In my classes I find many sincere whites confused, feeling left out, without authority to speak on matters of race and social justice. White males often feel they are automatically seen as oppressors, rather than as individuals. I am not just talking about their resentment of affirmative action, but of the yearnings many liberal whites (and conservative ones often too) have to know and to relate to Blacks, Asians, and Latinos as individuals rather than as members of a group.[7]

That sharp contrast between colonized and immigrant minorities underlies the strong approach to affirmative action along racial lines. So my own support of affirmative action is more measured, my position more complex than it was two decades ago. I take seriously the concern of critics about affirmative action's political divisiveness and I see nothing wrong with pragmatically assessing its utility in specific situations. But I do not agree with D'Souza and others who argue that affirmative action has reduced the quality of education at universities such as Berkeley. In my classes, more than a few of the brightest students—those with the freshest, most original approaches to the subject matter—are Black or Latino or Asian, groups that were virtually absent on campus when I began teaching. The situation may be different in other fields. I may attract students whose political commitment and life experience give them a special edge. But when I visit other major universities today, the whiteness of their student bodies comes as a shock and makes me appreciate how Berkeley's ethnic mixture is a very special education in itself.

Still, I would not dismiss the ideal of "color-blindness" as archly as I did in my earlier writings. I respect more today this basis of opposition to affirmative action. Yet I think critics like William Wilson and Paul Starr are wrong when they say its impact has been inconsequential, helping only the already qualified, the prepared, the middle class. I don't consider the Blacks and Latinos who work in the building trades and in such municipal jobs as police and fire fighting to be middle-class. They are working-class, and their numbers are significant. But I have long felt that the predominant emphasis on affirmative action as the single solution to racial equality has had negative political conse- quences and needs to be reassessed. I would like more emphasis on exploring and overturning traditional modes of discrimination, which, because of all the fanfare about affirmative action, most whites in the United States no longer think significantly affect racial minorities.

I have also been reassessing the racism concept. I now feel that it was premature to imply, as I did in my earlier writings, that its old-fashioned expressions—bigotry and discrimination—were on their way out, no longer necessary to maintain a racially stratified society that could rely better on a more impersonal institutionalized racism. During the sixties and seventies there was this strong tendency to privilege structural explanations of all types and to downplay—almost with scorn—the relevance of cultural values or the importance of racial prejudice. From the people in my book I have learned a new respect for the power of beliefs, which in the racial area are very deep-seated but also capable of change. And in racism's resurgence these past years, most prominent have been the old-fashioned forms of bigotry and hate crimes—even lynchings, in their northern (baseball bats replacing rope) version.

In my classes I've noticed how whites and minorities talk past one another, almost if there are two languages of race. When Blacks or Asians are being "ethnic," celebrating their distinctiveness, whites see them as being racial. Blacks and whites operate with different defini- tions of racism. The latter hold to older meanings, before the 1960s expanded the concept's purview: systematic ideologies of white su- premacy, feelings of prejudice, acts of discrimination. People of color are more attuned to newer definitions: institutional racism, the "atmo- spheric racism" of particular social milieux, and even what I have termed "racism as result," seeing the society or a particular segment of it as racist simply because nonwhites do not share equally in participation or power.[8] Operating with their more restricted meanings and turned off by the overheated racism discourse, many whites have come to see the "reverse racism" of affirmative action as the most important racism. What heartened me about the response to the Rodney King beating and verdict is that it marked the first time since Martin Luther King's assassination in 1968 that significant numbers of European Americans had been shocked by an incident of white racism against an African American or other person of color. There is an opportunity now for whites to begin to learn what minorities already know, that acts of racism are not isolated "aberrations," but part of a systematic pattern. Perhaps by listening respectfully to both Black and white definitions, we can begin to bridge the gap in the language of race.

In 1970, David Wellman and I wrote an article on the "decolonization" of social research that addressed the role of whites in the race relations field. We argued that certain aspects of racial phenomena—for example, culture and group ethos, the meaning of oppression, and the experiential aspects of everyday racism—"were difficult if not impossible for a member of the oppressing group to grasp empirically and formulate conceptually." We suggested that the most valuable contribution white scholars could make would be to bring minorities into graduate schools to make it possible for researchers of color to produce the ethnographies of their communities and the studies of their culture and politics that were so needed. While minority scholars should have free rein to tackle any problem, white sociologists "might well eschew focusing on Black and other Third World communities" and instead investigate "the ways that racist practices are embedded in particular institutions, and the permeation of assumptions of white superiority in American culture and personality as well as the special situation and problems of white ethnic groups and working-class people."

Today I would not call so starkly for such a "racial division of research labor." The very language suggests too much an apartheidlike arrangement, and of course I no longer write in that incisive style that suggests such confident solutions to problems I have come to see as most complex. And yet I find myself agreeing in general with this formulation of 20 years ago. To some degree there has been the development of a certain consensus on this kind of division of labor, but one of its consequences seems to be that fewer and fewer white graduate students have chosen race as their major field. To do so is seen as a bad move on the job market, so whites tend to connect such a strong interest to another specialization, perhaps gender, white ethnicity, or even historical sociology.

The issue of the role of whites in the era of affirmative action came to a head recently in the controversy over hiring Loic Wacquant in the Sociology Department at Berkeley. Though I admired Wacquant and his work and wanted him to join our department, I spoke against the appointment and warned my colleagues that the students' unprecedented opposition—manifested so forcefully during their appearance earlier at our meeting—was based on feelings of being twice betrayed: first by the denial of tenure to Tomás Almaguer and second by our dismissal of their objections to Wacquant. I went on to say that I could understand why the Democratic party might want to downplay affirmative action because it divides their constituency, but the Department of Sociology at Berkeley in voting for a position in race relations?

In retrospect, I believe I raised too strongly the question of Wacquant's whiteness, because the real issue—for me and I believe for the students— was the question of field. For 20 years the position had been a Chicano studies one, so I felt that it should be used either in that capacity or for the sociology of Asian Americans, another unrepresented area in our department. I would like to think that all of us would have welcomed certain whites: someone whose work was close to Latino or Asian communities and whose ideas were at least in part informed by their perspectives—a latter-day version of Carey McWilliams, in other words. I would be the last person to argue that whites cannot teach or do good research in race relations.[9]

Still I was and remain discouraged by my sense that members of my department (leftists as well as centrists) have given up much of their commitment to the affirmative action that has been a part of our culture for so many years. With my arguments for the first time falling on deaf ears, I sensed a complacency about our progress—and we do have considerably more women and minorities than most departments at Berkeley.

The student boycott may have ended that complacency, but I take little comfort in the overturn of the hiring decision because such legalistic bureaucratic concerns give affirmative action a bad name. And I see my department's priorities today as primarily focused on the enhancement of its prestige in the profession rather than on social and political change or a liberal arts teaching mission. And, pointedly not considered by the search committee for that race relations position, I felt my own marginality once again.

In *Black Live, White Lives,* there is a white woman I call Virginia Lawrence whose long commitment to "an integrated life" set her off from the rest of the people in the book. I cannot honestly say my own life has been thoroughly integrated, even though over the years people of color have usually made up more than half of the entries in my address books. But most have been work associates, students, and acquaintances rather than intimate friends. With the important exception of two men in my men's group, my closest friends have been white, reflecting the fact that most social worlds remain separate in our society. And in my various periods of singlehood I had never gone out with a Black American. At times I shied away from a possible relationship because I did not want to be part of a historical legacy of sexual exploitation, until 1988, when I began a very important relationship with an African American woman, a scholar in a distant but still related field. I was more optimistic than she was about overcoming the difficulties of an interracial relationship, as well as reconciling our personal and cultural differences. Though our romantic connection lasted only two or three years, it was a deeply meaningful one. I learned much about myself in relation to Black people, including the fact that much of my "knowledge" about African Americans had been abstract book knowledge, based on a kind of intellectual or political identification. With more firsthand experience it became clear that although I admire Black culture, it is not really my own.

My relationship with this woman began just before my book was published, and perhaps the timing was not accidental. But on the level of my psyche, I may have been trying to heal the nation's historic and continuing chasm between Black and white. From this standpoint, it is interesting that the woman I now love, and to whom I am now married, was born in Germany. She has innumerable inimitable qualities, besides the fact that she is deeply spiritual and an artist—traits that have become much more important to me as I enter my older years. But the German connection cannot be accidental either. Growing up in the aftermath of World War II, Karina has worked, through her poetry and performances, to confront the meaning of the Holocaust and the war, those very historical experiences that most formed me—and have long remained unresolved on some deeper level. So our meeting must be—among many other things—about healing a number of splits in my consciousness: that of my European and American heritages and that between Jew and Gentile that so marked my childhood.

Thus Karina and I have been partners in a mutual project of exploring the meaning of Jewishness in each of our lives. Yet even before I met her new rumblings of ethnic identity were rising within me. Though unlike many of my more strongly Jewish- and Israeli-identified friends, I unequivocally opposed the Gulf War, I still felt some (unexpected) sympathy with Israelis under siege. At a meeting to discuss relations between Jews and non-Jews in the antiwar movement, I felt frightened on a visceral level by some of the rage expressed toward Jewish students. It was my first experience since childhood with raw anti-Semitism, and it scared me. I thought about studying Yiddish and planned to go that summer to Israel, where a paper of mine had been accepted at a conference. Neither the language nor the trip has yet come off, but when I taught a course in Berkeley's new American cultures curriculum, I chose Jews as one of the three groups I covered.

At this late date I am not likely to become a strongly identified or active Jew. But I am no longer resisting my heritage as insistently and no longer need that earlier identification with African Americans to fill the vacuums of ethnic identity, manhood, and meaning in my life. At the same time, many of my life's endeavors—the political choices, the sociology, the writing—were responses to those older dynamics. And it is this that I can now look back on, not without some regret, but in general with a sense of satisfaction that the result is a lifework that has been meaningful to me and, I would hope, valuable to others.

A Final Note

An earlier and much shorter version of this piece was written as an epilogue to *Black Lives, White Lives.* My editors rejected it out of a fear that my candor about my political past would prejudice potential readers and reviewers, branding the book's author as an ex-Communist 1960s Berkeley radical. Though I disagreed, I did not argue with a press that had been so supportive and patient in waiting for my manuscript all those years. Biding my time until the book was well launched, I persuaded them to include it in the second printing.

It seemed important to me then that a book of "racial life histories"— as I call the personal accounts in that work—should include the author's own story, particularly when that author is white. Today, young people, particularly African American young people, have few models of whites who are engaged or otherwise care passionately about racial justice.

Nothing impressed this on me as clearly as an interview with a young journalist a few years ago. She never could get past her first question: "Why did you, a white man, write a book about race and Black people?" She was convinced I must have witnessed a lynching or something just as extreme at an impressionable age. This essay has been an attempt to answer that reporter's question, as much to my own satisfaction as to hers or to anyone else's. In a lifetime in which I have indulged in much self-reflection, tasted many varieties of psychotherapy and other explorations of consciousness, and undoubtedly wasted too much time in obsessive brooding, I have never satisfactorily figured out the mystery of this enduring theme of my life. And if in this piece I have engaged in much psychologizing, I hope I have also made it clear that my commitments to race and radicalism have not been determined simply by accidents of personal biography but also have been principled political and moral responses to the realities of American life.

Notes

1. "The Russians are pigs too," I whispered to attorney Faye Stender as the judge brought the court to order the morning after Soviet tanks rolled into Czechoslovakia, crushing the Prague Spring.

2. The essay was to be a review of Jackson's moving *Soledad Brother,* a book of prison letters published in 1971, supplemented by an account of my visit with him at San Quentin a few months before he was killed.

3. This is the no-win situation of the "left colonizer" that Albert Memmi has so brilliantly described in his *The Colonizer and the Colonized* (1991).

4. One 1972 chapter, "Marxism, Nationalism, and Colonialism," enjoyed quite an underground circulation during the 1970s, and I intend to publish it in a new book of essays.

5. This was thanks in part to its inclusion in Ronald Takaki's 1987 anthology, *From Different Shores.* I have no idea whether it is related to the new race relations situation since the mid-1980s, but in the last several years I have seen a renewed interest in my writings on internal colonialism. During the 1970s and early 1980s, many sociologists, including people with similar views, seemed loath even to footnote me.

6. For an earlier brief comment on "the declining significance of race" and the class-race issue, see Blauner (1989, p. 170).

7. I suspect the absence of a felt place for white males today in the "identity politics" that so dominates liberal and progressive circles is one reason for the emergence of a "men's movement" in the past few years. Despite obvious differences, there is a parallel to the women's movement's emergence in the late 1960s and the 1970s, when white women (for the most part) developed feminism after the nationalism of the civil rights movement and the sexism of the antiwar movement left them without a political home.

8. In a recent article I elaborate these different meanings of racism as well as the distinction between race and ethnicity (see Blauner, 1992).

9. In 30 years, my legitimacy on this matter has been challenged at most two or three times: in the late 1960s by a Black professor in a professional school and in the early 1970s by one or two undergraduates.

References

Blauner, B. (1964). *Alienation and freedom: The factory worker and his industry.* Chicago: University of Chicago Press.

Blauner, B. (1972). *Racial oppression in America.* New York: HarperCollins.

Blauner, B. (1987). Colonized and immigrant minorities. In R. Takaki (Ed.), *From different shores: Perspectives on race and ethnicity in America.* New York: Oxford University Press. (Original work published 1971)

Blauner, B. (1989). *Black lives, white lives: Three decades of race relations in America.* Berkeley: University of California Press.

Blauner, B. (1992). Talking past one another: Black and white languages of race. *American Prospect, 11,* 56-65.

Memmi, A. (1991). *The colonizer and the colonized* (rev. ed.). Boston: Beacon.

Myrdal, G., with Sterner, R., & Rose, A. (1944). *An American dilemma: The Negro problem and modern democracy.* New York: Harper & Row.

Rich, A. (1985). Split at the root. In U. Owen (Ed.), *Fathers: Reflections by daughters.* New York: Pantheon.

Styron, W. (1967). *The confessions of Nat Turner.* New York: Random House.

Terkel, S. (1974). *Working.* New York: Ballantine.

Wellman, D., & Blauner, B. (1970). Toward the decolonization of social research. In J. Ladner (Ed.), *The death of white sociology.* New York: Random House.

2

Studying the Ghetto Economy

DANIEL R. FUSFELD

How It All Began

It was a telephone call from Fred Hoehler, who was then running labor education programs for the Labor and Industrial Relations Center at Michigan State University. I don't remember the date and I can't look it up, because the economics building at the University of Michigan burned down some years later and most of my records turned to ashes or water-soaked pulp. But it was sometime in the late summer or early fall of 1967, shortly after the Black riots in Detroit and Newark.

Hoehler asked me if I would be willing to give a lecture to a group of union people on the economic costs of the recent riots. "Sure," I responded, thinking I could go to the library, cannibalize some data, string them together with some analysis and anecdotes, and have my lecture. But when I went to the library I found that there were no data. Furthermore, the economics profession had absolutely nothing to say at that time about the economics of the inner-city ghettos or how they fit into the complex modern economy.

The Seminar

So I put a notice on the department bulletin board:

WANTED: ONE GRADUATE STUDENT TO WRITE A DOCTORAL DIS-
SERTATION ON THE ECONOMIC COSTS OF THE URBAN RIOTS. SEE
PROF. FUSFELD.

Twelve graduate students applied, so I organized a seminar. It was
outside the department's regular program, so no course credit was
given, and it was over and above my regular teaching load. Nevertheless, we met once a week for the next five years or so. We read widely
in the works of historians, sociologists, psychologists, and other social
scientists that dealt with the urban ghettos, their history, and the people
there, and even found some publications by economists. We delved into
census reports and population studies; the effects of migration, immigration, and technological change; discrimination and racism; the effects
of slavery and other forms of constrained labor. We looked intensively at
theories of exploitation and uneven economic development, from Marx
through Myrdal to writers on imperialism—and much more. Some of
the works that affected our thinking most heavily were by Gunnar Myrdal
(1968, app. 2, secs. 2, 4, 5, 8-11) on circular causation with cumulative
effects, F. Y. Edgeworth (1922) and Barbara Bergmann (1971) on labor
market crowding, Richard Day (1967) on technological change in southern
agriculture, and Charles Killingsworth (1968) on Blacks in the changing
labor market. You may note that none of these ideas were to be found in
the mainstream of economic thinking, either then or now.

One result of our work was an early version of the theory of structured
labor markets—that the low-wage workers of the inner cities functioned
in a sector of the labor market quite different from the mainstream labor
market. This analysis appeared at about the same time as the work of
Peter Doeringer and Michael Piore on internal labor markets.

I am sometimes given credit as one of the originators of the structured
labor market theory (e.g., Vietorisz & Harrison, 1973, review the
literature on segmented labor markets to the early 1970s), which was
included in some of my early papers on the ghetto economy. That's
wrong. It was the collective work of the members of the seminar,
particularly Barry Bluestone. I merely wrote it up out of the seminar's
discussions.

I can't recall all the names and my records are gone, but the group
included Howard Wachtel, Larry Sawers, Mary Huff Stephenson, Michael
Zwieg, and John Weeks, among others whose names have fled my aging
and cluttered memory. Some four or five doctoral dissertations related
directly to the work of the seminar, or influenced by it, came out of our

group, along with a number of papers of my own. My chief function in the seminar was to synthesize and summarize the work we were doing. Most of my early publications in this area were the result of the joint work of the members of the seminar.

What We Found

We discovered a portion of the economic world that lay outside the mainstream economy. Urban ghettos are a world apart that does not share in the affluence and technical progress of the mainstream. Their populations are analogous to, but different from, the marginal populations of the Third World. Permanent economic depression prevails, with high unemployment rates even in the best of times, a high incidence of poverty, and a population imbued with hostility, anger, apathy, and hopelessness.

Yet this subsector of American society performs an important function. It is a source of low-wage labor that provides cheap services and products to the mainstream economy. The chief beneficiaries are the more affluent middle-income families outside the ghetto who buy the products and services produced by low-wage labor. This is one reason we lack programs that would eliminate or significantly reduce the ghetto poverty that is the source of this low-wage labor. There are too many relatively affluent voters outside the ghetto who benefit from the poverty there and would have to pay taxes to support such programs.

Perhaps our most important finding concerned the flow of resources out of and into the urban ghettos. First, there is a continuous flow of resources from the urban ghetto into the mainstream economy. Savings move into financial institutions outside the ghetto for loans outside. Capital moves out in the form of deteriorating housing and public facilities. Human capital moves out, as many of the best and brightest escape the ghetto into the mainstream economy. Income flows out through purchases of goods and services produced outside the ghetto in stores owned outside the ghetto whose employees live outside.

Second, these outflows of funds and resources are balanced by large inflows of income from government services and transfer payments. Earnings by people living in the urban ghetto are not large enough to balance the ghetto economy's outflow. Without government transfers there would be a continuing decline in the level of life in the ghetto until the outflows fell to equality with the inflows.

Inner-city poverty generates crime, drug use, single-parent families, and other "social pathologies," as they have come to be called. We deal with them not only through government services and income transfers but also with law enforcement and jail terms. These methods compound the problem: Police records and jail terms keep men and women out of the mainstream labor market, forcing them permanently into the low-wage sector or the criminal portion of the underground economy. This is a good example of Myrdal's circular causation with cumulative effects.

Law enforcement in the inner city has a further implication. It is one of the chief means by which ghetto discontent is held in check. We stabilize the ghettos partly through bribery (government services and transfer payments) and partly through force (law enforcement, courts, and jails). When all the rhetoric is stripped away, that is exactly what our public policies amount to.

Another example of circular causation with cumulative effects is the reduction of funds available to inner-city schools because of the exodus of middle-income families to the suburbs and the consequent decline in tax revenues for the support of education. At the same time, the need for educational funds is increased because of difficulties in educating poor children. Children of poverty need more educational funds per pupil than children of affluence, but the outflow of resources from the inner city means that they get less. The result is another generation largely condemned to poverty.

We were also able to add a pattern of population dynamics to our conceptual framework. The number of people in the urban ghettos is increased by population growth. It is also increased by people moving into the ghettos from outside: immigration from other countries, people displaced by economic and technological change (such as the great Black migration to the North in the late 1940s and early 1950s), and people discharged from jails or mental hospitals. At the same time, the ghetto population declines as people overcome the barriers to exit and move out, are sentenced to prison, or return to their countries of origin. The size of the ghetto population rises or falls in response to these movements of people.

We also found that economic development and technological change do not solve the problems of the ghettos. Several major technological changes associated with economic development helped create and pre-serve the urban ghettos. One was the technological transformation of southern agriculture after World War II. This included mechanized planting, cultivating, and harvesting of cotton, and the substitution of soybeans for corn. The demand for labor fell drastically. Black labor was dispensed with, leading to a massive migration to the North between about 1947 and 1953.

A second technological change was the shift of industry from city to suburb in the North, which began at about the same time as the great migration of 1947-1953. This shift was driven by technology. New automated production methods required continuous-flow processes, which required single-story factories spread over many acres, as well as large parking areas. The old-fashioned, multistory factories of the crowded cities could not take full advantage of the new methods or the shift to automobile and truck transportation.

As jobs moved to the suburbs, the new residential areas there were off-limits to Blacks and Hispanics. These restrictions were not eased until the 1970s and 1980s. By then, the Black migrants from the South and Hispanics from Latin America were ghettoized in poverty, unable to take advantage of the reduced housing segregation in the suburbs.

A related technological change was the shift from public transportation in the cities, which enabled workers to get to jobs in the urban factories, to automobile transportation, which workers in the new suburban factories used. This shift made it difficult and expensive for urban workers who lost jobs in the urban factories to get to the new jobs available in the suburbs. In the 1940s the population of the urban ghettos included a significant number of high-wage employees in the automobile, steel, and rubber industries, among others. By the 1990s this group had largely disappeared from the inner cities, partly because jobs were lost and partly through moves to the suburbs as housing restrictions diminished. The inner cities were left poorer.

More economic change came in the 1970s and 1980s. As the economy shifted to electronics and processing of data and information, new jobs opened up. These jobs required more educational skills than the older factory jobs, were located largely in the suburbs and exurbs, and were filled in large part by young white men and women. Blacks and Hispanics in the inner cities could not get to them because of a lack of public transportation, and the schools of the inner cities did not provide the necessary educational skills.

A startling proposition emerges: Economic development involves technological change, and technological change creates poverty. Some jobs are destroyed, the locations of jobs shift, and the skills required change. These changes are felt particularly severely in the low-wage sector of the economy, where workers are less able to adapt to economic and technical change. The low-wage sector is also the recipient of many workers displaced by a changing economy.

I have said little, to this point, about racism and the historical heritage of Blacks in the United States. These factors are terribly important, of course. Our seminar had little to add to the huge amount of scholarship devoted to these topics. We did, however, develop a general concept that helped us understand the linkages in the long history of Blacks from slavery to the modern urban ghetto: constrained labor. Slavery is a classic case of human labor forced by law into economic exploitation. After slavery was ended in 1865, it was replaced by sharecropping and debt peonage enforced by law and custom in a South controlled politically and economically by whites, especially after the "compromise of 1876," which gave Hayes the presidency over Tilden. The combination of sharecropping and debt peonage was another form of constrained labor, but without the legal bonds of slavery. Then came the great depression of the 1890s, in which skilled Black workers (carpenters, longshoremen, barbers, and so on) were largely driven from their jobs, chiefly in southern cities, and forced into low-wage jobs. This was also the period in which the political disenfranchisement of southern Blacks was completed, and in which the U.S. Supreme Court upheld the so-called separate but equal doctrine. Segregation was legalized, including the terribly unequal education system of the South, and in some parts of the North, that left Black children with few choices beyond the exploitative systems of sharecropping and debt peonage in rural areas or low-wage employment in cities. The Black middle class was often able to escape these forms of constrained labor, but the vast majority of Blacks could not.

Crowding of Blacks into low-wage employment meant that wages in those jobs were pushed below the levels they would have reached without crowding. Wage levels in those sectors were pushed even lower by the huge northern migration of 1947-1953, which also triggered a huge increase in Black unemployment. In 1940 the Black unemployment rate was less than that of whites, largely because many Blacks were employed in southern agriculture. By 1955, after the migration, the Black unemployment rate was double that of whites, and it has remained there to the present. Crowding of Blacks in low-wage occupations also resulted in somewhat higher wages for whites in the other occupations, because of reduced competition for jobs there. White workers were among the beneficiaries of the way labor markets were structured.

We found, then, that Blacks were still being exploited in a system of constrained labor. Labor market crowding, unlike the quasi-legal patterns of sharecropping and debt peonage or the formal institution of slavery, is an informal system centering in the structure of labor markets. But it is constrained labor nevertheless. It remains today in the form of the structure and dynamics of the ghetto economy, which continually recreates and reinforces a marginal population excluded from mainstream society and economy. Some call it "institutionalized racism."

A Note on Method

I have just described a pattern model. It begins with descriptive data derived from empirical studies of the real world. The observed data are then linked together to form a group of unifying concepts, which together form a conceptual framework. The conceptual framework has two parts. One part explains the institutional structure of the phenomenon under investigation; the other explains the processes operating within the institutional structure and its connection with other structures. The conceptual framework can then be modified or amended as further empirical data are obtained, as conditions change, and as the perspective widens.

Pattern models have great advantages. They rest upon empirical data throughout, not upon initial assumptions that may or may not be empirically verified. The unifying concepts that create the larger conceptual framework can be modified as further data are accumulated. The conceptual framework itself is open-ended, in the sense that it can be modified to accommodate changes over time. It can also be enlarged as empirical studies extend its scope. Pattern models, then, are never complete or definitive, but they enable investigators to develop a continually deepening understanding of the phenomena under study.

The proposition that there is a steady outflow of resources from the ghetto is a good example of a unifying concept derived from empirical data. Our seminar found individual studies that showed outward flows of capital through deterioration of housing and public facilities, outward flow of savings through financial institutions, outward flow of income through retail sales, and outward flow of human capital as better educated and more capable individuals were able to escape the ghetto and enter the mainstream economy. Putting these empirical studies together led to the unifying concept of a general outflow of resources.

This generalization was confirmed not by the seminar, but by a comprehensive study done elsewhere of a Black ghetto in Brooklyn, New York, and a nearby middle-income neighborhood. The study was designed to test whether the ghetto had a larger overall deficit in its flows of capital, income, and savings. It showed that was indeed the case, whereas the inward and outward flows in the middle-income neighborhood largely balanced (Schaffer, 1973).

Once the outflow concept was established, it was easy to fit government services and transfer payments into the model as the balancing flow that stabilized the system. It then followed that the larger the inflow of transfer payments, the larger would be the outflow out of the higher income. The level of life within the ghetto would be raised, but no process of internal economic development would start. The ghetto would remain a poor, economically backward area with a marginal population largely outside the mainstream economy and society. Eliminating the ghetto would require new institutional structures to reduce or eliminate the outflow of income, savings, physical capital, and human capital.

Unfortunately, just the opposite has happened, and conditions within the inner cities have deteriorated further. The introduction of crack cocaine in the mid-1980s both accelerated the outflow of income to pay for the new import and significantly altered the use of income and the direction of its flow. My own rough estimate—or guess, if you wish—is that by 1989 purchases of crack and other drugs by residents of the urban ghettos amounted to some 25-40% of the value of government transfer payments into the ghetto, with the percentage varying from one city or neighborhood to the next. Government transfer payments are a significant source of spending for drugs.

The flight of the Black middle class also had a devastating effect on the urban ghettos. It was made possible by the breakup of housing segregation in the suburbs, the opening of jobs in government and private enterprise, and a variety of affirmative action programs in government, business, and educational institutions. Many of the best and the brightest were able to leave inner-city poverty areas to find better and safer lives elsewhere. They took with them, however, a great deal of human capital and leadership. Not all of the Black or Hispanic middle class left for the suburbs, but even those who remained moved out the areas of concentrated poverty. Changes that benefited a minority worsened conditions for the majority.

An aside: How many universities, busily engaged in recruiting Blacks and Hispanics from the inner-cities, have programs to help the ghettos overcome the loss of human capital and potential leadership? That question is seldom asked, because we tend to think of inner-city poverty areas within the framework of methodological individualism: All actions are individual actions and result from individual motivations. This viewpoint leads to policies that seek to change individuals: education, better health care, training for job skills, and so on. Many of these programs may help individuals escape the ghetto, but they do little to change the institutional structure and processes of the ghetto economy. And although some are able to move up and out of the ghetto, others are moving down and in, impelled by economic and technical change, or released from prisons or mental institutions, or coming as immigrants from abroad.

All actions may well be traceable to individual behavior—but what of the functionally illiterate 24-year-old Black man who could read, write, add, and subtract when he graduated from high school at 19? In the intervening years he didn't have to use those skills, and his store of human capital withered away. A pattern model focusing on institutions and processes helps us understand his case, and much more, better than the implicit assumptions and political agenda of methodological individualism.

The Intellectual and Political Environment

The conceptual framework of the ghetto economy sketched here was not developed in isolation. It was born during a period of turmoil within academia generated by outside events: the civil rights movement, the Vietnam War, the women's movement, the sexual revolution of the 1960s, and the killings at Jackson State and Kent State, as well as the urban riots.

Many of the members of my seminar, probably most, were radicalized by those events. So was I. I would describe myself, as of 1965, as a liberal Keynesian economist opposed to big business oligopoly, supportive of labor unions, and in favor of a more egalitarian distribution of income. I didn't like the way the federal government was wasting the nation's resources on a futile arms race with the Soviet Union or supporting authoritarian governments in the Third World. I voted Democratic, although sometimes I had to close my eyes and hold my nose when pulling some of the levers in the voting booth.

By 1970, events had pushed me toward the left. I reread Marx after many years, and Veblen as well. I began teaching classes in Marxist economics, being careful to point out that Soviet Stalinism was a far cry from Marx's brilliant critique of classical economics and incisive analysis of the industrial capitalism of his day. I participated in the organization of the Union for Radical Political Economics (URPE). I supported the Black action movement at the University of Michigan and the opposition on campus to the Vietnam War—causing several of my departmental colleagues to stop speaking to me for some years afterward. I supported the drive to get the university to sell its investments in firms doing business in South Africa. Academically, I moved further and further away from the applied mathematics of general equilibrium theory, which had come to dominate mainstream economics.

My first paper on the economics of the urban ghetto, titled "The Basic Economics of the Urban and Racial Crisis," was presented at the first annual conference of the Union for Radical Political Economics (Fusfeld, 1968a), as was my first paper analyzing the economic and political forces that brought the United States into the Vietnam quagmire. That paper was titled "Fascist Democracy in the United States," later modified and toned down as "The Rise of the Corporate State in America" (see Fusfeld, 1968b). My work on the ghetto economy was one product of a liberal economist who had been radicalized by events.

The idea that a ghetto economy and marginal population is a functional (or should I say dysfunctional) element in a private enterprise economy, and is the direct result of the way that economy functions, is indeed a radical concept. The proposition that many in the private sector benefit directly or indirectly from the ghetto economy and exploitation of the marginal population is equally radical. So is the policy conclusion that major changes will have to occur if those conditions are to be altered. One implication of the analysis is that elimination of the ghetto economy, its poverty and backwardness, will provide a larger share of the nation's goods to those who are now poor and a smaller share to those who are now affluent. That is why it won't happen without some "revolutionary" changes.

"Just Shut Up!"

"The Basic Economics of the Urban and Racial Crisis" was distributed in part at the National Black Economic Development Conference in Detroit in 1969. I was proud of that. The participants were given three items: a speech by John F. Kennedy, a speech by Malcolm X, and my paper. You may recall that the conference called for reparations to Blacks for decades of repression and exploitation.

A few days after the conference—I wasn't invited and didn't attend— I was at a meeting in Ann Arbor that discussed problems of Black employment. A Black carpenter who had attended the Detroit conference gave a summary of my analysis of the ghetto economy, but with a few inaccuracies. I spoke up: "That's a pretty good summary, but you didn't get it quite right." He angrily shot back: "I was at the conference and you weren't, so just shut up." I shut up.

Postgenesis

Our analysis of the ghetto economy was well received by Blacks, and it stimulated considerable interest. URPE published it as a pamphlet. A somewhat expanded version was in the first issue of the *Review of Black Political Economy,* an augmented version was published in *The Michigan Academician,* and variations on the theme were published elsewhere (see Fusfeld, 1969, 1970a, 1970b, 1970c, 1973b, 1975, 1980, 1981).

However, the analysis was never accepted by economists and social scientists in general. It was largely ignored by academics, with some exceptions. I think there were several reasons for that. First, we argued that the urban ghettos were inherent in American attitudes and economic institutions. Ghettos were not an aberration that could be eliminated by an antipoverty program or other reforms. A serious rethinking and remodeling of basic economic relationships was required, including fundamental changes in the distribution of income and the structure and locus of power. The entire analysis was a challenge to things as they were. Themes of that sort were not highly popular among academics during the Cold War era.

Second, the idea that economic factors were at the heart of the ghetto problem was not compatible with the received wisdom of either liberal reformers or stand-pat conservatives. It was a lot easier to attribute the existence of urban ghettos to racist attitudes or the heritage of the past. Thus Gary Becker (1957), then at Princeton, could publish the idea that whites had a "taste for discrimination." The fault was not with our economic institutions, but with the attitudes of whites, which could be changed by the proper types of education, along with a gradually

increasing pattern of white-Black interaction. This nonsense was actually taken seriously by economists.[1]

I felt, too, that the general rejection of theories of economic determinism, which was one result of the Cold War and scholarly rejection
of Marxism, also worked against our analysis. Economic relationships
were certainly at the heart of our work on the ghetto economy, but we
had carefully steered clear of a class analysis or class theory. It just did
not fit the facts.

Finally, the analysis was not based on the assumption of individual
economic rationality, nor was it expressed in the mathematical form that
had become the dominant style in economic discourse. The analysis was
far too complex to be presented in the relatively simple mathematics
available to economists. It would be compromised by the simplifying
assumptions needed to fit the reality to the mathematics and the analysis
to the individual rationality assumption.

Nevertheless, there was a great deal of concern about the urban
ghettos in the early 1970s, so I put together a small book to take
advantage of what looked like a good potential market (Fusfeld, 1973a).
It was merely a pastiche of what our seminar and some others had found,
and made no scholarly contribution whatever, but it was quickly accepted by a publisher. Unfortunately, the publisher went through a
series of reorganizations, the manuscript was apparently mislaid, and
three years went by before the book saw the light of day. It was printed
in tiny type on cheap paper, and given absolutely no marketing push.
By then there was little general interest in the topic. I learned two
lessons: Don't prostitute your scholarship in an effort to make a fast
buck and, if you do, make sure you get a big advance—it will sustain
the publisher's interest in the project.

Turmoil in the inner cities had died down by the early 1970s. The
revolt of the late 1960s had been calmed and turned inward by large
increases in welfare and other transfer payments, and by increased law
enforcement. Public policy focused on a strategy of fostering the advancement of individuals through education, affirmative action, elimination of housing and school segregation, and opening the political
process to minorities. The economic basis of poverty and ghettoization
was largely ignored.

By the mid-1970s my own interests were turning elsewhere: toward
worker-managed enterprises, the corporate state in America, and theoretical and methodological problems of mainstream economics. My
interest in the ghetto economy remained, but it was secondary to a larger

critique of the America political economy and its economic rationale. I was moving from a critical analysis of the urban ghetto to a larger critical analysis of the American political economy.

Then I got another push from outside, this time from Timothy Bates, then at the University of Vermont, in the winter of 1980. Bates had been doing some path-breaking work on business enterprise in the urban ghetto and some related topics. He had used some of my papers on the economics of the urban ghetto in his teaching and liked the analysis. He proposed that we combine our talents to produce an up-to-date historical, empirical, and theoretical analysis of the inner-city ghettos. Why not? I thought; it was obvious that the policy strategies of the 1970s did little to change the situation in the inner cities. Maybe a new look would make a contribution. So we became coauthors and found a publisher. The result was *The Political Economy of the Urban Ghetto* (Fusfeld & Bates, 1984). It was successful enough for the publisher to ask us to work on a revised and updated version. We hope to submit a manuscript in 1993.

In Retrospect

Studying the ghetto economy has been a frustrating experience. Although I learned a great deal about the American underclass and its relationship to the national economy, I also learned that the American political system is unprepared and unwilling to take the steps necessary to change things significantly. Indeed, conditions in the poverty areas have become worse, despite programs designed to help.

The violence of the riots of the 1960s was ended and the ghettos were stabilized by a strategy that combined income payments and law enforcement. One result was that the violence and frustration were turned inward toward crime and drugs, which resulted in escalating costs of law enforcement and prisons on the one hand and further disintegration of inner-city communities and family structure on the other.

Another arm of the policy strategy, designed to open job opportunities, education, and housing, benefited primarily the Black and Hispanic middle class, but deprived the inner cities of leadership, capital, and purchasing power. As whites and middle-class Blacks fled the inner cities, Blacks and Hispanics took over many city governments, creating a new middle class centering in public employment and other activities related to government services. But tax receipts fell and city services deteriorated as the proportion of poor Blacks and Hispanics rose.

Meanwhile, relatively high-wage employment in manufacturing industries fell substantially under the impact of international competition. The new jobs in other manufacturing and service industries appeared in the suburbs and exurbs, rather than in the inner cities. Uneven economic development helped worsen the problems of poverty and unemployment in the inner cities.

In another, almost unstudied, development, low-wage industries were helped by government policies that encouraged immigration, allowed the real value of the minimum wage to deteriorate, and cut back on enforcement of a variety of worker-protection laws and regulations.

By the early 1990s it became clear that the United States had a permanent marginal population embedded in the inner cities, largely isolated from the economic forces that lead to economic development and affluence, and excluded from the mainstream of society. We bemoan its existence but do little to mitigate its worsening condition.[2] When will it next explode?

Notes

1. The reasons Becker's theory is nonsense are explained in Fusfeld and Bates (1984, pp. 174-177).

2. You will have to wait for the revised edition of *The Political Economy of the Urban Ghetto* to find out what Bates and I propose. This essay already exceeds the editor's limits.

References

Becker, G. S. (1957). *The economics of discrimination*. Chicago: University of Chicago Press.

Bergmann, B. (1971). Effect on white incomes of discrimination in employment. *Journal of Political Economy, 29*, 294-313.

Day, R. (1967). The economics of technological change and the demise of the sharecropper. *American Economic Review, 57*, 427-438.

Edgeworth, F. Y. (1922). Equal pay to men and women for equal work. *Economic Journal, 31*, 431-457.

Fusfeld, D. R. (1968a). The basic economics of the urban and racial crisis. In *Conference papers of the Union for Radical Political Economics, December 1968*. Ann Arbor, MI: Union for Radical Political Economics.

Fusfeld, D. R. (1968b). Fascist democracy in the United States. In *Conference papers of the Union for Radical Political Economics, December 1968*. Ann Arbor, MI: Union for Radical Political Economics.

Fusfeld, D. R. (1969). Anatomy of the ghetto economy. *New Generation, 51*(2), 2-6.

Fusfeld, D. R. (1970a). The basic economics of the urban and racial crisis. *Review of Black Political Economy, 1,* 58-63.

Fusfeld, D. R. (1970b). The basic economics of the urban and racial crisis. *Michigan Academician, 2*(3), 3-34.

Fusfeld, D. R. (1970c). The economy of the urban ghetto. In J. P. Crecine (Ed.), *Financing the metropolis.* Beverly Hills, CA: Sage.

Fusfeld, D. R. (1973a). *The basic economics of the urban racial crisis.* New York: Holt, Rinehart & Winston.

Fusfeld, D. R. (1973b). Welfare payments and the ghetto economy. In K. E. Boulding, M. Pfaff, & A. B. Pfaff (Eds.), *Transfers in an urbanized economy* (pp. 78-92). Belmont, CA: Wadsworth.

Fusfeld, D. R. (1975). The economics of the inner city ghetto. In W. F. Owen & H. Ulveling (Eds.), *Selected readings from the Economics Institute's Special Lecture Series* (pp. 261-272). Boulder: University of Colorado, Economics Institute.

Fusfeld, D. R. (1980). Capitalist exploitation and Black labor: An extended conceptual framework. *Review of Black Political Economy, 10,* 244-246.

Fusfeld, D. R. (1981). The ghetto economy. In J. E. Darden (Ed.), *The ghetto: Readings with interpretations* (pp. 131-156). Port Washington, NY: Kennikat.

Fusfeld, D. R., & Bates, T. (1984). *The political economy of the urban ghetto.* Carbondale: Southern Illinois University Press.

Killingsworth, C. C. (1968). *Jobs and incomes for Negroes.* Ann Arbor: University of Michigan, Institute for Labor and Industrial Relations.

Myrdal, G. (1968). *Asian drama* (Vol. 3). New York: Random House.

Schaffer, R. L. (1973). *Income flows in urban poverty areas: A comparison of the community income accounts of Bedford-Stuyvesant and Borough Park.* Lexington, MA: Lexington.

Vietorisz, T., & Harrison, B. (1973). Labor market segmentation: Positive feedback and divergent development. *American Economic Review, 63,* 366-376.

3

From Assimilation
to Human Nature (and Back)

MILTON M. GORDON

I came to study racial and ethnic relations and found that, some successes aside, I needed to study the human being and society instead. Although such an epigrammatic statement vastly oversimplifies, there is enough truth in it to allow me to state that it is basically the theme of this chapter. But let us go back to the beginning.

I was born, the son of immigrant Jewish parents from Russia, in a small town on the banks of the Kennebec River in inland Maine. Why my parents had gone to Maine after arriving in the United States, rather than settling with most of their fellow Jewish immigrants in New York or Boston, I, to this day, do not really know. But there they were, and there I grew up, subject to the influences of two cultures: the immigrant Jewish in the home, and the Yankee Protestant—liberally leavened with working-class French Canadian and Irish Catholic—in the community. There were perhaps a half dozen other Jewish families in the town, but these were ecologically dispersed, and most of the children I played with were the sons and daughters of Yankee farmers and shopkeepers and French Canadian and Irish factory workers.

AUTHOR'S NOTE: This chapter is a revised and updated version of my article, "Linking Sociology and Psychology: What's a Nice Cultural Determinist Like You Doing in a Place Like Human Nature?" *Society,* Vol. 17, No. 4 (May-June 1980), pp. 56-62 © Transaction Publishers. Used by permission.

My father had started out as a manual laborer, cutting ice on the local river in winter, then turned to peddling, and finally, through very hard work and ability, had become a successful small-town businessman. However, as was customary with immigrants, when he became more prosperous he continued to live and maintain his family in one of the poorest sections of the town, literally on the wrong side of the railroad tracks. Anti-Semitism, albeit not of crisis proportions, was predictably present on occasion, although I do not recall any such manifestation from my teachers in the public schools. I was definitely, however, a classic case of the marginal man—or, more accurately, the marginal boy—in this case, marginal in terms of both ethnic group and social class.

When I was 13 years old, my family was broken by divorce and I moved with my mother to the largest city in Maine—Portland. There, for the first time, I became part of an organized and reasonably numerous Jewish subcommunity and discovered the comforts and solace of operating within its boundaries. There had evolved among the Jewish high school students a rather elaborate system of fraternities and sororities, ethnically confined and divided by social class. On Sunday nights, the Jewish fraternities and sororities met separately in members' homes for their portentous business and arcane rites. After the meetings, the sorority girls held open house for the boys. The boys from the middle-class fraternities appeared at the middle-class sorority girls' homes, and the boys from the working class found their way to the homes of the corresponding class of sorority girls. It was quite a lesson in sociology. Some of my readers will perhaps recognize therein the origins of the concept of *ethclass,* which figures prominently in my later work.

After high school, I went to Bowdoin College in my native state. Bowdoin was then, and is now, an excellent undergraduate academic institution, with a cultural ethos embracing both "little Ivy League" values and loyalty to the sturdy, unpretentious folk of the state of Maine. The student fraternity system was overwhelming in strength and discriminatory against Jews and the few Blacks who were then present in the college. To my knowledge, only two Jews were invited to join a fraternity during my four years there. One was an all-New England guard on the football team; the other was very wealthy, came from the Midwest, and was probably of German rather than Eastern European origin. Needless to say, I qualified on none of these counts. My companions were largely the other Jewish boys of modest background from Maine and the rest of New England. I received a very fine education in the liberal arts and further exposure to the problematics of ethnicity and social class.

My sociology mentor at Bowdoin was a prince among men—Elbridge Sibley. He was a Columbia Ph.D., and my first textbook in sociology was MacIver's *Society* (1937). Lynd and Lynd's (1937) second Middletown study appeared during my undergraduate years. There was no question that I would aim for Columbia for my graduate study. I was accepted, and arrived in New York City in the fall of 1939 equipped with a Bowdoin A.B., *magna cum laude,* a Phi Beta Kappa key, and a Maine accent, eager to experience the delights—intellectual and otherwise—of this great metropolitan universe that promised so much. I was not disappointed!

Studying sociology at Columbia in the late 1930s and early 1940s was an extraordinarily exciting and rewarding experience. In addition to courses with MacIver and Lynd, I learned research logic from Paul Lazarsfeld, who had recently joined the department, and ran punch cards and compiled contingency tables in his newly instituted research arm—called then the Office of Radio Research, later to become the famous "Bureau." Robert Merton joined the department as a young, brilliant theorist from Harvard, by way of Tulane, whose work already augured great things. In adjacent Schermerhorn Hall, Ruth Benedict and Ralph Linton taught cultural anthropology, and some of us took their courses and read their books. Willard Waller, Theodore Abel, and Charles Page, before he joined the service, were among those who imparted their knowledge and their wisdom. It was a heady time, shadowed, however, by the clouds of war, already raining their destruction on Europe, and by the diabolical ideology of Hitler's Nazism.

In New York City, I found, both inside and outside Columbia, the exhilarating outlines of the social world I was later to call the *intellectual subsociety* and *intellectual subculture.* Here, friendships could be formed, and romantic entanglements entered, freely and easily across the boundaries of ethnicity or social class origin. Pairs of tickets to concerts at Carnegie Hall or Lewisohn Stadium, or to modern dance recitals at small studios in Greenwich Village, did not ask for strict homogeneity in their bearers. The cozy tables in John Jay Hall's Lion's Den or International House's Waffle Wing encouraged the sharing of contemporary experiences in intimate and animated conversation, quite oblivious to the varying sociological backgrounds of the participants. It was an expanding and liberating milieu for a young Jewish boy fresh from the American provinces.

In my intellectual studies, one of the most salient themes I encountered, and that meshed perfectly with my own previously formed orientations, was the overwhelming importance of culture and social institutions in shaping human behavior. Benedict's *Patterns of Culture* (1934) and Linton's *The Study of Man* (1936) both emphasized behavioral variability among human groups as the result of cultural antecedents; the work and classroom impact of MacIver and Lynd, although stemming from different methodological styles, led to similar conclusions. In fact, the entire corpus of historically developing sociological thought, from Comte to Durkheim and Sumner and beyond, appeared to point unmistakably in the direction of a cultural interpretation of human behavior, at least in its group aspects. The long-standing structure of American racism, directed most devastatingly at Blacks, but operating also against Asians, Jews, and Catholic immigrants from Europe, now joined by the virulent specter of Nazi anti-Semitism, made it apparent that all the resources of a cultural interpretation of behavior must be used to battle the pernicious and destructive doctrine that the many races and ethnic groups of humankind were biologically unequal in intellectual and emotional capacities. MacIver's *The More Perfect Union* (1948), Benedict's *Race: Science and Politics* (1940), Otto Klineberg's *Race Differences* (1935), and Jacques Barzun's *Race: A Study in Modern Superstition* (1937) were all contributions by Columbia academics during this period—paralleled and augmented, of course, by the work of social scientists from other institutions—designed to combat the idea of racial supremacy. I believed then, and I believe now, that this effort was intellectually justified and morally right, and constitutes one of the noblest chapters in the history of the social sciences.

I had begun to develop pacifist views in my undergraduate years at Bowdoin, and both my senior thesis and master's essay at Columbia were concerned with sociological analyses of the religious pacifist movement at various points in American history. I spent nearly four years during World War II as a conscientious objector in forestry camps set up by the government and administered by the Quakers. When I began my teaching career, after the war, at the University of Pennsylvania, I was intellectually at home in most of the mainstream assumptions of contemporary sociology and carrying out my own work basically within their framework. My first book, *Social Class in American Sociology,* was essentially a cumulative and analytic review of the social class literature—theoretical and empirical—based on a multidimensional view of stratification traceable in scholarly provenance to Max Weber (see Gordon, 1958). Other work on social class I published in that period emphasized the cultural effects of being socialized into a particular portion of the class structure—a sociological phenomenon that fascinated me then and continues to do so to this day. In both functional and moral terms, it was apparent to me that the differential disadvantages and advantages of initial class position were of a double nature: objective in the area of direct access to life chances, subjective and behavioral in connection with culturally based class behavior patterns. Never far from my mind or work, however, was the subject of ethnicity. I was not satisfied with the theoretical orientation to ethnic group assimilation and ethnic group contacts that was still dominated by Robert Park's "assimilation cycle" hypothesis. Nor was I convinced that emphasis on personality structure as the key to understanding the formation of racial and ethnic prejudice, stemming from the work of Adorno and others, was maximally fruitful. The cumulative experiences of my life had prepared me for an attempt to put the field of racial and ethnic group relations into a distinctly sociological framework, one that emphasized both the structural and cultural aspects of group living arrangements that made even industrialized societies a mosaic of subsocieties and subcultures that produced differential behaviors, thus limiting and defining social contacts. The nature, frequency, and absence or presence of those contacts, in turn, were presumed to have a decisive effect on intergroup attitudes—a point of view that was then receiving some empirical and theoretical support in the published literature.

Incorporating the above ideas and developing a multidimensional approach that factored the assimilation process into seven subprocesses, of which the distinction between behavioral and structural was the most crucial, my book *Assimilation in American Life* made its appearance in 1964.[1] Hypotheses were also developed about the chronological relationships among these subprocesses. With these theoretical tools, I was able to analyze the concepts of the melting pot, Anglo-conformity, and cultural pluralism and put them in a precise sociological perspective. I was also able to characterize the American historical experience in ethnic group relations as one of, progressively, structural rather than cultural pluralism, and to emphasize the existing variability in cultural traits, with some exceptions, as a function of social class rather than ethnicity. Among other ideas developed in the book, as mentioned earlier, were the concepts of ethclass and the intellectual subsociety. In the year following its publication, *Assimilation in American Life* won two national prizes: the Anisfield-Wolf Award in Race Relations and the Brotherhood Award of the National Conference of Christians and Jews. It progressively became a staple of assigned reading in college courses in intergroup relations throughout the country and was widely cited in research reports and theoretical discussions in scholarly and scientific journals.[2]

Several years before the publication of *Assimilation in American Life* I had come to the University of Massachusetts at Amherst as professor of sociology. Here I had for the first time in my professional career the opportunity to teach in a developing graduate program. Two of my graduate students carried out dissertation projects in the middle and late 1960s that studied my thesis that an American intellectual subsociety had formed, particularly in academic circles, in which issues of ethnicity in its various forms were largely ignored in the structuring of friendships of both a close and a general kind. Charles H. Anderson (1966, 1971) found substantial verification of this hypothesis with regard to religious lines for a sample of Protestant and Jewish academicians at four nonsectarian institutions in New England, and John D. Murray (1969, 1971) found the hypothesis essentially verified with regard to the religious factor for a sample of Catholic academicians teaching in four nonsectarian institutions in New England, but contradicted for Catholic faculty members teaching in two Catholic colleges in the New England area.

In the middle 1960s, probably as a result of the growing impact of *Assimilation in American Life,* I was approached by the publishing firm of Prentice-Hall and invited to become general editor of a series of books on American racial, religious, and national origins groups aimed primarily, although not exclusively, at adoptions in the college market. I accepted, and the Prentice-Hall Ethnic Groups in American Life Series was born. As I pointed out in my foreword to the series, each book was meant to provide both a descriptive and an analytic overview of the particular group under study, and the series as a whole was designed to provide its readers with a picture of America as a multiethnic society and to aid in the effort to eliminate prejudice and discrimination. The authors of the individual books in the series varied considerably in the degree to which they drew on the theoretical paradigm I had presented in *Assimilation in American Life,* but whatever the varying theoretical orientations used by its authors, by virtually all accounts the series as a whole has been a successful one and has played a role in sensitizing some members of a generation of college students to the cultural diversity in the United States and the challenge of incorporating this diversity in a viable American society. Over the years, 11 books were published in the series, some going to multiple editions.

Some years later, I took on an additional editorial assignment by becoming special editor of a volume of the *Annals of the American Academy of Political and Social Science* consisting of papers on the various racial, religious, and national origins groups in the United States, together with some theoretical articles; the title of that volume was *America as a Multicultural Society* (Gordon, 1981). A "paper text edition" of this volume was subsequently issued, presumably because it had attracted attention not only as a scholarly resource but as an entity suitable and useful for course adoptions.

Although *Assimilation in American Life*'s highly favorable scholarly and scientific reception was gratifying, I do not believe that it had a major impact on policy developments in the United States subsequent to its publication. Its discussion of cultural pluralism probably helped to popularize the concept in American intellectual discourse, but its conception and delineation of the concept of *structural pluralism* was one of its crucial contributions, and its warning against the development of excessive structural separation among racial and ethnic groups on the grounds that such a high degree of structural separation would significantly increase tensions and conflict has hardly been heeded. On the one hand, the book took the position that structural pluralism on a racial and ethnic basis was the characteristic condition of American society and had some positive features in providing for the preservation of in-group cultural values, comfortable intragroup social relations, and group defense in case of civic attack. But it further argued that too high a degree of structural separation would exacerbate the tensions and conflicts between groups. Events in American intergroup relations that have occurred subsequent to the book's publication suggest that the question of what constitutes a desirable degree of structural separation and an excessive degree of such separation is worthy of serious attention.

The major criticism of *Assimilation in American Life,* which actually materialized some years after its publication, as a consequence of the racial unrest of the late sixties, was that it tended to ignore the issue of power. I accept this criticism as justified—particularly with development of my own hindsight—although I might rephrase it to say that the book took for granted the existing power relationships. My subsequent paper, "Toward a General Theory of Racial and Ethnic Group Relations," constituted an attempt to integrate power considerations with assimilation processes (Gordon, 1975). In this paper I also raised the issue of the role of individual motivations in group processes and related it for the first time in my work to the subject of basic human proclivities. I developed this last theme in the long introductory essay to my collection *Human Nature, Class, and Ethnicity* (Gordon, 1978) and presented a theory of basic human nature in that essay.

In the late 1970s I was elected to the presidency of the Eastern Sociological Society. My presidential address to the Society at its annual meeting in March 1979, held in New York City, emphasized the need for a human nature concept in sociological investigation and the desirability of linking sociology and psychology more closely.

In this new development I was not turning my back in any way on the orientation of my previous work, or rejecting modes of sociological analysis as currently understood. What I was doing was attempting to link sociological variables with psychological ones to present more complete explanations of human behavior than are customary in the sociological enterprise. I was finding that those psychological variables lead to rather basic questions concerning possible biological predispositions of human beings. The sociological variables explain differences among human groups and variations in social institutions, and constitute the cultural and subcultural givens that any cohort of people encounters upon birth. But sociological variables alone do not explain the *constant* aspects of human behavior—constant aspects that appear to me now as being in considerably greater abundance than they did when I first set foot on Morningside Heights more than a half century ago. In fact, the entire web of social reality appears to me at this point to be made up of a fiendishly complex system of intricate interactions between individual human motivations and social and cultural patterns; any attempt to explain that reality by exclusive resort to either sociological or psychological variables lands quite far from the mark. This statement, in turn, leads me to two areas of discourse: The first is why I came to this perspective; the second is a series of more technical professional issues.

First, I want to examine why my perspective has been modified—or, I should prefer to say, simply, deepened. We are all chronological denizens of the twentieth century. We have witnessed the two most destructive wars in history; the fanatical and methodical murder of 6 million Jews carried out by elected representatives of one of the most advanced, and presumably most civilized, nations on earth; the systematic oppression of Black people by a society only several generations away from having held their ancestors as slaves; the transformation of regimes brought into being by the promise of abolishing poverty and distributing resources more equitably into totalitarian dictatorships distinguished by calculated suppression, terror, and gulags. Before the recent upheaval in the Soviet Union two powerful nations sat for many years on opposite sides of a once great ocean—now made puny by rocketry—poised in readiness for the possibility of mutual and world destruction. Newspapers and the evening television screen bring us daily accounts of civil wars, bloody territorial disputes, ideological hatreds, terrorist and counterterrorist ambushes, not to mention the incessant reports of individual murders, maimings, and assaults of passion and profit to which our senses by now have become somewhat dulled. Continued reading of history has brought me to the strong suspicion that, apart from variations produced by more primitive technologies, the affairs of humankind have never been particularly different. In such a world, obscured to me as a young idealist shaped and molded by the principles and hopes of the Enlightenment, I, for one, can no longer believe that humans are rather amiable, infinitely malleable creatures, temporarily seduced by the wrong social institutions that we, as liberally oriented sociologists, have been set upon the earth to remedy and rectify with our conventional wisdom. It is all much more complex than that.

The social world of human beings is, always has been, and always will be one in which the emotions and passions of the individual actor interact with his or her cognitive faculties to provide "decisions to act" that have been affected by and that, in turn, affect the already crystallized sociological structures that we have in mind when we speak of social norms, cultural patterns, social sanctions, and social institutions. The indissoluble links between sociology and psychology, then, are at least three in nature:

1. Social norms and institutions are the products or residues of *past* interactions of myriad individual actors accreting through time.

2. The individuals of any given cohort have been socialized, albeit imperfectly, into particular cultural and subcultural value systems that they have in varying degree internalized, while at the same time they face a series of options and sanctions that are the dynamic aspects of the institutional structure based on those very cultures and subcultures.

3. The various portions of the institutional structure are manned (or womanned) and led by *particular individuals* whose own decision-making apparatus is governed by the same forces—emotional, cognitive, cultural—that apply to all individuals in the process of social interaction, but whose effect is considerably magnified by their positions of leadership and power.

Thus the circle is completed. No sociology without psychology. No psychology without sociology.

The significant developments in the area of racial and ethnic group relations that emerged in the middle 1960s and throughout the 1970s produced further reflection on my part concerning the nature of human nature and its role in societal outcomes. Racial turmoil in American cities, calls for social separatism by minorities themselves, the receding of racial and ethnic goals emphasizing integration and the minimization of differences, the extension of ideological programs of cultural pluralism, the rise of government measures to redress past discrimination with "affirmative action" policies, and the adverse reaction to those policies in many portions of the majority community—all these significant developments led me to ponder issues that clearly devolved on the nature of human interaction in the most basic sense. How deep in the individual human psyche did feelings of ethnic identification go? What were the lineaments of reaction to decades and even centuries of group oppression? How did majorities characteristically react to assertions of power by previously subordinate groups? How rational was the decision-making process in individuals caught up in the highly charged area of racial and ethnic conflict? How objective and disinterested could both leaders and followers in contending groups be in arriving at ideological goals that ensured a viable and equitable social structure when their own group interests seemed overwhelming in their salience? All of these questions impelled me in the direction of attempting to develop a model of decision making in the individual that clearly rested ultimately on a conception of the basic nature of the human being.

Let me flesh out this theoretical paradigm with another example. In the field of criminology, a currently salient topic is the role of threat of punishment in preventing crime. Deterrence theory, it is called. The resolution of pertinent issues in deterrence theory, it is quite clear, depends on the construction of an adequate model of the decision-making process among members of a given population as they confront norms and negative sanctions, at the same time that hypotheses deriving from this model are tested by observing varying rates of crime under variant deterrent conditions. Any total explanation of the operation of deterrence variables must clearly link the decision-making process in the individual with the sociological variables. Ego's perception of the nature of the deterrence threat; his estimate of the probability of apprehension, of conviction, of the severity of the penalty; his previous culturally induced value orientation; his perception of noncriminal options for realizing his goals; the strength of his emotional drives, his cognitive powers, and situational factors; in addition to the nature of the deterrence threat itself—all become indivisible causal links in the chain of causation that leads to particular outcomes. There is no feasible way of separating sociology and psychology here.

Thus we need to insert the individual, with his or her passions, his or her cognitive functioning, and his or her societally induced value systems, into sociological analysis, setting up models of the decision-making process and thus giving deepened meaning to the study of social interaction and social institutions. If this is the case, however, unless we are willing to accept an extreme version of cultural determinism, then we must begin to ask questions about the role of biological and genetic factors in the individual—factors to which we pay lip service in our introductory textbooks—that interact with the social and cultural environment to produce the person who makes the decisions that become a part of the social process. In other words, we must—whatever conclusions we finally come to—grapple with the question of human nature.

Where, then, do we go for evidence regarding human nature? Here, as elsewhere, I must indicate my lack of enthusiasm for the methods and assumptions of the growing subdiscipline of sociobiology as currently conceived. I do not believe that we will learn very much about human nature by studying ethology, primatology, the history of evolutionary development, or population genetics. Valuable as the findings from these areas are for their own disciplinary purposes, their extrapolation to human nature issues must, inevitably, involve long leaps of speculation that cannot be proven in their own terms. As ethologists themselves concede, all inherited behavioral tendencies are species specific and cannot, a priori, be projected from one species to another. Furthermore, the long periods of evolutionary development for each species provide no guarantee that consistent gradations in biological traits will appear from one species to another in evolutionary lines, even where those evolutionary lines are known (which in many cases they are not). And, finally, the attempt to reconstruct the biology and culture of early forms of humans is a highly speculative and inconclusive enterprise at best. I argue, then, that to turn to *Homo habilis, Homo erectus,* chimpanzees, or macaques for an understanding of *Homo sapiens* is to look in the wrong place. The proper study of *Homo sapiens* is ourselves—our own species—our history for the past 50,000 years or so, contemporary manifestations as gleaned from current events, the social psychology laboratory, the clinician's office, sociological studies of human interaction, social institutions, and social change, and indeed, our own private social worlds in which we are participant observers. When we find constant manifestations in these data that appear to be little subject to cultural variation, we will then be on sounder ground for hypothesizing the presence of constant biological predispositions that have produced those uniformities.

In a very basic sense, I see the human being in any society, with whatever culture, as a creature devoted to ego-enhancement and ego-defense.[3] Within that framework, in various ways, the individual balances and integrates emotional predispositions, cognitive perceptions, cognitive calculations, and physiological drives, particularly those concerned with sexuality and comfort as variously specified by such routine needs as food and alternations between privacy and sociality. These individual dynamics are, of course, exercised within a normative framework characterized by particular cultural and subcultural expectations. But these cultural frameworks do not extinguish or negate the thrust of the individual's strivings; rather, they provide the social and cultural *field* that dictates the tortuous and intricate paths through which the individual attempts to realize his or her goals. The fit between cultural prescriptions and ego-desires is never perfect or even close to perfection; ego-desires and wishes inevitably impinge upon the desires and wishes of other egos, and the cultural prescriptions themselves have arisen and crystallized in part as a functional response to the need for resolving a zero-sum game whose unregulated performance would lead to the breakup of any conceivable social order. This situation is magnified by the insatiable and theoretically unbounded nature of the human being's status striving in the ego-enhancement process, and the capacity and tendency to turn material goods into symbols of status. Thus the tension between ego and society is perpetual and ineradicable. It can be reduced—this, to me, is what social policy is all about—but it cannot be eliminated. It is built into the very fabric of the human condition.

The processes of ego-enhancement and ego-defense central to human nature take place at three levels, each level corresponding to a stage of chronological development, but all the stages functioning simultaneously and interactively in the mature adult. For shorthand purposes, we may refer to this theory of human nature as a *triple-layered and triple-stage theory of ego-welfare effectuation.* Stage 1 is simple hedonism, in which gratification of physiological needs and acting out of simple emotional responses (such as anger, rage, attachment, and dependency) are the paramount concern of the human organism. This stage is present in the infant prior to development of a sense of self and continues, under societal constraints and definitions of various sorts, in all subsequent stages of human development. Stage 2 appears after the sense of self has materialized, sometime during the first 18 months of life, and consists of defense of the self against adverse judgments by, and enhancement of the self in the opinions of, significant others. This is ego-defense and ego-enhancement as conventionally conceived by social psychologists, and becomes a permanent part of the human organism's subsequent response set. Stage 3 arrives when the child becomes aware of his or her own mortality and develops the fear of death. Although this awareness and fear undoubtedly arise at different times for different individuals, psychoanalyst Gregory Rochlin (1965), in *Griefs and Discontents,* estimates that they are present in the child by 3 years of age. Eventually, this fear of death is met by the development of what I call *immortality-granting belief systems,* or, more briefly, *immortality systems.* Most religious beliefs serve this function, among others, and strongly held political and social ideologies that promote the concept of "dying for a cause" are not totally unrelated to immortality systems, even though other motivational complexes based on a sense of outrage at the violation of justice norms are also surely involved. These three serially developing layers in the construction of a self devoted to the effectuation of ego-welfare, once in appearance, subsequently function together in intricate and complex ways to shape the characteristic responses and activities of the human being. They are at the core of human nature.

It will doubtless be noted that this view of the human condition appears to leave little room for validation of behavior that could be called genuinely altruistic. This appearance accurately reflects the nature of the theory. Some purportedly altruistic behavior reduces, I believe, to implementation of the norms of immortality systems, and, thus, is massively infused with considerations of self-interest. Other forms of altruistic actions—and, in this, I share the views of Gerhard Lenski (1966) as expressed in *Power and Privilege*—are similarly reducible to unspoken selfish motivations, confined to areas where little is at stake, or are addressed to primary group defense. Although this very last type poses further analytic questions, I am content for the moment to leave the area of primary group relations, as represented by the family or close-knit peer group, as the one sociological area where genuinely altruistic behavior is generated with any degree of frequency.

Such a view clearly does not project genuine altruism as a very powerful force, either in the relationships of everyday life or in the larger sweep of human affairs. It may be objected that I have presented an essentially mean-spirited picture of the human condition that denies what might be called "the better side" of human nature and actions as reflected in countless instances of benevolence, genuine cordiality, and affability that we have all observed and all felt. Let me hasten to redress the balance. The human being is clearly capable of acting and responding in the world of interpersonal relationships with generosity of spirit, affection, admiration, concern, warmth, and grace. I salute these qualities and rejoice in their appearance. None of this, however, negates the basic thrust of ego-welfare considerations in shaping the larger outlines of the social process.

I would like, now, to make a few comments on some of the basic capacities of the human being that fall into the realm of cognition. Humans' powerful brains allow and impel us to make extraordinarily fine distinctions in all areas of our existence. As I wrote in *Human Nature, Class, and Ethnicity*:

> Some people are taller, others shorter. Some individuals charm us by their personalities, others repel us. Some members of the opposite sex are more attractive physically, others less attractive, still others are not attractive to us at all. Some persons are highly intelligent, others are average, or below average in intellectual abilities. Some people impress us with their leadership and executive qualities, others do not. This listing of traits could obviously be extended indefinitely. (Gordon, 1978, p. 52)

What I am specifying here is the human propensity to *distinguish* and *evaluate* the characteristics of other human beings—a propensity that I believe is anchored in our biologically given cognitive apparatus and can be only modestly modified and channeled by any given cultural system. All human interaction is massively infused with a process of *mutual evaluation* that is partially obscured and kept within reasonable bounds of visibility and manifest expression by the norms and standards that govern ordinary role behavior and social discourse. But the underlying current of mutual evaluation is at least partially understood by all participants and is inevitably destined to set up ego-defensive reactions, particularly in those areas in which we do not shine—or, at least, where our interaction partners *think* we do not shine. Sometimes I think the amount of ego energy generated in this universal human process is enough to make the amount of physical energy produced by nuclear fission or fusion pale by comparison.

This constellation of cognitive processes leads inevitably to *rationalization*—the provision of socially acceptable reasons to explain and justify actions when the real reasons for the actions are negatively evaluated by group and societal norms. Thus we see that humankind's magnificent capacities for conceptualization and means-ends apprehension, which have brought such impressive results in science and technology over the centuries and millennia of human existence, are used extensively in social interaction as defensive tools in the service of the self. I believe this goes a long way toward explaining why the human race has been so successful in the first area and so relatively unsuccessful in the second.

I come now to the matter of aggression. Unlike the orthodox Freudians, and some of the ethologists, I do not regard aggression as an insistent instinctive force that exists like a head of steam in all individuals regardless of external circumstances and must perforce find an outlet or release, whether destructive or nondestructive. Unlike the extreme cultural determinists, I do not view aggression simply as a derivative of modeling behavior or socialization into the wrong institutions, and thus as essentially eradicable through correct social measures. Aggression arises from blockage of the individual's attempts to satisfy his or her ego-needs. This blockage may occur at any or all three of the levels of ego-welfare—that is, satisfaction of hedonistic drives, status defense or enhancement, and defense of immortality systems. Given that such blockage, to one degree or another, is bound to occur endlessly in much social interaction, the generating conditions for aggressive feelings are virtually omnipresent. Aggressive feelings, however, must be distinguished from aggressive behavior. Expression of aggressive behavior becomes a function of the individual's decision-making process and brings into play moral norms, force and authority sanctions, and relative deprivation considerations that frame our expectations, together with competing emotional states of need satisfaction and psychic euphoria. The analysis is made even more complex by the fact that aggressive behavior may be force or authority induced by social institutions, quite apart from the presence of emotional instigators—as, for instance, when the state demands violent behavior of its armed forces conscripts. Thus aggression is a highly complicated phenomenon, the understanding of which is poorly served by facile references to a so-called aggressive instinct or the easy triumph of alternative socialization procedures. Exactly the same kind of analytic complexity is necessary to explain the cooperative behavior that makes up a large and necessary part of the social process.

This theory or model projects a view of the human being that, when inserted into the equations of human social interaction and the functioning of social institutions, gives me a much better understanding of what is actually going on in the world. In the area of ethnic group relations it allows me to ask basic questions about the formation and sustenance of racial and ethnic prejudice and to suggest tentative answers to those questions. Specifically, it leads me to posit the existence of a low-level (and individually variable) tendency toward "ethnocentrism in collectivities" in the human psyche that is exacerbated under conditions of excessive social separation. Such conditions, I have come to believe, foster the development of stereotyping and prevent the development of social bonds that produce psychological defenses in individuals against prejudice and discriminatory behavior toward members of out-groups. Thus I have pointed to limits in the degree of structural pluralism that a society can tolerate without developing racial and ethnic tensions that cause the society to splinter or break apart. These matters are dealt with in some detail under the framework of "an integrated theory of racial and ethnic prejudice" in my latest book, *The Scope of Sociology* (Gordon, 1988, pp. 229-238).

In the last analysis, then, although I am usually identified as being an "assimilation theorist," my goal in social structure is to allow the individual the maximum amount of free choice in matters of cultural integration whether that results in close identification with, and participation, in racial and ethnic collectivities or broader contact in the society as a whole. Sociologically, however, my theoretical analysis points to the importance of the *structural* issue and the dangers of excessive structural separation. In my latest work I have linked the structural issue to individual psychological mechanisms and to human nature issues to warn against the development of a degree of structural pluralism that produces fragmentation in the society.

With regard to my general theory of human nature, or model of tendencies in the human being, I anticipate at least two types of objections. First, some will accuse me of setting up a "self-fulfilling prophecy"—that is, of engaging in a kind of labeling process that will actually make people worse than they might be because of the lowered expectations thus created. I deny this charge. In the first place, there is nothing in my theory that militates against development of a morality and ethics that emphasize decency, respect for the rights of others, concern for the welfare of the entire community, and, in general, the creation and preservation of a civilized societal framework that is, in fact, absolutely necessary for the emergence of our own and every other individual's healthy pursuit of life, liberty, and happiness. Indeed, the model clearly suggests that only in working toward a society that is carefully tuned to minimizing and containing the inevitable conflicts of human ego-wishes can the conditions for reasonable human happiness be constructed. Second, labeling effects constitute only one limited sector of the arc of stimuli that propel action, and thus operate within a total constellation of activating forces, many others of which are, in most situations, overriding. The human being's ego-demands will not go away because of, or be charmed into oblivion by, sociological sweet talk. Their existence is not a function of our recognition, nor will they wither because of our averted gaze. Instead, they form the central and ubiquitous thrust of the actor who is the essential building block of our social laws and plans for societal welfare. We ignore them at the peril of egregious error in our calculations and disastrous failure in our proffered remedies.

The second potential objection to this theory is that its social policy implications would appear to be politically conservative. In the first place, it is very difficult these days to know what social measures should be identified with the appellations of liberal, conservative, or radical. I would rather judge social remedies by their practical usefulness in improving the human condition without creating even greater problems than by their political labels of the moment. Second, as social scientists, we must confront stubborn reality and attempt to understand and utilize that reality to set and reach realizable goals in social arrangements. So far as I am aware, there is no "leftist," "rightist," or "centrist" chemistry, nor conservative or radical physics. We are at liberty to bay at the moon with ideological disputes, but actually getting there was accomplished by exquisite accuracy in understanding the principles of rocketry and allied scientific disciplines. To use an inadequate model of the nature of the human being in developing social programs designed to improve the general welfare is to build on sand and to invite the unanticipated consequences of purposive social action—a recipe for failure. The tides of change will not be harnessed by false hopes; so summoned, they will only wreak destruction in channels not thought of. Let my theory of human nature be studied and debated in the arenas of the social psychological laboratory and the sociological investigations of institutions and social change. If it turns out to be false, discard it; if it appears to be faulty in detail, modify it. But do not either condemn it or embrace it from the perspective of current political persuasion. It is true that this theory promises no utopias, presents no comforting Rousseauian view of the human condition, and has a keen respect for the fragility and precariousness of the social order that we all need in order to become human, to work, to achieve, to love, and to be useful, fulfilled, and creative actors in the human community. Such a social order is my goal for all men and for all women. Thus it was for the boy from Maine—it is no less for the man from Amherst.

Notes

1. I explored some of these concepts and analytic ideas in shorter form in earlier work (see Gordon, 1954, 1961). During the 1950s I also contributed in the affirmative to the national debate on the use of law to enforce nondiscrimination in the racial area by coauthoring with a political scientist the article "Can Morality Be Legislated?" which appeared in the *New York Times Magazine* and was widely reprinted (Roche & Gordon, 1955). I also published two articles during this period arising out of my work as a consultant to the city of Philadelphia in the legal battle over racial exclusion at Girard College, in which I supported the argument that the "equal protection of the laws" clause of the 14th Amendment to the Constitution could be used to banish racial segregation from institutions and situations infused with state action (Gordon, 1956, 1959).

2. For some comments on the role of *Assimilation in American Life* in the development of assimilation theory, see the entries "Assimilation and Pluralism" by Harold J. Abramson (1980) and "American Identity and Americanization" by Philip Gleason (1980) in the *Harvard Encyclopedia of American Ethnic Groups*.

3. For an important discussion of the dominant role of ego-defense in human behavior from a psychoanalytic perspective, see Rochlin (1973).

References

Abramson, H. J. (1980). Assimilation and pluralism. In S. Thernstrom, A. Orlov, & O. Handlin (Eds.), *Harvard encyclopedia of American ethnic groups* (pp. 150-160). Cambridge, MA: Harvard University Press.

Anderson, C. H. (1966). *The intellectual subsociety: An empirical test.* Unpublished doctoral dissertation, University of Massachusetts, Amherst.

Anderson, C. H. (1971). The intellectual subsociety hypothesis: An empirical test. In C. H. Anderson & J. D. Murray (Eds.), *The professors* (pp. 227-245). Cambridge, MA: Schenkman.

Barzun, J. (1937). *Race: A study in modern superstition.* New York: Harcourt, Brace.

Benedict, R. (1934). *Patterns of culture.* Boston: Houghton Mifflin.

Benedict, R. (1940). *Race: Science and politics.* New York: Modern Age.

Gleason, P. (1980). American identity and Americanization. In S. Thernstrom, A. Orlov, & O. Handlin (Eds.), *Harvard encyclopedia of American ethnic groups* (pp. 31-58). Cambridge, MA: Harvard University Press.

Gordon, M. M. (1954). Social structure and goals in group relations. In M. Berger, T. Abel, & C. H. Page (Eds.), *Freedom and control in modern society* (pp. 141-157). New York: Van Nostrand.

Gordon, M. M. (1956). The Girard College case: Desegregation and a municipal trust. *Annals of the American Academy of Political and Social Science, 304,* 53-61.

Gordon, M. M. (1958). *Social class in American sociology.* Durham, NC: Duke University Press.

Gordon, M. M. (1959). The Girard College case: Resolution and social significance. *Social Problems, 7,* 15-27.

Gordon, M. M. (1961). Assimilation in America: Theory and reality. *Daedalus, 90,* 263-285

Gordon, M. M. (1964). *Assimilation in American life.* New York: Oxford University Press.

Gordon, M. M. (1975). Toward a general theory of racial and ethnic group relations. In N. Glazer & D. P. Moynihan (Eds.), *Ethnicity: Theory and experience* (pp. 84-110). Cambridge, MA: Harvard University Press.

Gordon, M. M. (1978). *Human nature, class, and ethnicity.* New York: Oxford University Press.

Gordon, M. M. (Ed.). (1981). America as a multicultural society. *Annals of the American Academy of Political and Social Science, 454.*

Gordon, M. M. (1988). *The scope of sociology.* New York: Oxford University Press.

Klineberg, O. (1935). *Race differences.* New York: Harper & Brothers.

Lenski, G. E. (1966). *Power and privilege: A theory of social stratification.* New York: McGraw-Hill.

Linton, R. (1936). *The study of man.* New York: Appleton.

Lynd, R. S., & Lynd, H. M. (1937). *Middletown in transition.* New York: Harcourt, Brace.

MacIver, R. M. (1937). *Society: A textbook of sociology.* New York: Farrar & Rinehart.

MacIver, R. M. (1948). *The more perfect union.* New York: Macmillan.

Murray, J. D. (1969). *The American Catholic intellectual: An empirical test of the intellectual subsociety hypothesis.* Unpublished doctoral dissertation, University of Massachusetts, Amherst.

Murray, J. D. (1971). Catholic academicians and the intellectual subsociety hypothesis. In C. H. Anderson & J. D. Murray (Eds.), *The professors* (pp. 247-263). Cambridge, MA: Schenkman.

Roche, J. P., & Gordon, M. M. (1955, May 22). Can morality be legislated? *New York Times Magazine,* pp. 10, 42-49.

Rochlin, G. (1965). *Griefs and discontents.* Boston: Little, Brown.

Rochlin, G. (1973). *Man's aggression: The defense of the self.* Boston: Gambit.

4

"Friendly Margins"

A Wonderful Afternoon With Hylan Lewis

JOHN H. STANFIELD II

Lewis: I was always, even then, at 7, 8, 9, an active, mobile person with a wide range of persons with whom I had some connections, my boyhood friends—from the people who ran the market to the janitor. There was also the blind man who sold score cards and pencils at the American League baseball park and whom I led and worked with. One consequence was that at the beginning of games— or at the middle of the fourth inning—we would go and sit in the box seats; I saw all the great American League baseball players of that time. But it also was a period when I worked. I sold newspapers and I can still hear and repeat the street cries of the paperboys. I worked in the bowling alley, for which I would get 4 cents a game. I was very pleased with my prowess as a pinsetter. On holidays I worked full-time and would make $4.00 setting pins—that's 100 games—but any evening I would make 80 cents or $1.20. So I had a rather active time, and when I say active I mean I had many associates my age and older. I lived in a neighborhood that actually was mixed with whites and Blacks.

AUTHOR'S NOTE: Owing to illness, Professor Emeritus Hylan Lewis was unable to contribute a chapter to this volume, but he was generous enough to take the time to give this interview

Stanfield: And where was the neighborhood?

Lewis: In Washington, D.C. A part of my interest had to do with many, many connections I had with all kinds of people. I'll give you one indication of what a typical weekend for me might be.

I had a friend who was a Seventh-Day Adventist, so on Saturday I would go with him to Sabbath school. On Sunday morning I would go to Sunday school at the Episcopal church and in the evening to the BYPU at the Baptist church. There was that kind of range and I felt very comfortable doing that. Just to jump ahead a little bit—later on I worked for the Unitarian Service Committee. I had a discussion one time with some friends—theologians and others—and I jokingly told them about my weekends and they laughed and said, "That explains a lot about you" [laughter]. But my point is, I had many interests. I use the word *interest* to mean having curiosity about what was happening around me. On Sundays, when the weather permitted, I would put on my little pongee shirt and shorts and walk up to 7th Street in Northwest Washington, where the movie houses were located. On Sundays, the movie houses would show shoot-'em-ups and serials. I would go to all of them in the course of the day—the Dunbar, the S. H. Dudley, the Gem, the Alamo. At the time I also would listen to the street evangelists. I remember some of the groups that came, often from orphanages from the South. They featured musicians such as Louis Armstrong contemporaries, who would come and play on the streets. Washington at that time was a different place, with a number of different entities that were important, I think, to giving one a sense of oneself, if one responded. Well, the Washington, D.C., schools were available for Negroes or Colored and called Division 13. There were 13 divisions in the school system and Division 13 was under the direction of Negro assistant superintendents, principals, and teachers; and some of the schools were named after Negroes and some of their white benefactors. I went to Elijah P. Lovejoy. My father was a schoolteacher, so very early I was aware of people like Judge Terrell and Colonel Young, and historical figures like Phyllis Wheatley and Benjamin Banneker. I also was a pretty voracious reader and I would go to the library and always get three or four books each week, including some of the great adventure books including the Altschuler series. I also read things by Nick Carter and Horatio Alger, and I read my sister's

True Stories magazines. But at the same time I was working; I sold papers, worked in the bowling alley, I shined shoes in a white barber shop; and was pretty active, pretty happy. There was something about my life there then that was important that I have never lost to this day. My nickname was Rabbit—something of a clue to the fact that I moved fast and turned up in lots of different places [laughter]. In that sense when I do my autobiography, my working title will be *Friendly Margins.* I say that because—you are well aware—autobiographical statements are as much a search on the part of the person who is the "auto" for some sense and meaning about himself or herself, as they are a way of explaining oneself to others.

Stanfield: Right, certainly. You used the phrasing for a possible autobiography *Friendly Margins* . . .

Lewis: Yes, the metaphor, both the direct and the metaphorical meanings.

Stanfield: So your experience in marginality hasn't necessarily been a bad or negative experience?

Lewis: No, I think that the meaning and the experience of margins—notice I say *margins,* not *marginality,* although I make some small allowance here too—has not been explored as much as it might. Although, I suppose most autobiographers to some extent directly or indirectly deal with not so much the centers of human contact but the edges [laughter]. So how does one interrelate experiences to the centers? And what about dealing with the findings in each, and possibly seeing the differing and new reference points not as antagonistic necessarily, but as integral parts of a moving whole? Obviously, this too is a way of indicating what in retrospect one sees as changes in the temper, and the quality, and the essence, and the excitement, and the joy of life in relating these roundabout dimensions—this may seem contradictory—but one thinks of friendship. What is friendship? Friendship is both intense and is also edged in a sense; and true friendship, as old man Ellsworth Faris . . . used to say, "Friendship knows no rules." And here once again we begin by talking about margins: Each friend is a margin, which some think of as being not a compliment, but for me, friending brings in all kinds or aspects of them that one sees as meaningful experiences. Again I am roaming, with you I am just talking . . .

Stanfield: Sure.

Lewis: But I think this is important in examining the texture of one's life, and also very important again in getting at this conjunction of the biographical with the social.

Stanfield: Definitely. Well, you are doing fine. I was just going to raise another point, and that is, How has this philosophy of life influenced your concept of what a career is? Because it struck me, as I was looking at your CV, this is an individual who has done an incredible amount of different kinds of things and in many cases all at once [laughter].

Lewis: When I was at Atlanta University in the fifties and when Truman was about to come out with his pronouncement abolishing segregation in the armed forces, among the things that they thought to do was to send teams of social scientists to Korea and other places. So they called me from Washington very urgently and wanted to know would I be willing to go and I said, "Yeah," and they said, "Well could we get back to you in a few days after the FBI check" and things of that sort? And time went on and they never called me; later on I asked why and they told me that they looked at my vita, and they said, "You had been so many places that it would have taken too long to check you out" [laughter]. But there again, it's true, even though, somewhat unwitting. I didn't plan to live that way, but this is the way in which . . . this is where the margins have been and this is why I say some of the margins have been friendly in their effect on me. I give you another example, just to make the point here. When I left—I was at Howard University back then—Capstone—at that time certainly nobody ever left Howard University [laughter]. You were just there. So I was on leave of absence from Howard in Chicago at that time sitting in the stacks at the University of Chicago one day and someone said, "Would you mind coming upstairs? Dr. Gallagher wants to meet you," and Buell Gallagher, president of Talladega College, was in a sense seeking me out and making me an offer to come to Talladega College in Alabama. This was a very exciting offer to me at that time, for they were experimenting with different kinds of freshmen and sophomore comprehensive courses. They were using the layer-cake model and—you know that story—had experimented with a lot of different formats, interdisciplinary faculty groups, etc., and none of them worked. Gallagher said he had a different idea: He said, "I would like you to come down to

Talladega and all you will have to do is teach freshmen social science; you develop the course and all you do is that one course." It was an exciting idea; and just to jump ahead, it was really the most exciting and fulfilling experience I have had in my life as a teacher—I can show you my student notebooks from there. I never was as successful with any students, graduates included, as I was with those freshmen [laughter]. To get back to the point of change here, so before I went I talked with Ed Shils, a good friend from the University of Chicago. Shils said, "Well, you know you can do well what you are doing now; and you can always return to that. This is something new, why not try that?" I spoke with Charlie Johnson [at Fisk University] about it and Charlie in his way said, "Talladega's the best of our colleges. Mind you now, I said *colleges*." [laughter] At Howard a few of my senior colleagues along with Carter Woodson (who lived down the street) ate every evening at the YWCA at Ninth and Rhode Island Avenue. I ran into a few colleagues one day after supper at the YWCA, and one person said rather seriously, "I hear you are going to leave Howard University. You resigned to go someplace else. What you going to do, you going to be president?" He said, "Any man who leaves Howard University and goes someplace else must be going to be president" [laughter]. I was never fazed by that at all; but Talladega was new, and again, here's a margin. Again, I link these kinds of career job changes.

I'll go back to what you asked earlier—during the war I worked at the Office of War Information [OWI]—and we will talk about that in the same context of margins and friendly aspects of them. And after the war ended, Ralph Bridgman [Hampton Institute president] came to see me and offered me a faculty post in the same manner Gallagher had done.

Stanfield: Boy, what a life [laughter].

Lewis: And so I decided to leave Washington and went to Hampton; and the point I wanted to make is, this was 1945. Again, I had lots of friends at Howard—Eugene Holmes, Williston Loften, Harold Lewis—and they were fascinated by my move to Hampton since they were quite dissatisfied at Howard, as were Frazier and Harris and others. My younger colleagues were intrigued and interested. I always thought at that time if an offer had come their way, they would have been tempted to accept because postwar Hampton was new and alive. They all came to visit me [laughter]. I mention these things as further examples of "friendly margins."

Stanfield: Let's go back to Virginia Union, where you went to undergraduate school. What happened there; another example of friendly margins?

Lewis: Yeah, okay, you have read something of mine. I guess from there—can I show you something to read to give you a sense of my transition from high school? My freshman composition, my first composition I wrote as a freshman was autobiographical.

Stanfield: Okay.

Lewis: This is my first publication when I was in high school. I established this paper. I must have been a freshman or sophomore.

Stanfield: Oh, 1927, was it?

Lewis: Yeah, I was a junior then, but then that was high school, but this is my very first as a freshman at Union. But again, you must keep in mind, given my background, that at some points even though you are not self-centered, you do think about yourself. This is again the freshman composition [pause]. I am still answering your question. It seems like we are digressing a little bit, but I think the answer comes. . . . Just a year or so ago, I met some people who were in school when I was there—I finished Virginia Union in 1932—and when some see me they say, "Oh, Humpty Dumpty," a reference from the past. And why do they call me Humpty Dumpty? Well, this is the very first speech I made in college. I didn't read it but I wrote it out, I memorized it and made it to the whole campus . . . [pause]. I'll tell you what, to give you some sense of the context and also what I wanted to talk to . . . these are a collection of speeches I made in college and many relate to metaphors, for instance "Twinkle, Twinkle Little Star" and "The Giant and the Pygmy."

Stanfield: Were you a student body officer of some kind?

Lewis: No, Union was quite a place at this time and I will talk to you about it later. Well, I guess at some time I may have been president of a class—no, I wasn't, Picott was. I was very active on the debating team. As a freshman I did something that no freshman had done at the time, I was chosen with a senior to participate in the longest trip by a debating team in Union's history. Union had a very long tradition in debate. We had a debate scheduled in Texas—Marshall, Texas, at Wiley College—which was quite a plum. I was chosen with William Robinson who later on was state senator in Illinois. I was active on the campus and again, part of my high school and college related to my declamations and oratory.

You asked me a question about, well, about the people who influenced me. I go back again to my childhood and I could talk at great length about the range of people, such as Mr. Carter (the janitor), Mason (the market man). I had good close and trusting relationships with several; but the interesting paradox is: You can have good trusting and close relationships with people and still in some sense they don't know you and you don't know yourself. I worked with Abe Harris [at Howard] for many years—that's another margin we can tap into later on—and Abe and I were friends. Abe and I were quite close, yet, on one occasion he told an acquaintance who came to the office, "I don't know much more about him now than I did when I first knew him." I was startled once by my daughter four or five years ago, when at one point she said, "You know, Daddy, I don't know you." Again contextually, I realize what she was saying. It was that there are hidden and unclear aspects and dimensions of a person's life. One of my desires is to write or do something so that my daughter and my son will come to know me better. Ken Clark and I are close friends, and I told Ken, "Ken, you know what Carole, my daughter, said?" When I told him, he looked at me and said, "Okay, tell her to join the queue!" Again, this is kind of a joke, and I don't intend to hide, but one must take that into account. I think I have as wide a friendly network of people as anyone I know.

Stanfield: Well, you know, as George Simmel would put it: The more the better.

Lewis: Yes, if it were a "stranger" phenomenon, I really would be worried and concerned about it . . . I am aware of that.

Stanfield: But, you know, there is another aspect of Simmel that relates to what you are saying: The more networks one is part of, the more one becomes an individual.

Lewis: Yeah, okay, I'm an individual then.

Stanfield: Yeah.

Lewis: Yeah, that's very true, I hadn't remembered that from Simmel. Again just telling about . . .

Stanfield: I mean, most people aren't like that. Most people tend to find a little niche in a circle and become deeply knowable.

Lewis: Yeah, truly underground.

Stanfield: That's right. And people who are floaters so to speak, and I mean that in a positive sense, are individuals who many people think they don't know but they do know, but are just not used to that kind of personality.

Lewis: You are absolutely correct, you are right on target, you are very sensitive.

Stanfield: Uh-huh.

Lewis: And if I hadn't . . . had the sense of the knowledge of true friendship and trust of so many people I would have been concerned. I have a very good friend, Mary Strong, who's done a little book on friendship and friends—do you know Mary? . . . Mary and I are close friends, and I can name four or five others.

Stanfield: You know, at the very same time, there is a certain attraction to those kinds of individuals because of the fact they have a skill of being able to do well in a good number of groups and networks.

Lewis: Yeah, at the same time. Do you know Joe Himes?

Stanfield: Yes.

Lewis: Joe's a very close friend of mine, very close, and he said, "Hylan, you have been a chameleon" [laughter]. And if he weren't a friend, I would be very concerned, but I knew what he was saying.

Stanfield: Yeah, that is very interesting, because baby boomers who are like that are considered to be high-quality cultural capital, because we live in an era now where people who are skilled at crossing boundaries are those who are considered to be, you know, flexible. Well, where was it that you decided to pursue a career in sociology?

Lewis: All right, let's talk about that. I'm pretty sure that I was pursuing a career in sociology in some sense [laughter], in my sense, during much of my childhood and certainly a considerable part of high school. I could talk a great deal about my high school experience, how in some sense it was a laboratory; about how distinctive this high school was and the quality of the education there; about how a principal, Y. H. Thomas, and how two spinsters, old-maid sisters, Julia and Ollie Richmond, and Jessie Wyche made a big difference. A little personal background might be useful again: I lived in Jersey City with an elderly uncle and aunt for a while after my father died when I was 11, and my mother had been institutionalized. Anyway, I went back to Washington very briefly from Jersey City when I was 12. In April 1924 the question for my aunts, uncles, and grandmother was what the hell to do with Highland (the way I spelled my name then) and two brothers and one sister from a family with five kids [laughter]. After a complex series of discussions, I was sent to Hampton, Virginia, to live with a family with which none of us had any previous connection. That's how I became called "Bassette's boy." So, anyway, unaccredited Union High School in Hampton was where I went to high school in April. At that time school closed around the first of May. And during those days the Virginia elementary schools had seven grades; I came out of Washington and so I was literally in the eighth grade, but the eighth grade was the first year of high school in Hampton. I went in early April to the first year of high school and took exams in May, and I passed them. Miss Julia Richmond arbitrarily—but wisely—wouldn't let me go to the second year, she made me repeat the freshman year. She became one of the most important influences in my life. She would say, Okay, here, read this, memorize this, do something with this, here, take this part in the play—those kind of things. What is the question you asked first?

Stanfield: Where was it that you decided on a career in sociology?

Lewis: All right, okay. [Hands Stanfield a book.]

Stanfield: Is that a dedication?

Lewis: Yes, it's an answer to your question, but the dedication is the beginning of the answer to your question.

Stanfield: [reading] "Hylan Lewis, graduate of Bay Shore University, brilliant student, master teacher, and friend of all students."

Lewis: Yes, Bay Shore University—Arthur P. Davis—When I lived in Hampton, during the summers, during high school, I worked at Buckroe Beach's Bay Shore Hotel. Bay Shore was one of the resorts, one of the prime resorts, probably you don't remember it.

Stanfield: No.

Lewis: I know you don't remember it, but it was during the period when it was quite a place, a hotel with beachfront rooms and steeplechases and things of that sort and I worked there as a waiter; it was a prime example of an amenity, but also a prime example of enterprise among Negroes. Hampton itself is a very interesting, historical community—the town and the college.

Stanfield: Oh, yes.

Lewis: Anyway, I lived on the Bassette's farm at that point, but I also went every day to work at Bay Shore, and Bay Shore was like a university in terms of the people there, in terms of Arthur Davis, who was my boss, a young man, a few years older than I, and old man Banks and others from whom you learned a lot. G. James Fleming worked there for a while too. And Arthur was a very important influence as a teacher at Virginia Union, very important. I was lucky in high school and lucky in college in the teacher and peers I had—Arthur Davis, Henry McGuinn, Gordon Hancock, Rayford Logan, Elizabeth Johnson.

Stanfield: They were all at Virginia Union?

Lewis: Oh, sure.

Stanfield: I didn't realize that.

Lewis: Rayford Logan and I were very close friends.

Stanfield: I understand Gordon Hancock was quite a character.

Lewis: Gordon Hancock. Have you read the book about him?

Stanfield: No, no, but I read some archival materials about his role in the Rockefeller circles.

Lewis: When I finished, I mean high school at Union High in Hampton, Logan was the commencement speaker there. I didn't tell you—I was a boy orator, I was a great speaker, so I was entered into many state contests—there were three of us high school students always who were among the finalists! G. James Gilliam, from Portsmouth—he's in California; Rupert Picott—he died not too long ago—from Newport News; and I was from Hampton. The oratorial fight was always between Gilliam and me. We met for state championships first at Virginia Union—there were six of us competing there and Gilliam finished first and I finished second and Picott was third. I got eight points—we had a point system. And as it so happened, I should have finished first, because you had three judges, and you had six people, and so those you have for number one you give them a one—and one of the judges turned it upside down [laughter] and I had two ones and six, which gave me an eight. It didn't bother me a great deal. The three of us wound up at Virginia Union as students there. The second time that Gilliam and I went at it was at Newport News and I had a 45-minute speech, which I had memorized, and one of my coaches told me, "Well, you know, that is a long speech and what you should do in the middle of the thing is walk up and down to break the thing." So I spoke and in the middle of the thing, I stopped and I walked up and down and again I came in second, because the judges thought I had forgotten the speech [laughter].

Stanfield: Oh, mercy.

Lewis: So we are still great friends; and anyway the three of us wound up at Virginia Union, which had a great tradition—a small school and marvelous teachers, and among them was Pat McGuinn. And when I went for this first oratorical contest—he was a bachelor at that time—he took me down to the basement of a dormitory while he shaved, and we rehearsed my speech and he coached me. So when later we went to Union, we were very active and a bright bunch of kids. Logan was teaching history and political science, and McGuinn was teaching sociology and economics, and Hancock was teaching sociology and anthropology. It was very lively. I had in my background some economics, and the models of people like Abe Harris, Charles Johnson, and Chandler Owen. So I was really more interested in economics; and I took a lot of history and got a lot of credits. Hancock messed around with a little economics but didn't do very much except read us old notes he had gotten at Colgate or someplace like that.

McGuinn was a very important influence at Virginia Union, and he received his Ph.D. from Columbia. His great idol was MacIver. So when I came along to finish there two things opened to me: One was to work for Eugene Kinkle Jones of the Urban League. He wanted to give me a job working with the Urban League. Another offer was from Guadaloupe College, in Seguin, Texas. I received a letter from the president that said, "Dear Mr. Lewis, we would like to invite you to come to teach at Guadaloupe College here in Texas. We can offer you $28.00 a month and a horse" [laughter]. Choices were narrowing to work with the Urban League with Kinkle Jones—but Charlie Johnson came through. The Social Science Research Council was that year establishing an early affirmative action program. Due to Charles Johnson, they set up a special series of scholarships, southern scholarships—not white not Black, but southern—so there were three of us who got those fellowships, I from Virginia Union, Estelle Hill from Fisk, and Sarah Alice Mayfield—a white student—from Birmingham. She later married Stuart A. Rice who was filling in for Ogburn.

We all wound up at the University of Chicago. As I said, I would have preferred to go into economics for a number of reasons, among them I knew a great deal about Abram Harris, who was a Virginia Union grad and a distinguished economist; and I suppose in some way the toughness of economics attracted me too. But I was also attracted to sociology because of Charles Johnson and one of the Daniels and others who had gone that route, as well, and because the University of Chicago was well known, and so I signed up for sociology with a minor in economics. But again, I couldn't go into economics because I didn't have much strength and my courses were few and weren't really that good at Union. But throughout my graduate work I had a minor in labor and personnel and I did other work on the economics side. . . . I had courses with Harry Millis, Paul Douglas, and I actually took a course from Frank Knight—"Economics and Welfare"—but I didn't know what the hell it was all about. These again were influences that made that first year well spent. This was the Depression of 1932; I had a fellowship of $1,000 with which I was able to pay tuition, and room and board that was $20 a month. When the banks failed I was able to lend my landlord, Mr. Bland, the moving man, some money, which was very interesting. Among my teachers were Faris, Wirth, Ogburn, Rice, Burgess, Paul Douglas, Cottrell, Blumer. . .

Stanfield: What about Park?

Lewis: Park had just left. He would come in once in a while for a seminar.

Stanfield: You must have been in the same year as Horace Cayton.

Lewis: That was the next name I was going to mention. Horace and I were good friends. Horace Cayton, Ed Shils—Do you know Horace's *Long Dusty Road?*—and I were in classes together.

Stanfield: Yes, certainly. He never did get all the due credit he deserved for a lot of the work he did.

Lewis: Well, Horace was a character. I think yes and no. He got a lot of recognition because of the combination of Drake and Cayton; and don't forget Liz Johns who was a support behind everything, Drake's wife. I think Horace would agree with me, that Horace was a very important person and a very influential person, but, I think he would probably shrug and say, "You know, but I am really not a scholar," but he could do what scholars did. He was an important presence at the Parkway Community Center. He spent time at YADDO in Saratoga—I had a Saratoga connection too—and we would meet there while he was in residence. You are right in one way, he didn't get the credit, but he was an extraordinary and interesting person who I think was more involved in acting, organizing, and influencing. I think he gets a lot of credit down in *Who's Who.* But Horace was a good fellow. He wasn't as diligent about his classes. Oliver Cox was around at this same time too. Oliver was in economics and at that time it was alleged that economics faculty at Chicago would not admit Negroes; Cox took an M.A. That is why he ended in sociology. Back to Horace—in one sense he got credit and the luck was that he and Drake were able to combine and have Liz behind them. I think Horace was very important as an influence and manager, somewhat picturesque, and a very important figure who should be better remembered than he is. And things I am especially thankful for are his contributions to *Black Metropolis* [Drake & Cayton, 1945], his work with St. Clair Drake and Lloyd Warner in Chicago, and his collaboration with George Mitchell in an early study of industrial unionism.

Stanfield: Who at Chicago probably influenced you the most?

Lewis: The persons who influenced me the most in Chicago were Ogburn, Burgess, Blumer, Hughes, Wirth, Faris.

Stanfield: Who chaired your dissertation committee?

Lewis: Well, you really know how to go for the interesting questions [laughter]. I again am speaking about friendly margins; for both my M.A. and Ph.D., I had no committees or faculty advisers. I took in a finished project each time that I had worked on myself.

Stanfield: That's incredible. How . . .

Lewis: The Ph.D. dissertation was even more incredible because that was lost for two years. Louis Wirth lost it and Everett Hughes had to come down as an ambassador for the department and ask, "What can we do?" But I said I had another copy. Chicago at that time had its sort of farm schools—Tulane, Stanford, Carlton. Some students always would get jobs out there as instructors, but I never even thought of it, and in some sense I probably resented the fact, some of my schoolmates were probably not as good as I was, and some of whom I tutored. Through my own sense of perverse pride, I never signed up or put my name in the place where you put your name where students put their vita on file—the career place.

Stanfield: You could almost say, I was surprised to see you were a Chicago Ph.D. For some reason or another, I thought of you as being Columbia or Wisconsin, maybe because most of the official accounts of the Chicago school deal with students and faculty of the twenties and early thirties, and not of the late thirties, forties, and fifties.

Lewis: I was in and out. . . I was very close to Blumer, Ogburn, and Hughes. I think a couple of things might be pointed out: one, my work and influences at Howard, and the other the Rosenwald Foundation Fellowships in 1939 and 1940.

Stanfield: What years were you at Howard?

Lewis: I went to Howard in 1933. . . I worked with Abram Harris in economics. And I was there before Frazier, and when Frazier came I helped him get settled and I shifted and I worked with him in sociology. We fired Henry H. Donald, who was a disaster. The department before Frazier was Henry H. Donald, Kelly Miller, and Gold Refine Wilson. But again, while working at Howard I worked with the *Cost of Living Study* in the field for the U.S. Department of Labor. My ties with Chicago were firm but, in some sense, not consistently close, and a part of what happened or did not was a matter of my own choosing . . . in the sense was a matter of my activities. So when I got the Rosenwald . . .

Stanfield: Did you have to go for an interview for the Rosenwald?

Lewis: No, but that again is another story that again refers to the politics of the business. I was supposed to have gotten the Rosenwald the year before, and Frazier and Charlie fell out and . . .

Stanfield: Fell out for what reason?

Lewis: I've forgotten . . .

Stanfield: I have heard they were always falling out . . .

Lewis: Yes, their relationship was off and on; and they both apologized and so I got it in the successive years and here again in some sense . . . but again those years were very good ones because my colleagues were Arnold Rose, Lionel Florant, and Shirley Star and the whole *American Soldier* group. But here again in terms of linkages or any connections I was closer to Blumer and Wirth and Hughes. Stouffer had come in, and his accent was on statistics and so on. So when I think in terms of the kind of professor whom you get attached to, I realize some of this is accident, but I am just thinking back . . . When the war broke out I came back to Washington and that was a whole other set of linkages and friendly margins. But I just wanted to make the point, you are quite correct in identifying the kind of factors affecting my career may seem loose and may seem unstructured, but at some point the pieces fall in place, not in terms of a straight line but in terms of some sort of logic and momentum.

Stanfield: Could we go back to the thirties and reconstruct the chronology in terms of your major activities, from, say, 1932?

Lewis: I finished Union in '32. Let me go back to Virginia Union and the choices I had. There was a third choice I had that I didn't mention; in addition to the National Urban League and a fellowship from the Social Science Research Council, the other was to teach high school in Goochland County, Virginia, for $30.00 a month. So all right, I didn't want to do this . . . the Depression had a very interesting influence on me in terms of its economic pressure and in terms of the people—my foster family . . . money was scarce, so therefore a job was important. I would have rather stayed in Chicago the summer after that first year and hacked out my master's thesis, but Virginia Union called and McGuinn said, "Okay, we would like you to come back and teach summer school." So I went back and taught summer school, and at the end of summer school what are you going to do? At the end of summer school, luckily for me, Abram Harris at Howard said that he was working on a book on Negro capitalists and Negro banks and had a grant from the University of Pennsylvania to support a research assistant. So I did some statistical work for Abe, for the net sum of $30 a month. He probably had a grant for $1,000. So I stayed at my aunt's and I paid my aunt $28 or maybe $26 a month. But the next year I went on the Howard payroll as an assistant and worked with students and faculty in statistics and economics. So we are talking now 1933, 1934, probably 1935—the Cost of Living Study for Labor came on and I took leave: Edward E. Lewis was in economics and he and I became good friends and we decided to take a trip South. He had never been South and he wanted to see the farm towns and rural life and the economics of it. He had never had a real feel for it, so he said, "Okay, let's get a car," so we bought a 1933 or 1934 Ford roadster—and a real oil burner—and he and I went South. We traveled through Georgia, Alabama, Mississippi, and back up to New Hampshire, and so on. And while in New Orleans—and here again sometimes you do things that you just do and other people don't do, and this is 1933, 1934, and there was an announcement that the Department of Labor was looking for Junior Social Economists—I sent in my application and the examination for it came at a time when I was in the field, so I wouldn't be in Washington—so I asked if I could transfer the exam and they said yes. So I took the exam in the U. S. customs house in New Orleans. And I was the only Negro in a whole sea of about 60, 80, or 100 white kids; and as it turned out, I got a pretty good mark on the exam, and they called me; and that is another story. Again, you get these side stories that are part of me; and any one of them I could carry on with. So where shall we go . . . ?

Stanfield: I'm interested in having you give me some insights into the influence of Frazier and Johnson, but before we get there could you give me insight about your work during the war years?

Lewis: All right. I'm at Talladega and I get a letter or phone call from a man at the University of Pennsylvania and he says, "Would you like to consider taking a job in Washington? Ralph Bunche has recommended you. Would you come to Washington?" The guy— you would know him—he's an old-timer at the University of Pennsylvania, he wrote a book on race relations, and was connected with the Social Science Research Council and Russell Sage Foundation.

Stanfield: Donald Young?

Lewis: Yeah, Donald Young, that's right. Donald interviewed me; He was a dollar-a-year consultant with an office right near the White House. So we had the interview, and that went pretty well. As it turns out there were two jobs: One was a job at OWI and the other was a job in Army Intelligence, where you would get a commission as a captain. And later on Donald laughed and said, "Well, you know, we interviewed Hylan Lewis and he definitely was not cut our for the army." The person chosen for military intelligence was Bill Bryant, Judge Bryant, William B. Bryant, judge of the Federal Court in Washington; he was one of Bunche's protégés. So the question was, there were two jobs and they had to make the decision whether Bill got the intelligence job or I—so I went with OWI. This is how I got to play a role in the war; and it suggests interesting things about friendly margins. I left Talladega, and reluctantly so, because this was one of my great experiences in teaching.

Stanfield: What years were you there, again?

Lewis: I went to Talladega in September 1941; I remember I wasn't there a full year because the war broke out and I left Talladega, probably before the end of the term. And Buell Gallagher took my class over [laughter]. And this is an immodest statement, but one that is very moving, because when I left the students came out and said goodbye to me, and some were in tears.

Stanfield: That's very touching.

Lewis: It was touching to me because of the experiences I had in teaching those bright and responsive freshman. All right—Washington, I am coming back home. Getting out of Talladega is another story, I won't digress on that. So I am in Washington at OWI. I came at the time that they were undergoing a reorganization. If you know government circles, you know what that means—job eliminations. So, in a sense the job I was supposed to have was probably wiped out in the reorganization, but luckily Clyde Hart was there (from the University of Iowa), as was Philleo Nash, the anthropologist, with whom I came to work. The stress of the reorganization brought out a small feud between Clyde and Philleo. Anyway, Clyde looked at my resumé and said, "Well, you have had some economics and you have had some labor and personnel work in Chicago, and we are setting up a research section, and I think you could handle the labor and personnel section. Just have patience and hold on." So I sat around waiting for the reorganization to go on—and part of the breaking-up process meant that secretaries get fired and the other guys "go upstairs." And Philleo "went upstairs" and eventually ended up in the White House to work with Jonathan Daniels and President Roosevelt. I'll show you some papers on that. Anyway, finally my appointment came through and I had the labor portfolio and became a colleague of Betsy Herzog, one of my great friends. Eventually I wrote and did backdrop research for the wartime domestic advertising, and so on; and later with Betsy and others I began doing content analysis. I would do analysis of newspaper and magazine editorials, and my analysis of editorials from the nation's newspapers would be distributed daily to government officials, including those in the White House. I learned a lot doing that. Herb Blumer came later on. He too became a member of a wonderful weekly salon that Betsy used to have. It included Harold Lasswell, Herbert Blumer, Ruth Benedict, and numerous others. Ruth Benedict was having a difficult time at Columbia, and when she was angry would charge Columbia with being very sexist, not to mention racist. She was angry because people like her weren't getting promotions, and she literally asked me how you organize a union. Well, she knew—again another digression that is important— that at Howard I was a charter member of AFT and later on the CIO Teachers Union, along with Callis, Frazier, Wilkerson, Hunton, and some other faculty people. That's another interesting story, but anyway, the salons of OWI people and wartime Washington associates and friends were the most remarkable Sunday afternoons we would spend there. Betsy Herzog and I were great friends and very, very close. She committed suicide years later. She had cancer of the pancreas. I went down to see her just before she died. The point is, again, Here was one of the major influences on my life. I have been very lucky . . .

Stanfield: What happened in her career—after the war, what did she do?

Lewis: Betsy? Betsy came to New York and worked for welfare and service agencies here. She married Ralph White, a social psychologist at George Washington University. As I say, I have been lucky, extremely lucky to have been close to people like Betsy. . . . She was an extraordinary writer and we collaborated; we did some pieces together. The Children's Bureau—she and Helen Witmer ran its research division and that is where she was in Washington after the war.

Stanfield: It looks like no matter where you have been, you managed to surround yourself with humanists. People who are humanistic and . . .

Lewis: Again I always tell my students you are not a good sociologist unless you have some sense of the humanities, and history is one of humanities, and that knowing and acting on this is some of the best sociology.

Stanfield: You said something about studying the wartime riots for OWI.

Lewis: Yes, I'll pull out some of these reports while I am thinking about it.

Stanfield: Were they ever published?

Lewis: No, they are presumably still confidential. I mentioned that Philleo Nash went upstairs to work there for a while, and when Jonathan Daniels came to Washington as Roosevelt's assistant for domestic affairs, Philleo went over to work with Jonathan and we kept our friendship, and so on. And so when we had the New York riots and the Detroit riots . . . they tapped me to come to New York to see what was happening and I worked with Herbert Hyman, a social psychologist at Columbia who recently died. Anyway we teamed up together, but we had a clash in the beginning because he was from Columbia and he wanted to tell me how to do field research, you know [laughter]. Later, though, we became very good friends. He died in China on a visit a few years ago. . . . Okay, here are some of the papers on the riot in question. Some are collaborative and some I wrote completely.

Stanfield: Did you have any interaction with Robin Williams?

Lewis: Robin comes later. He comes in on my Cornell days.

Stanfield: Oh. Well, was there any other Black social scientist or historian doing this kind of war work?

Lewis: Yes, Ken Clark worked for OWI in New York, and Lewis Jones and Ted Poston did in Washington. Ted Poston was on the OWI Negro desk, Bunche at the Office of Facts and Figures, later CIA. Also there were Harold O. Lewis and Clinton Knox, historians. And Ulysses Lee, as a captain in the army, worked on a history of the Negro soldier. He was recruited by Philleo Nash and me.

Stanfield: I am surprised that Charles Johnson wasn't called to Washington during those years. I would have thought he would be a natural. Maybe it was because of the fact he was a Republican.

Lewis: I think there were lots of reasons why Johnson was not called to Washington.

Stanfield: Okay, after the war you go on to Hampton.

Lewis: The war ends and I am transferred to the Bureau of the Budget, sort of a caretaker agency that was designed to dissolve wartime agencies, and "K. C." Blackburn, a woman who worked with Roosevelt when he was governor of New York, was head of that. So I had offices there in the Triangle on Pennsylvania Avenue, and this is when Ralph Bridgman popped on the scenes: So I went to Hampton to teach. You can look at these OWI reports sometime.

Stanfield: Thank you. I would imagine that somehow under the Freedom of Information Act now they could be released.

Lewis: I am sure.

Stanfield: So Bridgman popped in . . . You were in Hampton for a couple of years, right?

Lewis: I was in Hampton from '45 to '47. I guess I was there for a couple of years. In '47 I left to do the South Carolina community study—*Blackways of Kent,* and that gave me the opportunity to work on my dissertation. After all these years I was working exclusively on something, but you know . . . that's another story.

Stanfield: Now at Hampton you were one of the teachers of O. Rudolph Aggrey. You maintained a long continuous friendship with him.

Lewis: Oh yes.

Stanfield: Were there any other students at Hampton?

Lewis: Aggrey is the one that stands out that I have maintained this kind of relationship with over the years.

Stanfield: Did he minor or major in sociology?

Lewis: I think he majored in it.

Stanfield: Let's talk about *Blackways of Kent,* how you went about deciding on that research topic and how you gained access to the community.

Lewis: One day I had a phone call from John Gillin, the Chapel Hill anthropologist: He would like to come see me and talk with me. So he came and we talked; he really came to see if I had some students I could recommend. He had this proposed study and was looking for someone to do fieldwork, and, again, I suspect in the back of his mind he thought he might interest me, but ostensibly he was interested in my recommendation. So we talked at length and I finally said, "Well, I might be interested in that myself." I saw that as one way of getting the continuous time to do something, otherwise I would just limp along and never get back to my dissertation. To digress a little bit, Professor Earl Johnson at Chicago and I were good friends, and we pledged each other that we would not break the record for delay in finishing our dissertations, and we would also come to each other's commencement no matter what [laughter]. I think it was 10 years between my finishing up my work and I think for Earl it was a little longer. I actually finished in 1950. It wasn't difficult once I got into it. So how did I make my community contacts? I had the name of Isaac Wright—Isaac N. Wright, the undertaker there. You know how small towns are. I found out that Wright was a graduate of Johnson C. Smith and sort of a frustrated academic and scientist, who when his father died had to take over the undertaking business. But you know these guys—a small town, somewhat frustrated, making do, but also with interest and some wry but appreciative skepticism. But later we became very close friends. Here again was a situation where experienced locals might be tempted to think they know how to do your work better than you do, and with some justification. He was very nice and was quite concerned about getting a nice place for me to live. Among the choices for landlords were a town busybody and gossip and her daughter, . . . which would have been all right: then another choice . . . "Mammie" Neeley. "Mammie" Neeley was about at that time 70, a widow lady who lived by herself. She worked for white folks uptown and would leave at 7:00 p.m. and go spend the night with the white folks. And there was an outdoor toilet. Immediately I saw "Mammie" Neeley and saw the place, I said this was for me. So what I did quite deliberately was go against the grain of conventional fieldwork that says one should work from the top: My design was to go in from both the bottom and the top. If I had to make a choice, I was going from the bottom. But luckily, my ability to get along with "Mammie" Neeley paid off; she was cautious, but eventually she began to love me. We got along very well and when I left she would have left her property to me at her death, if she had had her wish.

Back to the OWI—just a general comment. I got into many situations where I was the only Negro in this setting and I wasn't characteristically a Negro representative. I was doing some things that were nonracial basically. In a lot of situations where I was the only and probably the first for many people and it might sometimes have involved their getting used to this sort of thing—although I was rarely acutely aware of this, there again this friendly margin bit was probably present. The only and the first phenomenon might illustrate a calculus of tolerance of the categorical others. You get whites who cannot fully tolerate more than two or three, it emphasizes the question, What use is one? That kind of thing. All my life I have had some degree of that feeling of being at the edges.

Stanfield: And, apparently, there is something about your technical competence, but also your personal management, that enablesyou to function quite well in settings without it becoming too self-conscious.

Lewis: Well, well, again, I want to give you this anecdote. Clyde Hart, who was later head of NORC—I first knew Clyde at OWI (again in this wartime period you had a proliferation of agencies and considerable shifting of people)—Clyde later on went to the Pentagon and after the war became head of NORC. As I said, Clyde and I were good friends, but Clyde said to me once, "Hylan, you know, I never think of you as a Negro." I tell this to my friends sometimes and they say, "What did you do?" I say, remember what the surgeons say, "Forgive and remember." And they say, "Well, he was being positive," and yes, he was, but that is the point. During my grant committee days I experienced a lot of anomalous situations involving race. I remember a grant proposal for something like a million and a half dollars coming from a prominent medical school. They had offered a project based on the fact that they had used Black women to get the preliminary data to plan and develop a program of research and treatment from which Black women were excluded. I protested and argued with these guys— some of the most distinguished guys in their fields. They would try to give you the line that it's possible to have research based on this kind of exclusion. I said, "No, no, this is not right," and I held it up. Later on they and the principals had to backtrack; and the proposal went back, for revision.

Stanfield: Before getting on to that, why don't we continue with discussion of your *Black Ways of Kin* research?

Lewis: So with regard to the entrance in the field here, the point I want to make is that I was able to move easily at all levels simultaneously. There was no sector that was closed to me or that I couldn't enter at some point. Some could be a little bit dangerous— the bootleggers, the jailbirds, the crooks—and some were a bit wary, some preachers, and the ministers. I suppose the anchors of my fieldwork were the old people. Again, in field research if you can get along with old folks and children, you've got it made [laughter]. Then there needs to be a little sense of humor but also, never take yourself too seriously in the sense that you think are "in" too much with the other: Act yourself. People would ask you, "You get around. What church do you belong to?" and I would say that I belong to all the churches. And one lady said, "No, you are out in the old field." Again it was that I became accepted. Ben

Williams ran the pool hall and filling station: I racked balls in the pool hall and helped at the filling station and helped with lots of things. A couple of guys tested me one night by asking me to go with them to the bootleggers' out in the country. Doing it scared me to death because this was a dry county and the cops would be waiting. I did it once just to test the level and prove myself. And again one interesting bit to illustrate how delicate the situation was: Ken Moreland was there studying the mill workers at the same time. We would meet in the post office. John Gillin said once that he would like to come down and visit with me, and I said, "Okay." At that time the Research Center at Chapel Hill had this big black station wagon. You can imagine this small town and these white guys coming in this big black van and parking it in "Mammie" Neeley's driveway. And we are sitting in my front bedroom and talking about field experiences and so on; and without my knowledge at some point these cops, led by this guy, Mr. Boyd—every town has a cop like this—that SOB was out there in the bushes, sneaking up to eavesdrop and to trap "the Communists" [laugh]. The chief of police, Mr. Turner, was friendly to me—Wright had introduced me. He said, "Don't fret about that Boyd, he's all right." Officer Boyd was skeptical, but I weathered that, but again you don't try that twice. Again, when you're in a tavern, how you get in and what you do, where do you stand, where do you sit, how do you get up, what happens when the cops come and make a sweep and carry guys to jail, what do you do? This was a very genuinely moving experience for me, but also in some sense you could always get out, leave town once in a while, you're mobile—and I could go see my friends, the Wrights and so on, but they also thought I was crazy [laughter].

Stanfield: How long did it take you to do your fieldwork and to write it up?

Lewis: Let's see, I wrote it up in the field. I was there about a year. Well, I went to the field in September and went back to teach in Atlanta University in August. One of the tricks of the trade you learn is that you make field progress reports that are more than progress reports. They become part of the full document. But again, speaking of my own personality, Audrey, my wife at the time, came to the field at the last part of the term; she was a very fair person, who drew stares when we walked the main drag. When we left the field at the end I stopped and talked with all the people

I knew, my friends, just to say hello and goodbye to them. Again, you know, even those close to you can be very cruel and cutting at times: When I got in the car the last time she excoriated me and said, "You hypocrite."

Stanfield: Your book was really the last of the great Afro-American community studies. How was your book reviewed in the fifties, when it came out? Do you remember?

Lewis: Very few reviews, not very many.

Stanfield: But it really represented a kind of sociology that was going off the scene. Perhaps that explains why there were so few reviews. The field was becoming more quantitative, large-scale data banks and more community-based qualitative studies were beginning to be . . .

Lewis: But I don't have a sense about that . . .

Stanfield: That's because you were so busy, you didn't have the time! So you moved from Hampton to Atlanta. Prior to your move did someone else pop in . . . ?

Lewis: Oh, from Hampton? Ah, yes.

Stanfield: Someone else popped in? Right?

Lewis: You got me. Every summer I was up here. I would always go to the Oyster Bar and one spring, maybe '47, Ira de Reid was there. He greeted me as a long-lost brother, and he said, "Hy, what are you doing this summer?" At that time he was teaching at NYU. He asked if I wanted to teach in Atlanta and I said sure; and I went down to teach summer school in Atlanta. I got to know Mozell Hill, Ira's successor as chair. You know the sequence: I went back to Hampton and that was the year I went into the field, and later I think I went to Atlanta after finishing in the field. I think that Mozell offered me a job. I know what it was, Ira left and Mozell became chairman.

Stanfield: Yeah, Ira went to Haverford.

Lewis: I think I went to Atlanta right after York. My getting linked up with Atlanta again is an aspect of my very good fortune. I have been a part of the academic communities at Howard, Atlanta, Talladega, and Hampton—where in each instance there was a flowering and a confluence of great spirits and great minds; and the interaction of these was so great and good, but it doesn't mean that there wasn't conflict.

Stanfield: Also, I don't know if you have thought about this or not, you probably have a great deal, but your career has also been at a point, let's say, at the apex of flowering. You moved from Howard to Hampton to Talladega, to Atlanta when things were developing . . . So you stayed in Atlanta for how many years and where did you move on to?

Lewis: Ah, yes. Friendly margins. In Atlanta at that time we had again the Ashmore Project and desegregation studies supported by Ford in that period. You know about that period?

Stanfield: There was something funded by the Ford Foundation?

Lewis: Yes, I was a participant in that with Mozell Hill, Harold Fleming, John Griffin, and Robin Williams.

Stanfield: Now that study took place in several cities, in Nashville, Atlanta.

Lewis: Yeah, various places around. Robin Williams and my good friend Marge Ryan wrote up this study.

Stanfield: How was that project organized?

Lewis: You had Harry Ashmore, who was editor of the *Arkansas Gazette*, as the point man. Harry depended very heavily upon Harold Fleming and John Griffin.

Stanfield: At that time Harold Fleming was with the Southern Regional Council?

Lewis: That's right. And George Mitchell was there. He and Horace did the book together.

Stanfield: Oh, yes, *Black Workers and the New Unions* [Cayton & Mitchell, n.d.].

Lewis: Anyway, I was there. But you see, Harry Ashmore was a very good journalist, but he was kind of skeptical and cynical about social science positions, like many hard journalists. So it depended a great deal on Harold Fleming. But anyway after the thing was over he needed someone to pull the stuff together and write it up and that's when he brought in Robin Williams and Marge Ryan from Cornell. How was it organized? I think in the main, again, you know what happens. Nothing changes a great deal. Blacks or Negroes are sort of attached and brought in selectively and never really given power. Mozell was linkage and Charlie Parrish was involved peripherally and a lot of things were filtered through us. We were associated with the project but never utilized as fully as we might have been or should have been, because, as Frazier used to say, "Hylan, white folks don't take Negroes seriously."

Stanfield: Some things never change.

Lewis: I say this again contextually, but again Negroes come out of it and you learn something. You learn, as I told a guy, you "forgive and remember."

Stanfield: Related to that, to go back a small bit, did you work on the *American Dilemma* project?

Lewis: No. Everything you ask, I'll give you a story. No, *American Dilemma* came, I'll tell you about it, that was 1939 and they brought Myrdal to the Howard campus and they were tapping people, but that's the time of my Rosenwald, 1939, so do I go to work for Myrdal when I've got Rosenwald? No, and I've got two years, but what I did, at Chicago—Ed Shils was a friend of mine so the project through him utilized a couple of term papers I completed. I was interested in intellectuals and professionals. I did the two papers on Negro intellectuals and professionals that Ed incorporated in terms of that component. So it was only to that extent.

Stanfield: Okay, now—when did you get from Atlanta to the CUNY Graduate School here?

Lewis: You mentioned how I got out of Atlanta?

Stanfield: Oh, I'm sorry.

Lewis: Matilda Moore of the Unitarian Service Committee had met Mozell Hill in Atlantic City at a conference and she had a bug in her bonnet that she wanted to establish a project that would facilitate integration, not desegregation, but integration in school—this again following the Ashmore report. So she asked Mozell to arrange a conference and she would come down with her staff. So Mozell asked me; and I actually did the organizing and arranging:

Among the people I brought in was Ken Clark. And that is when Ken Clark met Jeanette Hopkins, his editor and friend. The beginning of *Dark Ghetto* [Clark, 1989] comes out of that meeting.

Anyway, the conference went very well and I guess I was pretty active in it. And Matilda Moore in looking at it said, "Who is this guy Hylan Lewis?" In some sense, she conveyed that she wanted me to work with her. She asked if I would be a consultant. And so Ken and I became consultants to the Unitarian Service Committee. I traveled in and out of Atlanta, helping to set up a program and establish projects in Knoxville, Chicago, and Washington.

Stanfield: And is that where you also met Clark for the first time?

Lewis: I knew Ken Clark over many years. I was Clark's best man at his wedding. We worked at Howard together, where I taught Mamie, his wife and collaborator, before they married. Atlanta was where Clark first met Mozell and Whitney Young and a lot of other people. Anyway, to go back to my Service Committee activities, Tilly said, "I would like for you and Kenneth to do an intelligence trip in the South." Ken had never been South and I had, so we planned and then went to Mississippi and Alabama on what we called "the Lewis and Clark expedition." Those were the beginnings of a kind of constant involvement with the Service Committee; but later on, Tilly said, "But look, I want you to come and work with us in Boston. If you come I will make you associate director of the Service Committee." Again, this was one of those times. For a change anyway I left Atlanta for Boston.

Stanfield: What year was that?

Lewis: It was 1956, '57. I had the Ford Faculty Fellowship thing and had done Chapel Hill, Cornell, and Boston University. I also in the meantime had had my Africa bit. While at Atlanta, I had been tapped to be a consultant to the Gold Coast. Critical here was my record sheet that showed some consulting I had done for the Tennessee Valley Authority, and this was relevant to the Volta River Project. I went to West Africa to work for three months. When I came back, Emory University wanted someone from Atlanta University to teach a course; and so I was picked and I taught a course in sociological methods in 1954.

Stanfield: Was this during the academic year or during the summer?

Lewis: During the academic year—a regular course. Then, now, we return to the Service Committee: Again, I helped out with a project in Nigeria. I had met Ken Nzeribe, an economist, from Cornell; the Service Committee brought him in. He and I went to Eastern Nigeria to set up a development project. Later on, Ed Olds, who while working with the Health and Welfare Council in Washington read *Blackways of Kent,* and had the bright idea that if he could get someone to do a study, do research in the Washington community in the manner of *Blackways of Kent,* that would be a good base for policy-making and so on. Washington at that time was in the throes of being concerned about child dependency. So Ed got in touch with me and asked if I would come to Washington; I said yes and that was the beginning of my Child-Rearing Study in DC.

Stanfield: How long were you there?

Lewis: The Child-Rearing? Maybe two years. I left and again Howard was in the backdrop. I had a reincarnation at Howard. Jay Fishman wanted me to come to the medical school. Then President Jim Nabrit, a good friend, was having problems getting competent assistance in carrying out the university's community research projects. He came up with the idea to get someone in there who was experienced and strong. He offered the job to Nelson Jackson first, but Nelson turned it down. So Jay Fishman wanted me to come to the medical school and I was inclined to go and be a social scientist at the medical school. Nabrit cut in and, like Mephistopheles, offered me the world. He said, "Okay, come on in, you'll be professor of sociology and Director of Community Studies." I knew what kind of politics were involved, and bringing me in would have been all right—but I was only there a week or less, maybe a couple of weeks, when President Johnson asked Nabrit to be a delegate to the United Nations. That left me there with many of the campus wounds and the masters of "negative administration." I had a fairly rough time. Of course, nobody seemed interested except to keep me from doing the job. In the meantime, right after that came my selection as Chief Consultant to the Family Panel at the White House Conference. A bit later Ken [Clark] had gotten money from the Field and Ford Foundations for MARC, and so I commuted to New York for about six months or so to help him set up MARC [Metropolitan Applied Research Center]. I directed the Fellowship Program. Eventually we decided

I would come to New York and work full-time for MARC. When I became involved with MARC, Charlie Lawrence, the Sociology Chair from Brooklyn College, said, "Gee, you can come to Brooklyn College"—so again, "friendly margins."

Stanfield: What probably fascinates me the most about your career, the whole career, but particularly in the sixties, is that your work with government panels really did a number of things, in terms of developing the concept of the Black underclass. I am standing in the living room of the person who really helped develop that concept and the financing of research on it.

Lewis: I wouldn't take that as one of my . . .

Stanfield: I know, but I would [laughter], that is why I am standing right here, and you should get credit for that, but NIMH . . .

Lewis: Two things about NIMH. One, I was on several of their panels. I was a charter member of the Labor Department's Dissertation and Small Grants Program, and served for 20 years. At NIMH I was on the Delinquency Program Panel for several years before it changed to the social problems panel; and then I did an NIH stint and so on. In the meantime, when I directed the Child-Rearing Study, we turned in a report the first year that blew their minds at NIMH— they passed it all around. We should have published the damn thing then, but didn't; it was a cinch for a renewal grant. At that time the only two Negroes in the country who had control of significant public research money like that for projects were me in D.C. and Ken Clark in New York. Later on, before I left, I drew up plans for another project that called for a utilization grant. Luther Jackson came in and he and Pat Morisey took the findings of the Child-Rearing Study and utilized them in working with social workers and community groups in the DC area.

Stanfield: What were some of the other major publications, like *Tally's Corner* [Liebow, 1967], that came out of this work?

Lewis: Well, out of my project, one was *Living Poor,* a book by Camille Jeffers. Camille is dead now. Camille was really the strength of my staff . . . She was a social worker teaching at Atlanta University School of Social Work. I learned about her and I sought her and asked her if she wanted to come because I thought she could do the kind of fieldwork that had to be done. What I had in mind was living in a housing project. I negotiated with Walter Washington, who was head of housing, to provide her with an apartment for her and her son, and so she lived in the apartment for a full year and the book that she did was called *Living Poor.*

Stanfield: Was this sort of like the predecessor to Joyce Ladner's *Tomorrow's Tomorrow* [1971]?

Lewis: Well, in a sense, yes, but . . . Ladner and colleagues took off from *Blackways of Kent* in their St. Louis housing project studies. Camille showed my CRS staff the way fieldwork should be done: For the other persons doing fieldwork I would beat them over the head and say if you don't write it down it didn't happen [laughter]. James Comer, the Yale psychiatrist, was very much struck with her work and would always fuss and ask why didn't Camille get more play.

Stanfield: Frankly, you know, I don't remember that work.

Lewis: *Living Poor.* Well, this is another story . . . there was some negotiation to publish it first with a university press that fell through, but anyway it came out later, published by a small press.

Stanfield: If you were to sketch out the paradigm that you constructed and were interested in scholars taking an interest in regard to the poor, the underclass, what was it?

Lewis: That's an interesting question, I haven't thought about that. Let me go back again, we're talking in context of times. You see when I came to Washington to do this study, *poor* was not even in the contemporary vocabulary. They were using "dressed up" terms like *low income,* and this is just before, again, '59. Harrington came in the early sixties. What I sought to do at that time, one of my first papers said it very well, was to bring about this morganatic marriage between sociology and social work: to do research that was respectable, but at the same time useful to policymakers concerned with the problems of dependency and low-income, poor families— and so that was the big area [hands Stanfield a copy of the study].

Stanfield: Members of your generation save everything. I don't know how you do it.

Lewis: This comes out of one of the utilization projects, Luther put these together.

Stanfield: *Culture, Class, and Poverty.*

Lewis: Do you know this? This will tell you at that time what my approach was.

Stanfield: Was Ophelia Settle . . . ?

Lewis: Again you've touched on a story. Frazier and I were together in sociology at Howard. I helped Frazier in a small way to set up the School of Social Work at Howard University and we taught together in one of the first courses. We brought Inabel Lindsay and Ruth Jackson and later on Ophelia Settle into the social work faculty.

My wonderful interview with Hylan Lewis ended officially on that note, though we did go on talking off the record. The precious moments I spent gave me profound insights into the struggles of productive Afro-American social scientists active during the 1950s and 1960s. More than that, through Hylan's openness, I learned a great deal about networks and about the politics and sociology of mentorship. During the time of the great vacuum in post-World War II Afro-American public participation in social science research, scholars in policy circles such as Lewis and Clark worked diligently to shape race relations thinking in significant policy arenas. Their influence was in their ability to shape research agendas emerging on the scene in government and academic circles.

When the 1970s and 1980s came around, the entrenchment of conservative views in policy circles made the views of Lewis marginal. But by that time he had already paved the way for a cohort of scholars that included Joyce Ladner and Elliot Liebow, who published scholarship that will serve as a lasting memorial of a most humane way to understand the poor, particularly those of darker hue.

References

Cayton, H., & Mitchell, G. (n.d.). *Black workers and the new unions.*Salem, NH: Ayer.
Clark, K. (1989). *Dark ghetto: Dilemmas of social power* (2nd ed.). Hanover, NH: University Press of New England.

Drake, S. C., & Cayton, H. (1945). *Black metropolis: A study of Negro life in a northern city*. New York: Harcourt, Brace.

Ladner, J. A. (1971). *Tomorrow's tomorrow*. Garden City, NY: Doubleday.

Lewis, H. (1955). *Blackways of Kent*. Chapel Hill: University of North Carolina Press.

Liebow, E. (1967). *Tally's corner: A study of Negro street corner men*. Boston: Little, Brown.

5

A Sociologist Prospers in the Race Relations Industry

LEWIS M. KILLIAN

My first research in race relations was done in 1941 for my master's thesis, under a Phelps-Stoke Fellowship at the University of Georgia. I continued work in this field at the University of Chicago between 1946 and 1949, where I studied for my Ph.D. aided by a Rosenwald Fellowship. In 1954, now a faculty member at Florida State University, I conducted a study of readiness and resistance to school desegregation for the state attorney general. Thus from the earliest stages of my career as a sociologist I was committed to ethnic relations as my major interest.

It was not until 1975 that I encountered the notion of a "race relations industry." I was doing research on race relations in England under a Guggenheim Fellowship and found that this term was often used critically by a right-wing columnist for a London daily newspaper. I did not realize its applicability to me until a Black community relations officer told me, "I'm part of the race relations industry and so are you—we are both making our living off the race problem."

The London journalist had written sarcastically that in England "shares of all the big race relations consortia had moved up on the ethical stock exchange." In the United States the race relations industry,

AUTHOR'S NOTE: The original version of this chapter, titled "Prospering in the Race Relations Industry," is to appear in my book *The Civil Rights Crusade: Reflections of a White Southern Sociologist,* to be published in 1993 by General Hall, Inc. Used by permission.

104

professionals dealing with this major social problem, certainly bur-geoned after the 1954 school desegregation decision of the Supreme Court. I was one of the social scientists who profited from the increased investment by foundations and the government, for from 1957 until 1965 I engaged in a great deal of sponsored research. I became a "grantsman," albeit on a rather small scale. The experience of obtaining the grants and the behind-the-scenes story of how the research was done still overshadow in my mind the findings and the publications that resulted.

A Small Beginning

My first grant, obtained from the Social Science Research Council in 1957, was ridiculously small—less than $300. I could have done the research without it, but having sponsorship gave me a sense of obliga-tion that kept me from putting the task aside in the face of other demands on my time. This resulted in a study of Black leadership that C. U. Smith, of Florida A&M University, and I published in 1960.

Journey to Olympus

Following Governor LeRoy Collins's call for cities throughout Flor-ida to establish biracial committees, a colleague at Florida State Uni-versity, Charles Grigg, and I decided that these new bodies would be good subjects for research. Somehow we learned that the Field Foun-dation, located in New York but funded by the Marshall Field family of Chicago, was awarding grants for research that had implications for application. Leslie Dunbar, whom I had known when he was executive for the Southern Regional Council, was now with Field.

Grigg and I devised a very imaginative experimental research design to compare two cities, one with a biracial committee and one without. Apparently it seemed reasonable to someone on the foundation staff, for I was invited to meet with the board of directors to discuss our application. All my expenses for travel to New York would be paid and a room was reserved for me at the Waldorf, just across the street from the Field Foundation office.

My reunion with Les Dunbar was just that—a pleasant visit with some discussion of changes in the South since he had left. We discussed very few details of the research design and the grant application. The crucial event was to be my meeting with the board that evening during their dinner meeting at the apartment of Mrs. Marshall Field, Jr., on Park Avenue. To me, this would be a journey to Olympus.

When I passed building security and stepped off the elevator into the foyer of Mrs. Field's apartment I entered a world that I had seen only in movies. My dinner companions included, among others, Adlai Stevenson, chairman of the board; Otto Klineberg, whose research on the intelligence of whites and Blacks had been so important in my education; and Ralph Bunche, at the peak of his career as a member of the United Nations staff. I was enjoying dinner with celebrities who were also some of the "big mules" of the race relations industry.

Another guest was a man whose fame, or notoriety, was quite familiar to me—Myles Horton, of Highlander Folk School. He was applying for a grant to help support his work, which had already played a crucial role in the practical education of civil rights leaders, including Martin Luther King, Jr. I found him delightfully humorous even when he was recounting incidents in which he had been cruelly persecuted by the Tennessee police. He said he wasn't sure whether or not it represented progress when his enemies started calling him a "Communist" instead of just a "nigger lover"!

The main thing I remember about the conversation was the stream of jokes told by Stevenson, one of the wittiest politicians in our history. After dinner we got down to business, but again I was asked little about the proposed research. Apparently the board members simply wanted to find out what sort of people Myles and I were. They were particularly interested in my experience in teaching race relations to white southern students, and encouraged me to speculate about what I had accomplished by requiring each one to write an autobiographical account of the development of his or her attitudes toward Blacks.

I left Park Avenue not knowing whether we would receive our grant or not, but soon after my return to Tallahassee, Grigg and I were notified that we had been awarded $25,000.

Politics and Research

As it turned out, very few communities appointed biracial committees, and Charles Grigg and I were lucky to find even one city where we could gain entrée. A special assistant on Governor Collins's staff had been working with a committee in Daytona Beach and introduced us to the chairman, a local undertaker, and the members. They had no objection to our attending their meetings and studying their work, but it was necessary to have the approval of the mayor and the city commission. This was particularly important, as we wanted to do survey research in both the white and Black sectors of the community, and we proposed to employ both Black and white interviewers. For their own protection they would require clearance by the police. Once again I was thrust into the political arena, challenged to sell research to elected officials.

The mayor proved easy to work with, and he and I established a pleasant relationship. Another of my stereotypes was destroyed in the process. He operated a personal finance or small loan company. I learned from him that a so-called loan shark could be a very decent person who actually provided a much-needed service for people who could not get conventional loans. Perhaps the fact that many of his clients were Black accounted for his relatively liberal position on race relations.

The city commission was a very different proposition. So frightened were they of the issue of race relations that they violated the Florida "sunshine law" by having a secret meeting with me before our proposal was submitted for action at a public meeting. Two members gave me a very hard time. One was a Republican, representing many wealthy, conservative constituents. He was not only conservative in his views on race, but also held a deep mistrust of social scientists. He stated that he felt the sort of research we wanted to do would not only be meaningless, but also might stir up trouble in the community. As soon as he stated his position, he was joined by another member, a crude, conservative Democrat who had once been convicted of election fraud and had to have his civil rights restored in order to run for office again. Without explanation, he exclaimed, "I wouldn't touch this with a 10-foot pole!"

The other members, fortunately a majority, were not hostile, but instead asked reasonable questions about just what it was we wanted to do. I did not know what the outcome would be when I left the illegal, secret meeting, but it turned out to be favorable. When the Commission held its official, public meeting, I presented our request and the commission approved it with almost no discussion.

Once under way, our research went well. In interviews with members of the biracial committee and while recruiting interviewers for our survey, I became acquainted with faculty and students at historic Bethune-Cookman College. One of our interviewers was the son of Mary McLeod Bethune. As I visited the campus, I was amazed to discover how the spirit of this great Black woman haunted the campus, almost as if she were still the president. On every hand there were memorials to her; it seemed to me that nearly every classroom held a picture of her.

Raising the Stakes

Even before all the results of our research were in, Grigg and I went after a larger grant. We went to New York to lay a proposal for a $100,000 grant before the Rockefeller Foundation. Success! We received the grant and went after our next research target, Jacksonville. It had not appointed a biracial committee, but negotiations were beginning between two leadership groups, one white and one Black.

Jacksonville's approach stemmed from the initiative of two people in the Chamber of Commerce—it was a project of the business community, not of the politicians. While the president of the chamber was on vacation in Scotland, he read in the British newspapers of racial disorders in his home city. His reaction was the same as that eventually shared by many white southern business leaders: "What is this kind of publicity going to do to business?" On his return he conferred with a very shrewd and experienced staff member named E. Howard Hill. The two men came up with a plan to stimulate the formation of negotiating teams in the two communities, with Hill to be the liaison. The Chamber of Commerce board went along. When we came in with our sumptuous grant, we were able to work out a nice symbiotic relationship. We rented and furnished an office in downtown Jacksonville that would serve as a neutral ground for conferences between white and Black leaders. At the same time it would serve as our research headquarters while we observed the interactions between the leaders and carried out surveys in the city. For two years we kept a graduate research assistant in that office full-time, first William Stacey and then Henry Stewart. Both have had fruitful careers in sociology since those early days of their training.

Our subjects in Jacksonville were significantly different from the members of the biracial committee in Daytona Beach. They were not politically appointed and they held no formal positions. Many of the Whites were very powerful men who came in and out of the negotiating process in response to threatened crises. The Blacks, although hardly radical, were nevertheless the people who were creating the crises by their demands. One was the president of the Youth Council of the Jacksonville NAACP; whenever Blacks demonstrated, he would be in the vanguard. The young executive of the Jacksonville Urban League was active in a different way, but in spirit was no less militant. He labored to solicit the financial support of the business community. He monitored the day-to-day needs of Black citizens, and he sought to direct the efforts of the social welfare bureaucracy toward them. He also undertook to see that gains won by demonstrators were not lost. He once remarked, "I'm about to develop an ulcer eating hamburgers at integrated lunch counters!"

These two research projects resulted in a number of articles and a book; their success astounded Grigg and me. One article I can only regard as a "sleeper." In one of our attitude surveys in Jacksonville we included the Srole anomia scale; at the same time we did a similar survey with a sample in Monticello, a small tobacco town not far from Tallahassee. The results, published in an article titled "Urbanism, Race, and Anomia" in the *American Journal of Sociology* (Killian & Grigg, 1962), received a lot of attention from sociologists because of our finding that Blacks in the rural community had higher anomia scores than did those in Jacksonville, contrary to previous theories about the effects of urbanization on anomia. The recognition was gratifying, but I have often felt that this little project may have been a prime example of the questionable validity of much of sociological research. First, despite its popularity, I had serious doubts about just what the anomia scale really represented. Second, as I spent most of my time in Tallahassee designing research and constructing instruments to be administered by interviewers whom I would never see, I wondered, as I do about most survey research, How closely did the people in the field actually adhere to the sample design? Did they conduct the interviews the way I meant for them to? Did they actually do all the interviews? I remembered the chagrin of a famous sociologist I had known early in my career who discovered by accident that one of his field people in a large survey had faked all of her interviews. He had to drop these protocols and complete the research with a flawed sample. The study was still published as a book that was highly acclaimed by other sociologists.

Despite the overwhelming popularity of survey research based on large samples, I have never been able to feel comfortable with data I did not collect myself, in the field. Obviously, this bias has placed severe limitations on the kind of research I would do, and rendered me perforce a "soft sociologist" in a discipline in which large samples and quantification often seem to be considered the only certain basis of knowledge.

The Big Payoff

As we began to get well into the Jacksonville research, Grigg and I saw the makings of a book summarizing what we felt we had learned so far. It started out almost as a "cut and paste" job. We planned to incorporate two already published articles and sections of several research reports we had done. The task of putting it all together fell to me. I was the chief writer in our team; Charlie was the statistician. He used to joke, "Lewis writes the conclusions and then I produce the statistics to support them!" As I started putting the materials together, I found myself writing more and more original text with a theme that became the title of our book, *Racial Crisis in America* (Killian & Grigg, 1964). The first chapter was titled "Race Relations: An Era of Struggle," and the last turned out to have the ominous heading, "The Specter of Conflict." The trend these two brackets enclosed reflected the pessimism that I had felt more and more since the hope-filled days following the *Brown* decision. Perhaps it was because of this pessimism, out of tune with the still-sanguine ideas of most of my fellow sociologists, that the book received so much attention. Some personal connections also helped, however. The first review was a lengthy article in the *New York Times* magazine section, written by one of their leading southern correspondents, Claude Sitton. He would later become editor of the *Raleigh News and Observer,* the paper that had become a symbol of southern liberalism under the editorship of Jonathan Daniels. The book came to Sitton's attention because of John A. Griffin, a friend on President Robert Strozier's staff at Florida State University.

John had been an invaluable editorial consultant while Grigg and I were writing the book. Shortly before it was published he had a memorable party at his farm outside Tallahassee. He had assembled a group of eminent journalists to cut a tape for an educational radio program to be titled, "Is There a New South?" John favored Charlie and me with an invitation to mix informally with a gathering that included Sitton; John Popham of the *Chattanooga Times*; Harry Ashmore, famous for his leadership in Little Rock; Harold Fleming, now with the Taconic Foundation; Bill Emerson of *Newsweek*; and Ralph McGill, editor of the *Atlanta Constitution* and one of the most famous of the white southern liberals. Harold Martin tells of this party in his 1973 biography of McGill, including the fact that Ralph slipped away early because of discomfort, which proved to be the harbinger of a fatal heart condition.

Claude Sitton was lavish in his praise of our work. He found the pessimistic position we took convincing and recommended the book as a timely and much-needed warning that the course of racial integration was not going to be as steady and free of conflict as many observers believed. Harry Ashmore, who reviewed *Racial Crisis* in the *Washington Post,* was very critical, however. He found our pessimism unwarranted and alarmist; he implied that we were a couple of "nervous Nellies" who had just discovered that all progress involves some conflict.

What was it that was so pessimistic about our conclusions? The sentiment was really mine more than Grigg's—I don't believe he ever shared it fully, even after the violent racial clashes of the late sixties lent support to my predictions. After witnessing and studying the ameliorative efforts at conflict resolution of the Southern Regional Council, Governor Collins, and biracial committees, I had become a conflict theorist against all my liberal inclinations. I could not forget the statement made by one mayor in reply to a regionwide survey we conducted to find out how widespread biracial committees had become. He wrote, "We are not appointing a biracial committee because we are already negotiating with Black leaders. If they have no power, putting them on a committee won't give them any more. If they do have it, you don't need the committee."

In my research in Daytona I had concluded that where biracial committees existed, they served what I called a "buffer function." If Blacks created a crisis by challenging traditional practices, one way to defuse the crisis was to appoint a biracial committee and assure the Black leaders that their demands would be discussed. A primary condition, however, was that they stop pressing their demands through demonstrations. Thus the biracial committee was more likely to block or limit change than to produce progress.

This conclusion had a corollary with broader implications. I had been enthralled by the philosophy and practice of nonviolent resistance to evil preached by Martin Luther King, Jr. His call to "love your enemies into submission" seemed to epitomize a Christian strategy for social change. Yet as I studied community strife in race relations, firsthand or through the press, I had a growing conviction that King's philosophy was not working as he hoped and perhaps believed. It appeared instead that it was the threat of creating disorder and thus hurting business that really moved white southern leaders to contemplate changes to meet the demands of Blacks. Power was the principal asset in this game, and the ability to disrupt a community and give it bad press through demonstrations, no matter how nonviolent, was a form of power possessed by militant Blacks. Those die-hard white resisters who met nonviolence with violence were unwitting allies of the Blacks in such conflict. White moderates who sought to cool the conflict by entering into negotiations and making minor concessions while avoiding larger, graver issues were their most effective opponents. One of the things learned by many white leaders, such as those in Jacksonville, was the value of restraining white counterdemonstrators who could make headline news out of a parade or demonstration that might otherwise go unnoticed on the national scene. Hence I concluded that what we were witnessing in the South was indeed conflict, even when it was muted, nonviolent, and triggered by actions allegedly inspired only by Christian love and a desire for justice.

Finally, our survey research in Daytona Beach led to a change in my thinking about integration as the paramount issue in the racial crisis of which we wrote. In our survey instrument we had an open-ended question asking people to say what they thought were the greatest needs of the community and to rank these needs in importance. Both Grigg and I were truly surprised to find that although integration of the schools, public facilities, theaters, and the beach were mentioned by many Black subjects, these were not what they saw as the greatest needs. The things they ranked highest were economic and material—more industry, higher wages, more jobs, better schools whether integrated or not, better roads in their neighborhoods, better housing, even "better Negro facilities." This strengthened my incipient belief that in the last analysis the problem of race relations in the United States was one of economic inequality, not of color prejudice. I began to understand the profound truth embodied in the question, first raised by Dick Gregory but taken up by King, "What good does it do a Black to be able to sit at a lunch counter if he doesn't have the money to buy a hamburger?" While not relenting at all in my opposition to segregation, I began to see that the issue was primarily symbolic and of minor importance compared with the greater problem of class. It would be many years before I found much company in this position among Blacks and white liberals, including many sociologists.

Our presentation of this part of our findings stimulated criticism in a review of our book by Tom Pettigrew, a friend and a social scientist philosophically dedicated to the notion that integration was a value with which there must be no compromise. He questioned the validity of our findings and suggested that we probably had not used Black interviewers with Black subjects and hence could not have expected them to come out strongly for integration. We were insulted by the naiveté that he, from the empyreal heights of Harvard University, imputed to us. In ensuing years I would disagree with Tom many times on such topics as Black power, school busing, and affirmative action. Yet I feel that we were able to remain friends and even allies in the struggle for racial democracy, despite our theoretical differences.

I also began to realize something even more important about integration as an overriding goal for Blacks in the United States. As it was being preached, it constituted what Milton Gordon, in his book *Assimilation in American Life* (1964), showed to be assimilation through "Anglo-conformity." We white liberals were arguing that Blacks could and would become like middle-class white Americans if only the barrier of segregation were removed, as Gunnar Myrdal had proposed in *An American Dilemma* (1944). There was a trace of bitterness in the words we wrote about the complexity of integration as a goal:

> The Negro is still faced with his ancient problem, the problem of being a black man in America, a white man's world. Here there is a rarely noticed identity between the premises of both white segregationists and white integrationists. The segregationist recognizes that it is a white man's world and frankly proposes to bar the Negro's entrance into it. The integrationist invites the Negro to enter it, but assumes that it will remain the same white man's world. . . . At the present time, integration as a solution to the race problem demands that the Negro forswear his identity as a Negro. (Killian & Grigg, 1964, p. 107)

I had no idea that events would soon prove the validity of the last observation as the Black power movement erupted to overshadow the assimilationist civil rights movement. In their book *Black Power,* Stokely Carmichael and Charles V. Hamilton (1967, p. 32) quoted this passage from *Racial Crisis in America* with approbation in their analysis of the profound effects of white power, not just of segregation, on the Black person's psyche.

Thus, although our little book received mixed reviews, it gained us ample publicity and consequent opportunities to be even more active in the field of race relations during the tense, uncertain early years of the sixties. Charles Grigg and I, along with C. U. Smith, learned to play "the consultant game." In spite of the growing cynicism and despair expressed in my writings, I continued to play the role of a missionary preaching integration to white audiences.

On the Circuit for Integration

The Southern Regional Council continued to call on me occasionally as one of its stable of consultants available to communities wanting advice on desegregation and tensions related to it. I particularly remember one session with a group in Columbia, South Carolina. It was the first time I can recall encountering the misconception, held even by some white liberals, that the NAACP constituted an "extremist" group equivalent to the Ku Klux Klan, at the other end of the spectrum. Apparently these people were quite unaware of the Black Muslims and did not know that SNCC arose in part out of what many young Black activists regarded as the overcautious conservatism of the NAACP.

Grigg and I were also invited to serve as members of a consulting service provided by the National Association of City Managers. Sometimes we would team up with C. U. Smith and put on a three-man performance for conventions of city managers. Whether our "show" caused them to change their policies or not, we certainly entertained them. Charlie and I would speak as sober, concerned white sociologists, giving them the benefit of the research we had done on problems of desegregation. Smith, very tall, handsome, and a humorous as well as dynamic speaker, talked from the perspective of a Black man, saying, in effect, "Look, fellows, what we're asking for isn't really so much." One of his most effective illustrations was that of the Black garbage collector who for years had ridden on the back of the truck, assisting a white driver. His punch line was, "Can you really blame this man for wanting to be able at last to ride in the cab?"

At first we would have Grigg or me speak first, with Smith taking the middle spot. Soon we realized that C. U. was so effective and entertaining that whatever followed was anticlimactic. After that we insisted that he be the final speaker.

One of the most interesting of the consulting jobs was one I did alone. I was sent to Tampa by the city managers' association to advise the biracial committee that the city had finally set up. This committee had gone so far as to employ a staff member to work full-time on anticipating and, if possible, reducing racial tensions in the city. They hired a young Black businessman who headed a small but successful air-conditioning firm. He was a college graduate and had been an army officer during the Korean conflict. After I was on the ground in Tampa I deduced that he had asked the committee to hire me not so much to give advice but, as an outside expert, to urge on them some of his ideas.

Knowing this made me feel better about some remarks made by a Black member of the committee, Perry Harvey, who was also a member of Governor Collins's statewide biracial committee. Harvey, a huge, fat, but powerful man, was the business manager of a longshoremen's union. I talked to him privately in his office, prior to meeting with the committee. The reception he gave me was a painful reminder that I was indeed working in the race relations industry. His first remark was, "I don't know why we're paying you $75 a day to come down here and tell us stuff I could tell the committee myself." Throughout our discussion he dropped several hints about how many better uses he could find for the money the committee was paying me.

The real goal of my visit proved to be to encourage the committee to ask the city council for money to fund a plan that their own community relations worker had already proposed. Alarmed by hostility to whites that he saw rising among Black youths, he wanted authorization to recruit and pay a corps of responsible young Black men who would identify and help him cool potential hot spots. They would be on the alert for allegations that the police were not acting properly; they would cope with rumors. After listening patiently to him and to me, the majority of the committee members still decided that things weren't really that bad in Tampa and that they couldn't justify a request for the money needed.

Only a little over a year later the committee was forced to eat its words. Racial violence did break out, for the reasons and in the areas where the staff member had foreseen it might. He received national publicity for organizing a corps of Black youth called "white hats" because he gave them white construction helmets to wear on the streets. The city ended up paying much more for the "white hats" and the cost of the miniriots than they were asked to put up in the first place.

My only direct challenge to segregation—not a bold or dramatic one—took place during a speaking engagement in Miami. This time an association of nurses had asked me, C. U. Smith, and Victoria Warner, also of the Florida A&M faculty, to present a panel discussion on desegregation during one of the sessions at their annual convention. The three of us were good friends.

Although the Civil Rights Act of 1964 was still in the future, some hotels on the perimeter of the South were beginning to relax their rules against having Black guests. Therefore, Chuck, Vicky and I all had rooms reserved for us at the convention hotel. We checked in just after lunch, gave our program during the afternoon, and returned to our rooms after agreeing to meet in the dining room for dinner. A few minutes later, Chuck called me in my room to say, "Lewis, we've got a problem." He explained, "The hotel was sold recently and the new owners have told the nurses they'll honor our room reservations but aren't ready to serve Blacks in the dining room. The association is protesting, and Vicky and I are going to wait for the outcome." He concluded, "You can go on and eat if you want to." I immediately replied, "I'll wait with you." He then said, "Come on down to my room, we've got a bottle of bourbon to enjoy while we wait!"

We waited and waited; it must have been nearly three hours, perhaps more. It is fortunate that we were not too drunk to get to the dining room when a call finally came informing us that the hotel management had relented: we were expected in the dining room. When we got to the door, it became obvious that it was Smith and Warner who were expected, not me. The headwaiter, correct but unsmiling, led them to a table without noticing that I was trailing behind. When we reached the table, he exclaimed, "You can't eat with them!" Chuck said, "Either he does or we don't eat." The manager must have been watching from the entrance, for he quickly appeared and precluded a "scene" by telling the headwaiter to seat us. We all ordered big, luscious steaks. I had never felt closer to my Black friends than I did as we enjoyed our meal, trying to appear as casual as possible while conscious of the stares of the other diners. As we walked out of the dining room, Chuck remarked, "I hadn't thought of making a federal case out of eating here, but that steak would have been worth one!"

I thought of that headwaiter's exclamation, "You can't eat with them!" many times after the Civil Rights Act forced many more reluctant restaurateurs to serve Black patrons. A story circulated, and I'm not sure it was apocryphal, of the Black man and his white friend who took a seat in a restaurant. The manager came over to their booth and declared, "I'll serve the nigger because the law says so, but it doesn't say I have to serve nigger lovers!"

The tremendous problem of the bad fit between changing national policies and local attitudes and practices was impressed on me when I served on a panel at an AFL-CIO regional meeting in Miami. Don Slaymon, educational director for the national union, presided. The other panelist was one of my heroes, Charles Morgan, Jr., already famous for having been ostracized and run out of Birmingham for taking a moderate position during the intense controversies there. The audience comprised business managers and officers of union locals from all over the South. Our task was to convince these local leaders that it was both feasible and in the best interests of their members to conform to the national union's liberal, inclusive policy on race. I don't think we were very persuasive, even though the audience was interested and courteous, as well as highly amused by Charles Morgan's folksy, southern style of speaking. Again it took the Civil Rights Act to provide these leaders with an incentive to catch up with their national leadership.

Writing on Black Leadership

With C. U. Smith, I embarked in 1964 on a project, sponsored and funded by the Committee on Sociological Resources for Secondary Schools of the American Sociological Association, to produce a teaching unit titled "Leadership in American Society: A Case Study of Black Leadership." It was one of a number of units designed for use in American high schools. To develop our unit we enlisted the aid of social studies teachers in the FSU and FAMU demonstration schools. There were some rumblings of discontent in the predominantly white high school when students were given material portraying Frederick Douglass, Booker T. Washington, W. E. B. Du Bois, and Martin Luther King, Jr., as examples of great American leaders. The test of the materials went on, however, and our unit, completed with the aid of James M. Fendrich, a colleague at FSU who took over my role when I went on leave to UCLA in 1965, proved to be one of the most successful in nationwide tests. It was especially effective in stimulating interest among Black students.

Whitney Young, Race, and Poverty

Just two months before the course of race relations would be changed by the passage of the 1964 Civil Rights Act, I was invited to be on the program of the annual forum of the National Conference on Social Welfare. The meeting was in Los Angeles. My topic was hardly specific—"Current Issues in Civil Rights." Already, however, I was beginning to foresee the changing nature of the problem and the issues. Foreseeing the imminent triumph of the civil rights movement, I declared, "There is growing evidence that no matter how successful the 'Black bourgeoisie' may be in breaking down legal and traditional forms of segregation, the Negro masses are in danger of becoming an urban proletariat trapped behind economic and educational barriers." I did not realize then how great this danger was, and the term *underclass* had not achieved currency, but I was talking about what would be the racial crisis of the 1980s.

One of the most memorable parts of my visit to Los Angeles was a luncheon for some of the speakers hosted by Nathan Cohen, president of the National Conference. One of the guests was Whitney M. Young, Jr., recently appointed executive director of the National Urban League. I had first met Whitney when he was dean of the School of Social Work at Atlanta University. During one of my visits to AU he had given me a guided tour of the Black belt of Atlanta and filled me in on the Black power structure in the city. After he went with the Urban League he had visited our FSU research office in Jacksonville during a fund-raising campaign among the white businessmen of that city.

Just before going to the Los Angeles conference, Whit had been testifying before congressional committees at hearings on the legislation that would become the foundation of President Johnson's War on Poverty. We were all impressed by his observation that one of his hardest tasks was to convince the congressmen that they should think of this legislation not as laws just to help Black people but rather to help all poor people. In a few months "Appalachian whites" would come to symbolize the poor white people he was talking about.

Whit also told an amusing and illuminating story of his introduction to New Rochelle, New York, where he and his wife Margaret moved when he took the job with the Urban League. Prior to taking office, he was featured as the "man of the day" by the *New York Times*. A few days later, a delegation of white citizens of New Rochelle called on him to invite him to buy a house in that suburb. In spite of the fact that he realized they really wanted to use him as a very acceptable token, he did buy in a previously all-white neighborhood. After moving in, he was horrified one evening when a strange white man came to his door and asked if he would be interested in joining the "white birch society." Conscious of the then prominent John Birch Society, his first reaction was that this must be an especially racist local branch whose representative had thought he was white. He was greatly relieved when the solicitor explained that the society was devoted to saving the white birch trees in the region!

The Industry Goes Federal

In July 1964, Congress passed the most far-reaching civil rights act in the history of the nation. It and the events of the next two years would change both the pattern of race relations in the United States and my personal diagnosis of the course of Black protest and white resistance.

At first I shared with many other supporters of the civil rights movement the feelings of triumph at the passage of the act. I rejoiced to see segregation in public accommodations begin to crumble, at least in the urban South. I fervently hoped that the equal-opportunity provisions of the law would quickly lead to more than token employment of Blacks, particularly in academia.

One part of the act had a very personal impact on me. The noncontroversial Title X created a federal Community Relations Service. Its mission was one of education and conciliation. Representatives would go into communities threatened by tension over desegregation and work quietly, often behind the scenes, to rally the forces advocating obedience to the law. Often individuals who desired peaceful progress toward compliance were so intimidated that they did not know who their allies were—CRS representatives would try to get them together. The service was placed in the Department of Commerce, not the Department of Justice, to convince people that it was not a law enforcement agency, but a conciliation service.

President Johnson asked Florida's former governor, LeRoy Collins, to be the director of this agency. Collins accepted, even though he was well aware that doing so might prove to be a political liability if he reentered Florida politics. He asked my old friend John A. Griffin to serve as his assistant. Immediately John started recruiting a corps of consultants to the Service. Charles Grigg, C. U. Smith, and I were among them.

Early in the autumn of 1964 this group of consultants met in Washington for an orientation and training session. This turned out to be another thrilling experience for me. When we all came together the first morning I met people I had known of for years as "white liberals," struggling to bring both peace and justice to the South, but stigmatized by both their neighbors and the federal government. I felt almost as if I were part of an underground that had suddenly emerged from hiding. I knew that for many years J. Edgar Hoover's FBI and various intelligence agencies of the federal government had viewed the liberalism of any white southerner as a possible indication of subversive tendencies. While doing disaster research I had been required to obtain the highest levels of security clearance for the Department of Defense and the Atomic Energy Commission. Friends who had been questioned by agents investigating me would tell me of the intense interest displayed in my interracial activities and my liberal views. According to some friends, even my wife was suspect. Now, however, the federal government was paying the expenses of scores of people like myself to come to Washington and promised to pay us consultant fees and per diem for going into communities to represent it. Although we would not work under the Department of Justice and were forbidden by law to reveal anything we discovered in a community to law enforcement agencies, the Civil Rights Division did send Burke Marshall and John Doar to speak to us about their role in enforcing the Civil Rights Act. With the victory of the civil rights movement, the race relations industry had become legitimate, no longer shady and suspect.

Knowing Fear

It was on my way home from this meeting that I came the closest I have in my life to knowing what it is to be Black in America. For some reason C. U. Smith and I were booked on the same flights to Atlanta and Tallahassee—Grigg didn't go back with us. During the flight to Atlanta we were concerned about reports of a hurricane that was approaching the Florida Gulf coast. When we landed about 7:00 p.m., there was a rainstorm over Atlanta and we learned that all flights south were canceled. The latest weather reports indicated that the hurricane might hit our hometown within the next hour or two.

Both of us had families waiting for us, and without hesitation we decided to rent a car and head south. As we drove further south in Georgia the night seemed to get darker and stormier. In a small town near Albany we stopped at a filling station to change drivers. C. U. took the wheel. A minute or two later, as we drove through pitch-black darkness, he said, "Lewis, I don't want to scare you, but a car full of white men has been following us ever since we stopped back there." He may not have wanted to frighten me, but he assuredly did. I suddenly experienced the fear that so many Black people, including my good friend, had known for so long. There was nothing we could do but proceed at a steady but legal speed while C. U. kept his eye on the rearview mirror. We both thanked God when the car turned down a side road a few miles further on. The rest of the journey was uneventful, but we remained tense. It was not until we drove into Tallahassee and learned that the hurricane had passed to the west of the city that we relaxed.

New Directions

Being as cynical as I am about sociology and its claims to being scientific, I have frequently felt that most of us complete research by reaffirming our preconceptions even though we may have stated them as hypotheses to be tested. Nevertheless, I feel that the studies I conducted between 1957 and 1965 did produce surprises that cumulatively led to a major change in my assumptions about race relations. This shift in my attitudes would be as great as the one that led to my "conversion" from being an orthodox cracker 25 years earlier. Now I would cease to be a liberal, optimistic integrationist and would view Black-white relations from a pessimistic, radical, and pluralist perspective.

The Impossible Revolution?

The idea of looking at the Black protest movement as truly a revolution came to me as I was preparing my notes for a class in race relations in the spring of 1965. Already intrigued by expressions of Black discontent with the amount of progress since the apparent victory of the civil rights movement, I noted that Martin Luther King, Jr., spoke increasingly of "appealing to a higher law." Higher than what? I asked myself. Higher than the Supreme Court and the Constitution? To appeal beyond these apparently sympathetic authorities was the language of revolution. Blacks were no longer simply asking that the nation "complete the unfinished business of the American Revolution" or that the wayward South rejoin the rest of the nation. They were challenging the values of all of white America and the authority of the federal government.

It was this insight that led me to write the book that I finally gave the title *The Impossible Revolution? Black Power and the American Dream,* published in 1968. The timing was opportune, for the Black power movement was in full stride and the rhetoric as well as the riots of the late 1960s were frightening white Americans. The reviews in sociological journals were skeptical if not critical because of my pessimism. Fortunately, sales did not follow the reviews—I was able to pay cash for a new Buick with my first royalty check. The book was used in undergraduate courses in many universities. According to William J. Wilson, who used it at the University of Massachusetts, many students thought I was Black.

I enjoyed my new reputation as a conflict theorist and the many invitations I received to speak, including being the author on the "Author Meets the Critics" session at the first meeting of the Eastern Sociological Society I ever attended. After I moved to the University of Massachusetts in 1969, I recognized that many people credited me with being far more radical than I actually was. Yet I rather enjoyed playing a new role after so many years of being cast as a white liberal.

This latest professional triumph was bittersweet, however. My sympathetic analysis of the Black power movement reflected the loss of my liberal, assimilationist optimism and even of my faith in human progress in "solving" social problems. I still cherished the ideal of a color-blind society that would embody Martin Luther King, Jr.'s dream of Black and white together; at heart I was still an integrationist. Even while writing an earlier book, *Racial Crisis in America,* I had realized, however, that even to most white liberals integration meant what my colleague Milton Gordon had called "Anglo-conformity." As I put it, it meant that Black Americans had to forswear their identity as Blacks, deny the worth of the culture of their ancestors in Africa, and devalue the new, adaptive culture that their forefathers had developed to cope with the strictures of slavery and segregation. Belatedly they had been assured that at last they were guaranteed the equal rights and the due process promised to all U.S. citizens; but at the same time it seemed clear that if they wanted to be treated as equal, they must act and even look as white as they could. If they would all become Lena Hornes or Sidney Poitiers, then whites would accept them; otherwise they would remain "niggers."

I could understand, then, what I perceived to be the message of Black power: We don't want your culture, your love, or your condescension; we want the power to control our own destiny even if it separates us even further from you. And for most Blacks in the United States the end of the loving era of the civil rights movement did mean greater separation, even though those "qualified Blacks" with the money to afford it could move far more freely and rise far higher than ever before. Even they remained exceptions in the eyes of most whites, and they were ever conscious that American society remained far from color-blind. The greater number of Blacks found the ghettos in which they lived becoming larger, denser, and poorer, and saw white fear and resentment of them symbolized by such political slogans as "law and order," "welfare bums," and "quotas."

My somewhat melodramatic prediction that the white response to Black demands for power and real progress would be greater repression, even white fascism, has not been borne out. I still tremble, however, at the popularity of David Duke, and even more so at the popularity of his ideas when voiced by more respectable politicians and columnists. My other predictions have, I feel, been validated by history. We have seen race relations fall in importance as a critical problem for the majority of white Americans, beginning with the preoccupation with the Vietnam War. We have seen the backlash represented by such questions as, Haven't we done enough for them? When are they going to start helping themselves?

Finally, in my writings during this period and up through the present I have attached far more significance to the Black power movement than do most social scientists. Although the movement was short-lived, even more so than was the civil rights movement, it gave voice to a tremendous spirit of disillusionment among Black Americans. The American dream lost much of its luster for them as they saw powerful white friends, from the White House down, promise them tradition civil rights as citizens and then renege on these promises. It was the Black power movement, not the civil rights movement, that advanced the concept of group rights based on ethnicity and a history of oppression and deprivation. Tenuously and uncertainly validated by the judiciary, compensatory treatment has been practiced by governments and private business under the vague rubric of affirmative action. I am among those analysts, white and Black, who find no convincing evidence that the benefits of affirmative action for Blacks, particularly for the ghetto poor, have been great enough to offset the tremendous cost of the support gained by white politicians who exploit the myth that reverse discrimination is rampant.

The source of my continuing pessimism as a sociologist and a citizen is the fear that the gulf I see widening between whites who feel themselves hard-pressed by a failing economy and Blacks who are suffering even more will eventually lead to a renewal of conflict and repression. Having witnessed the desperation and the courage of a small but valiant proportion of Blacks during what I termed the *first* phase of "the impossible revolution," I never cease to wonder that they seem to have no current counterparts ready to renew the struggle. I have yet to see indications of the emergence of a viable political alliance with white workers, who now must begin to ask what place there is for them in an economy that replaces them with computers and robots, or ships their jobs to countries where labor is cheap. What still seems more likely to me is that a more sophisticated white populist without the Klan background that burdens David Duke may arise to offer Black Americans as a scapegoat to bear into the wilderness the misfortunes and grievances of white Americans who themselves are victims.

References

Carmichael, S., & Hamilton, C. V. (1967). *Black power: The politics of liberation in America.* New York: Vintage.

Gordon, M. M. (1964). *Assimilation in American life.* New York: Oxford University Press.

Fendrich, J., Killian, L. M., & Smith, C. U. (1970). *Leadership in American society: A case study of Black leadership.* Boston: Allyn & Bacon.

Killian, L. M. (1968). *The impossible revolution? Black power and the American dream.* New York: Random House.

Killian, L. M., & Grigg, C. M. (1962). Urbanism, race, and anomia. *American Journal of Sociology, 67,* 661-665.

Killian, L. M., & Grigg, C. M. (1964). *Racial crisis in America.* Englewood Cliffs, NJ: Prentice-Hall.

Killian, L. M., & Smith, C. U. (1960). Negro protest leaders in a southern community. *Social Forces, 38,* 253-257.

Myrdal, G., with Sterner, R., & Rose, A. (1944). *An American dilemma: The Negro problem and modern democracy.* New York: Harper & Row.

6

In Search of an Identity

HARRY H. L. KITANO

Growing up as a Japanese American means a constant search for an identity. Even if one is monolingual and can speak only English, and knows nothing about the Japanese language and culture, one quickly learns that there are questions concerning one's American identity. Reminders that acculturation and identifying as an American are insufficient criteria for belonging to the host society often come in the form of questions: Where did you learn how to speak English so well? Why did your people bomb Pearl Harbor?

The reality of being different became clear very early in my life. My parents, who were from Japan, opened a hotel in San Francisco's Chinatown, so that in the beginning the differences they faced were not of race, but of nationality. China and Japan were enemies, ergo, the Chinese and the Japanese in the United States were also hostile to each other. When I attended elementary school, there was this very stout and, in my eyes, very unattractive Chinese girl, Dorothy Lee, who would mutter, "Jap," and try to pinch me. I learned to suffer these taunts in silence; I knew that my teachers would be of no help, and that my parents would only laugh and scoff at the idea that I was afraid of a Chinese girl. I was unaware of the word *prejudice* at that time, but whatever it was I was experiencing, it was uncomfortable. I tried to avoid any contact with Dorothy, and counted my days as successful if I could escape without being pinched.

There were only a few Japanese families living in or near Chinatown. They were concentrated in the small business sector: a dry cleaner's, an

125

art goods store, a pool hall, a restaurant, and small hotels and rooming houses. Most of their clientele were other minorities, especially Blacks, Filipinos, and other Asians. As far as I can remember, there were few of the racial tensions that are characteristic of present-day race relations among minority groups.

There was a closeness among the Japanese families, so that although we lived apart, we formed a community. One central gathering place was the Japanese school; most of the children attended this school after the regular school day. The Japanese classes met every day from 4:00 to 6:00, so that for most of us children it was an extremely long school day. However, it was not all work and study; on the contrary, it was often disorganized chaos. One lone teacher had to deal with more than 20 students ranging from the very young to some who were in high school. Motivation to learn was not very high; I found it a chance to meet with my peers, to tease and nag the teacher, and to behave in a way that would not be tolerated in the regular school. I was quiet, obedient, conforming, studious, and turned in my homework in the regular school—I was the opposite in the Japanese school.

It was a situational orientation; I learned early in life that at least for me and my peers, the situation shaped behavior. We learned that we were to behave with much more reserve when dealing with the dominant group, and less so among fellow ethnics. However, I deeply regret that I did not take the opportunity to learn the Japanese language more thoroughly; my attendance for more than 10 years was not a total waste, but, given that I can speak only limited Japanese, it was obviously not a total success.

The school involved the families, so that ceremonies, dinners, meetings, and speeches fostered community cohesion. There were year-end pictures, so that even today, looking back and wondering who went where on the basis of pictures taken more than 50 years ago, the experience remains a part of one's history. The school that I attended closed during World War II and never opened again.

The close network of the Japanese families constituted my first world. Parents would help each other; the reputations of all of the children were known, and the primary reference group was my family and the small Japanese American community in Chinatown. We shared experiences and were exposed to similar values, which were reinforced by the families and the ethnic community. Not all of us behaved according to these values, but we had a clear idea when norms were violated.

I don't remember any dramatic clashes between the ethnic way and the American way, primarily because of the situational orientation. I did things the American way when dealing with the host society, and the ethnic way when dealing within the family and community. This was not too difficult, as there was often a congruence between the two value systems.

I had minimal voluntary contact with those who were not fellow ethnics. I went to school with children of Chinese, Italian, and Mexican ancestry (in the North Beach area of San Francisco), but never got to know them intimately. The public school was integrated, but my early life was within a structurally pluralistic ethnic group. For example, I was never invited to visit or play at the homes of any children except Japanese Americans, and I never invited other than Japanese Americans to my home.

Growing Up in the 1930s and 1940s

Life for a Japanese American growing up in the 1930s and 1940s was, to use a current phrase, not a piece of cake. I remember discrimination and domination quite well. We lived just below Nob Hill in San Francisco. There was a public playground next to the Mark Hopkins Hotel on the hill, and I was told by my parents that I should not play there. No one would tell me why, so when I was about 8 years old, I trudged up the hill to the playground with several of my ethnic companions. We did this a few times and nothing happened, but one day, a stern white lady came up and said we could not play there. Her presence was dominating—we never questioned her authority and we hurriedly left. We thought that she was right; that the playground was reserved exclusively for the whites who lived on Nob Hill. This incident strengthened my belief in the wisdom of my parents, who knew that certain places were off-limits, and taught me that I shouldn't raise questions, especially when there were no appropriate answers.

Another incident that took place about the same time also remains strong in my memory. A close bachelor friend of the family used to take me and my brother fishing and to other activities. Once he took us to a swimming spa called Sutro Baths, which was purported to have both hot and cold swimming pools. We were extremely excited—we endured a long streetcar ride across the city to the baths. However, when we got there, the cashier evidently told my friend that "Japs weren't allowed." My friend looked embarrassed, never told us what was said, and muttered something about not wanting to go swimming anyway. I went along with his rationalization, even venturing that I didn't want to go swimming either, although I felt that the rejection had something to do with our ancestry.

Pearl Harbor and the Concentration Camps

If I had doubts that racism was a problem, they were quickly erased after the Japanese attack on Pearl Harbor in 1941. I had just entered Galileo High School; I remember attending the all-school assembly and hearing President Roosevelt's message to Congress, in which he spoke of the "day which will live in infamy" and the declaration of war against Japan. There were just a few Japanese American students; we glanced at each other furtively, feeling that all eyes were upon us. It was a trying moment; I felt confused and even guilty that Japan had attacked the United States. But nothing untoward happened; school continued and I thought that, aside from the war, I could live a relatively normal life.

However, soon afterward there appeared signs on the telephone poles addressed to persons of Japanese ancestry. The signs said that we were to register, assemble, and be prepared for removal to "relocation centers." Newspapers, especially those published by the Hearst Press, and politicians led the charge. They claimed that all Japanese were traitors, that we were dangerous to the war effort and so should be locked up and shipped to Japan. We were inundated by rumors about the relocation, ranging from stories of benign treatment by the authorities to permanent incarceration. It was an introduction to the next several years of my life, as rumors were an integral part of my wartime experience.

The FBI came and took my father away—a mixed blessing, because his being acknowledged as a community leader by the government gave him some status at the same time it forced him to leave his family under crisis conditions. We were not to see him for several years; later, he never talked about his experiences in his camp, which I believe was in Bismarck, North Dakota. One irony was that, because that was an "official" camp for prisoners of war, it came under the rules of the Geneva Convention, so that the food and treatment at the camp were better than what we were to experience.

Our worst fears were realized—all of us, whether citizens or aliens, were to be incarcerated. Disorganization was the order of the day. My mother, who had seldom been outside of the home, was left in charge, and she panicked. She was sure that we were going to be taken out and shot, and she was prepared to die (I should add that at the time of this writing, she has reached her 102nd birthday).

We heard a variety of rumors. One was that we were going to be shipped to Japan and traded for American prisoners of war; another, a more optimistic one, was that once the United States realized that it had made a mistake, the evacuation orders would be rescinded. We lived by rumors, primarily because the government provided very little information. Perhaps they didn't know what to do with us or, more likely, they kept secrets in the name of national security.

My family, along with all others of Japanese ancestry, was ordered to close our home, to sell or store our furniture and other valuables, to pack what we could carry, and to assemble at designated sites. Although my past experiences had shaken my faith in my American identity, the forced evacuation led to even more doubts about who I was. I still believed that I was an American; I belonged to the ROTC band at Galileo and played "The Stars and Stripes Forever," marched behind the flag, and had little identification with Japan. However, it was clear that my ancestry was viewed with suspicion, and that my government saw me, my family, and all members of my community as enemies; in simple terms, we were all "Japs."

To add to my discomfort, the initial assembly place was on Van Ness Avenue, just a few blocks from my high school. I tried to hide my face from the students who were walking by; several came over to express their sympathy, but others came at us making airplane noises, pretending "to kill the Japs."

An important-looking white man with a clipboard began calling out family names and we began to board the buses that were to take us to the train station. His poor pronunciation of Japanese surnames could have come as a source of comic relief if the occasion hadn't been so serious.

Life in a Concentration Camp

It is hard to recapture the feelings I experienced as we were herded into railroad cars. The shades were drawn and armed soldiers stood at every entrance—this especially disturbed me, given that more than half of the "prisoners" were women and children. We didn't know where we were going, how long the ride would be, or what would be at the end of the journey. My most vivid memories of that day are of crying children, confused parents, and the hot, stuffy car.

The train ride was from San Francisco to Santa Anita, the famous race track in Arcadia, near Los Angeles. My first impression as we left the train was that we were on an Indian reservation; all of the inmates at first looked like Indians to me. This was my first exposure to Southern California, where the Japanese Americans were much darker and had healthier-looking tans than those of us from much cooler Northern California.

We quickly adapted to camp norms. The young people formed youth groups, a euphemism for gangs, and I belonged to the San Francisco gang. There were already established gangs from various parts of Los Angeles, so that the primary identification for adolescents was with groups from their former area of residence. The change for me was that instead of identification with the family, my primary identification was with my gang.

Food was one of our highest priorities; my gang quickly learned that if we gulped down our food, we could run to another mess hall and eat another meal. Not that the food was of gourmet quality—we quickly labeled it "slop suey," but for a growing teenager a full stomach meant a degree of contentment.

The time I spent at Santa Anita represented a growing away from my family. Almost every facet of my waking time was spent with my peers; we got up, washed, ate, went to the bathroom, played, and argued together. The small, crowded barracks was for sleeping only, so the influence of the family became minimal. My primary identification was with the San Francisco group; we met other peers through their group identification, such as those from San Diego, Hawthorne, San Pedro, San Jose, and the numerous gangs from Los Angeles. I heard of a few fights between gangs, but my San Francisco group was known to be relatively peaceful, and we stayed out of any serious conflict.

However, I still remember one basketball game against a group from Los Angeles called the Exclusive Twenties. My group was ahead, but then the other team began to intimidate both us and the referee; we were manhandled and eventually lost. The next day, in the camp news sheets that were distributed to all residents, a commentary was printed emphasizing the need for fair play, even if only in a basketball game. The message, as I remember, was that there was no place to hide or to escape; we were all behind the barbed-wire fences, and losing a basketball game was trivial compared with living in fear of a gang that was much larger and more violent than ours.

Looking back, I marvel at the ability of the Japanese to organize a coherent community under concentration camp conditions. There were about 20,000 of us, hemmed in by barbed wire; the stay at Santa Anita was to be only temporary, until more permanent inland camps were developed. We all came from different parts of California, and yet the community was able to offer a semblance of coherent life. I don't know who provided the organizational impetus, but there were softball and basketball leagues, dances, talent shows, and other activities that kept our mind off of where we were living. There were some riots and some beatings, but Santa Anita was remarkably peaceful, given the unusual circumstances.

My adaptation was to *monku,* that is, to develop griping to an art. There was plenty to gripe about—the food, the smelly horse stalls, the bedding, standing in line, and, most important, the lack of freedom and the fact that we faced an uncertain future. My group argued constantly, even about whether jeans with a red tag (Levi's) were superior to those without a tag.

Camp life exposed me to a wide variety of identities. I met some people with a strong Japanese identity—so strong that they were convinced that Japan would win the war. They advised me to prepare myself for the future by learning to speak Japanese and to understand Japanese values and culture. One can't miss the irony of that advice—knowledge of Japan is extremely valuable today, but not because Japan was victorious in World War II. Then there were others who were 150% American, who felt it was our patriotic duty to cooperate with the U.S. government in order to win the war over fascist Japan, Germany, and Italy. I vacillated, most often leaning toward an American identity. But I found it hard to answer the question, If you are an American, why are you in the camp with the rest of us? My only weak rejoinder was that there were imperfections in any system.

Topaz

Although our stay in Santa Anita was short, from April to October 1942, I established some roots there. Even though we were to be there only temporarily, there was an attempt to start a school, but as it was not mandatory and there was little organization, I did not attend. Instead, I roamed around and played most of the day, made friends from other parts of California, and began to take an interest in girls. The news that we were to be separated from the new friends we had all made at Santa Anita and sent to different permanent camps was met with tears and frustration. We were again to be pawns of government decisions; the feeling of being utterly powerless reinforced the cynicism that was a strong part of camp philosophy.

Our move was to Topaz, a permanent camp set up in the middle of the desert in Utah. Here I got the feeling of being a real prisoner; at

Santa Anita, one could see cars moving along the outside streets, and some residents even had friends who would wave to them. But Topaz was in the middle of nowhere, and the perimeters were sealed with barbed-wire fences, guard towers, and armed soldiers.

I lived in Topaz from 1942 to 1945 and graduated from high school there. Now that I can look back with a little more knowledge concerning this period of my life, I find that Blauner's (1972) model of internal colonialism provides an insightful analysis of camp life. The four features discussed below are part of his model, and the camp experiences provide a good fit.

Entry is forced and involuntary. This was certainly true of the way we were herded into the camps; we had no choice but to comply with government orders. In fact, there were several moves: first to "assembly centers," then to more permanent camps.

The impact of the interaction is more dramatic than the slower process of acculturation. There were deliberate attempts to discourage the ethnic culture and to foster acculturation. Japanese cultural practices were discouraged and even banned; there was an emphasis on things American, and leadership was encouraged among the U.S.-born Nisei rather than the Japan-born Issei.

However, my acculturation was to camp norms, which often were at odds with both the past Japanese values and American middle-class values. For example, there was an attitude best described as "waste time," which meant that effort, responsibility, and productivity were unwarranted under camp conditions. The idea was to put in minimum effort: Why kill oneself with dedication and effort—what good would it do? Acculturation was also much more horizontal in nature—to one's peer culture and peer group.

Members of the colonized group tend to be administered by representatives of the dominant power. This was certainly true in Topaz. Caucasians were appointed to all of the administrative positions and made all of the major decisions. Government-appointed bureaucrats lived separately, had better food, and received regular salaries, whereas internees, often with superior training and credentials, received $16 or $19 per month. The outsiders had freedom of movement, whereas the internees were confined behind barbed wire and could leave only with government clearance. It was clearly a stratification system based on race; "they" were the dominators, "we" were the dominated. We adjusted to them; they ruled over us.

There is racism; one group is seen as inferior. This was clearly established in the incarceration of the Japanese. Germans and Italians, also a part of the enemy Axis alliance, were treated as individuals. As my historian colleague Roger Daniels used to say, there were "bad" individual Germans and Italians, but the entire Japanese race was "bad." A definition that I heard at a recent conference in Washington, D.C., concerning racism is appropriate in this context: Racism is "unconditional hostility," so that no matter what the individual of the pariah group does, it will be interpreted negatively. I remember many examples of this definition: If the Japanese worked hard, we were too pushy; if we worshipped separately, we were un-American; if we desired to compete and become part of the mainstream, we didn't know our place in the society. I remember that Earl Warren, later chief justice of the Supreme Court, when he was the attorney general of California, saying that because the Japanese in America had not committed any acts of sabotage, they were even more of a potential danger to the United States.

There was one element of our stay in Topaz that tested one's identification: the infamous "no, no" questionnaire that every internee had to answer. Basically, it meant that one's identifications were either with Japan or the United States, although there were many other issues involved. Responses of "yes, yes" were generally interpreted to mean that one identified with the United States, and "no, no" responses were generally interpreted to mean that one had stronger identification with Japan. There were heated discussions, meetings, and debates about what the questions meant and how individuals should answer. Different answers by family members had the potential of splitting families, because the "no, no's" were to be segregated and sent to a different camp.

At one of the meetings in my block, my older sister made an impassioned plea for objectivity, and for each individual deciding for him- or herself. This evidently was an unpopular suggestion among the kitchen crew in my block; at the next meal, they pointedly ignored serving any of our family. This went on for several meals—my uncle, who was a cook at another mess hall, fed us. Then, one of the kitchen crew must have mentioned that I was the captain of our high school football team (we actually played a schedule against surrounding Utah high schools), so regular service began again. I learned that identification as an athlete, even under primitive camp conditions, led to favorable treatment. I answered "yes, yes" on the questionnaire because I knew nothing about Japan, and I felt that my future was in America, no matter what the cost.

The relative shortness of the war meant that many of the things we learned in camp were not internalized and permanently incorporated into our life-styles. Nevertheless, many of the former residents still remember the feeling of being totally unwanted by the host society, and the hard struggle to reestablish themselves after the camps were closed in 1946.

It was in one of my high school classes that I first heard about sociology. In our many discussions on why we were thrown into the camps, one of my peers would very solemnly say that the reason was sociological, and we would all nod in agreement, although none of us knew what sociology was.

Release From Camp

There was a procedure through which, with government clearance, we were free to relocate anywhere in the United States aside from the barred zones along the Pacific Coast. After graduating from high school in 1945, and talking over the decision with the remnants of my family (three of my sisters and my older brother had already left camp), I decided to apply for my leave. Armed with something like $50, a high school diploma, a one-way train ticket, and some fear and anxiety, I left my "home" with a vague idea that I would go to Milwaukee. There was no logical reason I chose this city; I had no relatives, friends, or acquaintances there, although I could probably have said the same about wherever I chose to go. I sometimes wonder if I would have the courage to make a similar move today, leaving the relative safety of the camp to make my way in an unknown, but probably very hostile, society. But I was young, ignorant, and still believed in America.

I was extremely self-conscious when I boarded the train at Delta, Utah; I had not faced the outside world for more than three years, and the crowded train was filled with soldiers, sailors, and marines. I expected at any time to be spotted as a "Jap"; much to my surprise, I was totally ignored and even offered a seat. Everyone was more interested in their companions; some were even making love, which was a shock to one who had spent the last several years in a strict environment.

The War Relocation Authority had set up an employment office in Milwaukee, and they referred me to a farmer whose specialty was erecting silos. Aside from the fact that I disliked heights and hard physical labor, the job was mine for a short time. I remember several things from that experience: the enormous quantities of food, especially compared with camp fare, and the friendliness of the farm family. They were of German descent, and it was my impression that even with my doubts about America, I was much more American and patriotic than they. They had sons who were successful in avoiding the draft, while some evacuees, with parents behind barbed wire, were clamoring to join the army.

One of the things that I brought with me to camp was an old trombone, and I played in a number of dance bands that were organized in both Santa Anita and Topaz. I decided to try my hand at being a professional musician; I answered an ad in *Downbeat,* a magazine for musicians, and found myself traveling to Worthington, Minnesota, to play in the Tiny Little Orchestra. I was hired sight unseen, and I was given my two-weeks' notice (fired) the minute I was seen. The manager was nice enough to refer me to a new band that was being formed in Austin, and so I began my career as one of the few musicians of "Oriental" extraction playing in the Midwest. I had changed my name to Harry Lee, and I identified myself as of Chinese extraction from San Francisco. Aside from some skeptics who could not understand why anyone would leave California to play through a Minnesota winter, no one raised any questions about my identity, although I always feared being discovered. Occasionally some dancer would pull his eyes to achieve a slant and mouth the word "Jap," but such displays were few and far between.

There were a number of incidents that provided me with some insight into race, ethnicity, and stratification. In one band, I was told that I was hired to replace a Black musician—that musician was much more talented than I could ever be (Oscar Pettiford, who later played for Duke Ellington and was one of the foremost jazz bassists), so I was exposed to attitudes about a pariah group even more the target of prejudice and discrimination than mine. There were also heated discussions about Jewish musicians; one trumpet player I knew decided that Harry James was no longer his idol because he was Jewish. I suspect that when I was not around, Asians were also the target of snide remarks. In any case, I realized that there were also other groups that were not accepted. I strove very hard to belong; I dressed, talked, walked, acculturated, and identified as a jazz musician with a Chinese surname.

Berkeley

I returned to California to attend the University of California in 1946 and received my B.A., M.S.W., and Ph.D. in 1958. I continued as a part-time musician, and when I applied for membership in the San

Francisco Musician's Union, I was faced with a dilemma. There was a white union, I believe it was Local 6, and a Black union, Local 669: I had to make a choice. As it turned out, I joined Local 6 but then played primarily in Black bands.

One incident stands out in my mind. I played with an all-Black band that had a gig in Redding, in Central California. On the way, we stopped for something to eat. Imagine my surprise when they turned to me and said, "Lee, could you find out if they'll serve us?" Here I was with a group of talented musicians, acting as their spokesperson, even though I had only recently been released from a concentration camp. I think that the restaurant sold us sandwiches to go.

Academic Experiences

I regret being a quiet, nonaggressive student during my years at Berkeley. I stuck around mostly with fellow ethnics and did not participate in campus life. It was the post-World War II era, and all-white fraternities and sororities ruled campus social life. Asian Americans were viewed as outsiders. As a consequence, I felt that my role was to remain in the background and to be anonymous, even to professors. I was satisfied to sit and listen and not raise any questions. It was only after I graduated with my Ph.D. that I felt I had not taken full advantage of the opportunities that were available on the campus at Berkeley.

I was trained primarily as a psychologist, with a major interest in social psychology. An early mentor was social psychologist R. C. Tryon at Berkeley. In one course we were to survey a sample of Oakland residents concerning their political attitudes. Our results were certainly open to question; we predicted that Henry Wallace would be elected president.

In a course in clinical psychology, we were to write our own psychological histories; I don't remember the details, but I know that I wrote about myself without once mentioning my years in a concentration camp. I thought that such information would not be of interest to the professor, although by that time I was also acquainted with such terms as *repression* and *shame*.

The most influential professor during my years in Berkeley was Davis McEntire, a labor economist who also was my research professor in the School of Social Welfare. He gave me my first professional job in the field of social research; I developed a survey of Japanese Americans and their housing needs that eventually was published in a volume

titled *Studies in Housing and Minority Groups,* which McEntire edited
with Nathan Glazer (Kitano, 1960).

Employment

I held two jobs, prior to my appointment to UCLA in 1958, that were
important influences on my way of thinking. One was as a caseworker
at the International Institute in San Francisco, where the emphasis was
on working with immigrant groups and helping them adapt to the
American society. My major task was to work with a variety of Asian
immigrants, so that I developed a detailed knowledge of the kinds of
problems that are associated with moving to a new country and trying
to cope with only the values and experiences of the old country as
guidance. The problems of the children of these immigrants, the second
generation, were especially interesting, as I had also gone through these
conflicts in my own upbringing.

I also worked as a therapist in the Child Guidance Clinic of the San
Francisco Schools. Here I was exposed to psychoanalytic thinking; we
were supervised by consulting psychiatrists with a heavy psychoanalytic orientation. My clientele was made up of acting-out minority
children; although I would have preferred to work with Asian American
children, very few were referred to the clinic. It was exciting to deal
with some of the intricacies of psychoanalytic thinking, especially the
exploration of the development of personality, the use of dreams, and
the rich variety of symbolic interpretations connected with acting-out
behavior. However, variables such as discrimination and racism were
seldom given high priority in our psychiatric conferences, so that it was
difficult for me to believe that insight gained through verbal interaction
would lead to a significant change in the behavior of my acting-out
Black children.

Sociological input and sociological thinking came primarily after my
employment at UCLA. I received a grant to study Japanese American
crime and delinquency, and in that effort I worked closely with sociologists. Melvin Seeman served as one of my consultants. His paper on
alienation and his sociological perspectives opened up new ways of
thinking for me. The late Richard Morris worked closely with me and
also served as dean of the School of Social Welfare, where I was initially
employed. I received a joint appointment with sociology and taught
courses in ethnic groups and race relations.

I submitted a manuscript (I don't remember the publisher) about crime and delinquency among Japanese Americans, and received some extremely valuable comments from one of the readers, who turned out to be Frank Miyamoto, the University of Washington sociologist. Although the manuscript was rejected, it prepared me for writing my book on Japanese Americans. I also benefited from Miyamoto's (1939) monograph on social solidarity in the prewar Japanese American community.

The sociologist who most influenced me was Milton Gordon, who was also the editor of my book on Japanese Americans. His view of acculturation, expressed in his book *Assimilation in American Life* (1964), was extremely helpful in providing an organizational framework to my knowledge of my ethnic group. The concepts of "hyphenated" Americans, the different stages in acculturation, the effects of discrimination and prejudice, and the role of structural variables went far beyond the social psychological and psychoanalytic models that were a part of my early training.

Japanese Americans, published by Prentice-Hall in 1969, was a difficult book for me to write, because it was the first book about my ethnic group to be published after World War II, and there were no previous models. In preparing the book I found I had to learn a little bit about a lot of different things; it had to cover material from many disciplines—history, economics, psychology, anthropology, sociology, and psychiatry, to name a few, and yet provide a coherent account of the experiences of an ethnic group. Sociological perspectives provided the basic framework; my own life experiences were used to illustrate and add flesh to the frame.

The reaction to the book was very positive. I was especially pleased that members of my ethnic group reacted so well. Many called or wrote, some commenting that for the first time they had begun to understand something about their parents, themselves, and the Japanese American culture. The book provided the impetus for lectures throughout the United States. It was also translated into Japanese, and I found on visits to Japan that I enjoyed a degree of celebrity status.

I also was influenced by the historian Roger Daniels, who had written about the early Japanese immigrant experiences in his volume *The Politics of Prejudice* (1962). In many ways, Roger was much tougher in his indictment of the treatment of Japanese Americans than I (historians seem to know much more about influential politicians and their racist attitudes than do sociologists), and was able to provide names as well as documentation of some of the key actors who put the Japanese

Americans into the concentration camps. Roger and I have collaborated on a number of books (*American Racism,* Daniels & Kitano, 1970; *Asian Americans,* Kitano & Daniels, 1988; and *Japanese Americans: From Relocation to Redress,* Daniels, Taylor, & Kitano, 1986), and will continue to work together in the future.

Experiences Abroad

I had a number of teaching and research experiences abroad that were helpful in clarifying my ethnic identity. I served as the director of the University of California Tokyo Study Center at the International Christian University in the early 1970s. Aside from seeing the United States from a Japanese perspective, I quickly discovered that I was more American than Japanese. I was different from my Japanese colleagues, and during that stay of more than a year my American identity was reinforced. I walked, talked, dressed, and behaved more as an American than as a Japanese.

I also spent a summer with Professor Michael Banton at the University of Bristol in 1979. It was difficult to escape my ancestral heritage; questions about Japan were more common than questions about Los Angeles. The category of Japanese American was not readily understood; as a consequence, my identity as a Japanese, rather than as an American, was reinforced.

Domination

My past experiences and my own attempts to explain race relations led me to develop the domination model shown in Figure 6.1 (see Kitano, 1991, p. 49). I had been trying to make sense of what happened to the Japanese Americans, and to determine whether such an incident could happen again in a democratic society. In the model, the dominant group (D) has the power to erect barriers that limit the ability of the dominated group (d) to participate equally in the host society. The primary actions are prejudice, discrimination, and segregation, carried out through such mechanisms as stereotypes, laws, and norms that result in the dominated group being avoided, placed at a competitive disadvantage, and isolated. These are the shaping factors; the more severe actions, such as concentration camps, expulsion, and extermination, can

	BARRIERS		
	Actions	**Mechanism**	**Effects**
Common actions	1 Prejudice	Stereotypes	Avoidance
	2 Discrimination	Laws, norms	Disadvantage
	3 Segregation	Laws, norms	Isolation
More severe actions	4 Concentration camps	Crisis	Incarceration
	5 Expulsion	Crisis	Exile, refugees
	6 Extermination	Crisis	Genocide

Figure 6.1. Domination Model

best be explained when these prior actions have taken place. The more severe acts can occur when the host society perceives a crisis—fear that its very existence will be in danger unless more drastic steps are instituted. The Japanese attack on Pearl Harbor and World War II acted as such "triggers" for the action taken against those of Japanese ancestry residing in America.

Once a group is incarcerated, there is always the danger of expulsion, exile, and extermination. Some Japanese Americans were deported to Japan; there was talk of using the internees as guinea pigs for "experiments," such as lowering caloric requirements, and separating the sexes so that there would be no more "Jap bastards." Fortunately, saner and more humane forces prevailed.

It should also be noted that there is stratification in the lower part of the system (d). I have experienced these differences—specific dominated groups are less acceptable than others. These are the conditions that lead to "middleman minorities" (Kitano, 1974) and model minorities (Sue & Kitano, 1973).

Current Thoughts About Race Relations

It is difficult to make any simple comments on current race relations in the United States because of the complexity of the issues involved and their ever-changing nature. While I was serving as a visiting professor at Yamaguchi University in Japan during the spring of 1992, rioting broke out in Los Angeles. The view from Japan was dependent on media coverage, which focused primarily upon violence; once the violence subsided, news about the riots virtually disappeared from both television and newspapers. The view from overseas was that Americans were violent, and that there were deep racial divisions in the society. It is difficult to disagree with these observations, even though they do not address such major issues as inequality, racism, and historical tensions.

My own experiences indicate that if there is to be a major change concerning race relations, it will have to come from the dominant group. I remember the despair, the alienation, and the frustration among Japanese Americans prior to World War II. Although many of them were attending college and were college graduates, there were few opportunities for them outside of working in the ethnic community. I remember hearing my older sisters and their male friends talking about a hopeless future. Discrimination in jobs, housing, and entertainment meant living as second-class citizens. There was even a large research project that looked at the Japanese Americans as a problem group; it was published as *The Second Generation Japanese American Problem* (Strong, 1934). Contrast this to recent perceptions of Japanese Americans as constituting a "model minority" (Sue & Kitano, 1973).

The major changes I have seen have taken place in the dominant community: Discrimination and prejudice against Japanese Americans, although not entirely eliminated, have been significantly modified, so that the alienation and despair that were a part of the 1930s are no longer normative perceptions. But other minority groups, especially Blacks and Latinos, find that large numbers are hemmed in by discrimination, prejudice, and segregation. As Ogawa (1971) puts it, there has been a change from "Japs" to Japanese; however, other minority groups still face many barriers.

In summary, the model of domination was built upon my personal experiences and reflects what I went through. If the dominant society had remained closed—that is, if I were still a "Jap"—I suspect that I might be a discontented day laborer, even with a college degree, and ready to follow anyone who would advocate major changes in the society. But education has paid off, and at present I have become comfortable with all of my identities—as a Japanese American, a college professor, a member of the UCLA faculty, a Los Angeleno, and a Californian. I have lived in Japan, Great Britain, and Hawaii and my identity has retained some of all of them. My identity is a mixture of the semiprimordial (ancestry and visibility) and the functional. I suspect that if I were to write my headstone today, it would simply say, a Japanese American who served as a professor of social welfare and sociology at UCLA.

References

Blauner, R. (1972). *Racial oppression in America.* New York: Harper & Row.

Daniels, R. (1962). *The politics of prejudice.* Berkeley: University of California Press.

Daniels, R., & Kitano, H. H. L. (1970). *American racism.* Englewood Cliffs, NJ: Prentice-Hall.

Daniels, R., Taylor, S., & Kitano, H. H. L. (Eds.). (1986). *Japanese Americans: From relocation to redress.* Salt Lake City: University of Utah Press.

Gordon, M. M. (1964). *Assimilation in American life.* New York: Oxford University Press.

Kitano, H. H. L. (1960). Housing of Japanese Americans in the San Francisco Bay Area. In N. Glazer & D. McEntire (Eds.), *Studies in housing and minority groups* (pp. 178-197). Berkeley: University of California Press.

Kitano, H. H. L. (1969). *Japanese Americans: The evolution of a subculture.* Englewood Cliffs, NJ: Prentice-Hall.

Kitano, H. H. L. (1974). Japanese Americans: The development of a middleman minority. *Pacific Historical Review, 43,* 500-519.

Kitano, H. H. L. (1976). *Japanese Americans: The evolution of a subculture* (2nd ed.). Englewood Cliffs, NJ: Prentice-Hall.

Kitano, H. H. L. (1991). *Race relations.* Englewood Cliffs, NJ: Prentice-Hall.

Kitano, H. H. L., & Daniels, R. (1988). *Asian Americans.* Englewood Cliffs, NJ: Prentice-Hall.

Miyamoto, F. (1939). *Social solidarity among the Japanese in Seattle.* Seattle: University of Washington.

Ogawa, D. (1971). *From Japs to Japanese.* Berkeley: McCutchan.

Strong, E. K. (1934). *The second generation Japanese American problem.* Stanford, CA: Stanford University Press.

Sue, S., & Kitano, H. H. L. (1973). The model minorities. *Journal of Social Issues, 29*(2), 1-10.

7

Jews, Blacks, and
A Piece of the Pie

A Memoir

STANLEY LIEBERSON

A Piece of the Pie is neither an accidental nor an inevitable product of my background. As is the case for my earlier publications dealing with Blacks, it is the outcome of chance events interacting with a life history and a predisposition to think in a particular direction.[1] Once this linkage occurs, further work on Blacks, such as *A Piece of the Pie,* follows without any additional chance events. One is so wrapped up in the topic and exposed to so many stimuli that further interest is almost inevitable.

I will start with the earliest experiences that I believe are relevant, and will avoid either editing these memories to make me look better than I am or making fairly obvious social comments about them in other ways. Readers can do the latter without any help from me.

Brighton Beach

First, some simple facts: I was born in Montreal, Canada, in 1933, but grew up in Brooklyn, New York, my parents having moved to the United States when I was a toddler. I was living in the Brighton Beach area by the time I started kindergarten at PS 253. I never thought about Brighton being a voluntary ghetto, but it was overwhelmingly Jewish, with many being immigrants from various Eastern European countries. My mother was born and raised in Canada—her parents had immigrated from Lithuania—and my father was raised in Poland. Brighton was comfortable and very safe; one rarely saw police in a confrontational context. Beyond that, Brighton was comfortable because virtually everyone belonged to the same group and, although stories of hostility and discrimination in the larger world were widely known, it was not an issue where we lived. The customs of this population were much in evidence; for example, the main shopping street (which ran for perhaps 12 blocks) had literally no bars until the time of World War II (and then they catered to servicemen training at the Merchant Marine and Coast Guard stations not too far away). Supermarkets were present, but the many specialty food stores (often very crowded) meant that women would go from store to store, separately purchasing produce, dairy products, bread and cake, eggs, and so on. There were numerous kosher delicatessens and meat markets. There was a very small number of non-Jews—Italians and Irish, I remember—but I cannot recall ever encountering a Black student in any grade school class that I attended through the six years of PS 253. There are Yiddish words for non-Jews and for Blacks, neither with terribly favorable connotation, but I do not believe that the use of those words I was exposed to then reflected anything markedly more unfavorable for one than for the other.

The central in-group/out-group distinction for me was between Jews and Gentiles—whites who were not Jewish. For many years of my life, it was an automatic response for me to guess whether anyone I saw (almost all being white) was Jewish or not. At that point in my life, I never thought much about distinctions within the non-Jewish white population. For me, the question was whether they were Christian or not—differences between them were not particularly significant to me. I think I did this screening automatically: In a subway, for example, I would examine each person accordingly; on the beach, the people sitting around us were similarly categorized. For all purposes, *Christian* was not a religious term for me, but the name of an ethnic group, and it was a term that in effect incorporated all whites who were not Jewish. At least I think that was the basis of my thinking.

This focus on the Jewish/Gentile distinction was intense, accompanied by deep-seated feelings. During the spin-the-bottle stage of early exploration with girls, one of my friends had invited some Italian girls and an equal number of Jewish boys over to his house for a weekend evening. When the kissing games started, I experienced a feeling of revulsion at the thought of kissing these non-Jewish girls, for which there is a disparaging term in Yiddish. It meant crossing a line that was inherently wrong, that would violate some rule (they probably had similar feelings on the opposite side). I cannot say for sure, but I seem to remember other friends at the party having a similar reticence, at least compared with the enthusiasm that usually attended such parties with Jewish girls. It was a boundary that would later crumble, but not for years to come.

Blacks were *directly* relevant to me in only a peripheral way throughout my school days in Brooklyn, all the way through my first two years at Brooklyn College. After completing sixth grade at PS 253, a small number of us were sent to Junior High School 234 to participate in the rapid advance program, which meant skipping one semester during the ensuing two and one-half years. My other friends went to the dreaded PS 100 (rumor had it that it was 100 years old), which was more heterogeneous than the rapid advance program. There were some Blacks there, and fights would occur across the ethnic-race lines. I would hear about these scraps, and I must say it was scary. In point of fact, I cannot remember learning of anyone ever being seriously hurt on either side. In the local high school that I attended, Abraham Lincoln, there were probably no more than 20 Blacks. With a total enrollment of nearly 5,000, one would normally have minimal encounter with Blacks there as well. Again, I cannot remember ever being in a high school class with a Black student. If there were cross-ethnic fights or tensions, they were between Jews and Italians, and again these were not serious by the standards of the current times. Although fights occurred from time to time, verbal threats and exchanges were far more frequent.

I can still recall, however, a small number of interactions with Blacks during those days. The high school basketball team won the New York City Public High School Championship in 1949-1950, fielding an all-white and largely Jewish team. One of the playoff games was against a largely Black school, and there were some attacks after the game directed at Lincoln students. I can also remember taking the subway to Ebbets Field for Brooklyn Dodger baseball games. The best route involved a transfer to a line where almost all the passengers were Black (the main route from Brighton to Manhattan went through almost entirely white areas of Brooklyn). I remember my friends commenting about the fact that no trouble occurred, which I suppose means we had some stereotypes and expectations of what *might* happen. In my estimation, this white edginess about Blacks—fear particularly of teenage and young adult males—is in desperate need of further study. This mix of reality and unreality pervades our society and should be addressed.[2] It is a mistake to dismiss this as simply "blaming the victim" because, whatever the cause of this fear and no matter how overblown it is compared with reality, the fear is there and is of consequence for many features of race relations. For example, many years later, when I lived in Oakland, California, while bicycling through a park I remember seeing Black men standing around a table, dealing drugs—or so I thought. (When I got very close, I realized they were watching a chess game.) It is also the case that whites are largely unaware of the fears that many Blacks have of whites in a society that is essentially dominated by the latter. More than once, I have learned of neighborhoods and public facilities such as movie theaters that Blacks believe are best to avoid. It is also the case that many whites are unaware of how often they are perceived as brutal and untrustworthy.

Between high school and college I worked during the summer in a neighborhood grocery. Harry, a Black man in his early 20s, also worked in the grocery, and we got along fine. On busy Saturdays, we would make sandwiches at work to shorten the lunch break. I remember Harry once handing me some cheese he had sliced for my sandwich, and how for a moment I felt a certain aversion. I realized what was going on and, of course, took the cheese and had my sandwich. But it is curious to me how pervasive such a stigma can be, and how generalized such stigmas can become. Surely nobody ever told me not to take cheese handled by a perfectly decent man. Yet there must have been some chain of associations between a taboo about unclean food and a view of Blacks that contradicted that norm. It was an emotion that flashed before me, without any thought process whatsoever.

My father worked in the garment district in Manhattan. As I got older, I would visit him from time to time when school was out and he was working. There were two elevators in the building at 39 W. 38th Street; both were run by Black men, and my father had warned me the first time that they might be unpleasant. And indeed they were, often rather begrudging about taking me up to the floor where my father worked, preferring to ignore me and chat with each other on the ground floor until they were ready. Curiously, a similar type of event at this time would lead me to wonder if they were hostile to whites, but such a motive was never considered at that time.

Jackie Robinson became the first Black major league baseball player when he put on a Brooklyn Dodger uniform in 1947. He was extraordinary by any standard. What was obvious to an avid Dodger fan such as myself was that he had great playing skills, the most dramatic and exciting being his ability to steal bases. He took exceptionally long leads from whatever base he was on, and would often visibly distract and upset opposing pitchers. The most exciting of all was Robinson leading off from third base, dashing down the baseline toward home plate as the pitcher began to deliver. If memory serves me right, Robinson's running skills caused an exceptional number of balks. I had no idea of Robinson's even greater performance away from the baselines, taking abuse from other players, fans, and working under exceptional pressures. He was a man of rare courage (see Robinson, 1972, for an account of this remarkable man). Listening to radio broadcasts of road games, I remember hearing Robinson loudly booed whenever he came up to bat in St. Louis against the Cardinals, but among Brooklyn fans—and the vast majority in attendance at the games were white—he was popular. To be sure, there were now far more Black fans at Ebbets Field, the Dodgers' ballpark, than before. They were there to root for him: Extraordinary cheers would go up when Robinson came to bat— not just the first time, but every time. I found myself pulling for him even more than I normally did for a Dodger, simply because it was clear how much he meant to these Black fans—even though at that stage I had no understanding of why, nor did I appreciate what a significant moment it represented in Blacks' painfully slow movement away from a life of extraordinary segregation and second-class citizenship. I suppose this sounds strange to a reader now, when there are many Black athletes in baseball, but at that point I could tell how painful it would have been for these fans were Robinson to have a bad game.

I once actually saw the importance Robinson held for Blacks. As part of the stream of fans leaving the ballpark on a sunny afternoon, I noticed various fans ahead of me who were now looking back and in my direction. I realized that they were looking at Robinson, who was walking in the crowd. He would not sign any autographs and he seemed somewhat chilly, but it did not matter. One could see a look of deep pleasure and joy on the faces of Black fans in the crowd as they stood and smiled at him.

Mostly, my memories of Blacks are minimal and impersonal:

- Several times during the winter, and again once in the summer, a large coal truck would back up to the front of the apartment building where we lived. A chute would be inserted through a window into the basement, where the coal was stored for the furnace. For most of a day, several husky Black men wearing caps and no obvious expressions would fill upright barrels with coal from the truck and wheel them over to the chute.

- During World War II, Blacks began to drive the old double-ended trolley cars that ran along the street in front of where we lived. It was only when they began to drive the cars that I realized I had never seen them doing this job before. The change was a sign of the "desperation" caused by the war.

- A public beach runs for miles along the Atlantic Ocean from Brighton Beach to Coney Island. It was simply packed in the summer, with subway train after subway train delivering people from all over New York for a day of water, sunbathing, eating, and the rides and games that made at least the Coney Island part famous throughout the nation. Rarely did one see Blacks on the beach in Brighton. Coney Island was then largely white, although Blacks were present in modest numbers. However, there was a sparsely occupied stretch of beach between Brighton and Coney Island that was essentially Black (the lack of crowding was a very attractive feature during the peak of the summer, when the rest of the beach was "mobbed," particularly on weekends). I have no idea what caused this odd de facto segregation pattern on the beach—how much it was a matter of preference as opposed to imposition.[3]

There is a paradox here. During the period from my earliest recollections through my two years at Brooklyn College (ending in 1952), Blacks were of minor consequence to me in terms of either interpersonal interaction or as part of the core of my deepest (and most emotional) feelings. Yet, on the other hand, Blacks were important in an abstract way. This was a period during which Jews and many white Roman Catholic groups were considered minorities. It was a period in which there was a certain sense of a bond with Blacks, empathy for what one only vaguely imagined they were going through. The focus was on the South in this period. One heard of lynchings; Jim Crow in all public facilities, from separate water fountains to hospitals to seating in buses; poll taxes; the Klan; separate schools mandated by law; the southern legal system; laws prohibiting intermarriage; sharecropping; people living without hope or opportunity, and expected to be totally servile. Events in the North were totally overshadowed.

This was a period during which there was a certain sense of sharing common risks, dangers, and threats. Discrimination in employment, in social clubs, in college admissions, and in fraternities was often addressed toward both Jews and Blacks. We both experienced the casual use of stereotypes and open expressions of prejudice. The sting of being called a kike was no different from the sting of being called a nigger. This was a period when there were arguments for "tolerance"—which now must sound so unassertive and demeaning, pleading for what is, after all, one's rights. So there was a certain bond; we were both minorities and both vulnerable to whims of powers beyond our control.

Chicago

In the early fall of 1952, at age 19, I boarded a Greyhound bus in Manhattan for a 20-hour trip to Chicago. I was leaving Brooklyn College after my sophomore year and was about to start graduate school in sociology at the University of Chicago.[4] This was my first experience living away from home for any length of time, with the usual pains and pleasures that come with it. It was also my first introduction to a different kind of ghetto from that I had known in Brighton. The bus arrived in the old Greyhound terminal on Wabash Avenue in downtown Chicago (the Loop). Loaded up with my luggage, temporarily storing the remainder in a locker at the terminal, I got on a trolley headed for Hyde Park on the South Side of Chicago, where the university was located. Although the trolley was packed—it was the evening rush hour—I noticed that were only two whites present, myself and the driver. This was my introduction to the huge Black ghetto on the South Side of Chicago and to life on the University of Chicago's racially mixed island located within it.[5]

It was essentially impossible for me or anyone else to be unaware of racial matters in that setting. The Black population of Chicago was large and growing very rapidly, thanks to a migration stream from the South. Chicago was a city of neighborhoods; for example, politics was organized around the ward (the name of the Democratic ward committeeman was widely known). There were angry whites, distressed at seeing their neighborhoods change, or worried about them changing in short order, as the Black ghetto expanded. If you asked a white about a given neighborhood and the response was that it was "gone," although you might picture a huge hole resembling the Grand Canyon, what this meant was that Blacks lived there and whites no longer did. One had to think about Black bars and white bars, of places to go and not to go, of safety and danger, of daylight and nighttime, of police, of good and bad streets to walk on, of riding public transportation, of work that Blacks did, of work that they were kept from doing.

There were, of course, angry Blacks as well as angry whites. Because of a restricted housing market, Blacks were intensely segregated residentially. They were forced to overpay for the right to live in substandard housing located in dangerous areas patrolled by police who themselves were as likely as not to be an added source of danger. Local stores were overpriced, all sorts of work was closed off, and Blacks learned to take "hate looks" from whites as a more or less inevitable part of life in the North. Just to add insult to injury, the slum housing was often owned by whites—it was a "wonderful" investment because even minimal upkeep was unnecessary. Building inspectors were only a minor problem, and the excess of demand over supply ensured full occupancy almost irrespective of the level of dilapidation. As was the case in other large cities, many of the local businesses in the ghettos were then owned by whites. Nothing could be taken for granted. In Chicago, for example, it took active efforts via a boycott to get breweries to hire Blacks for trucks delivering beer to the Black ghetto. There were uncomfortable and stressful situations, and anger was oozing out. Nevertheless, after I acclimated myself to Chicago, I thought nothing of bicycling through the Black ghetto.

I will not dwell on the University of Chicago in great detail. However, the racial composition of the neighborhoods to the west, south, and north of the university were becoming increasingly Black when I moved to Hyde Park in 1952 (Lake Michigan is to the east of the university). It was impossible for any whites or Blacks at the university, regardless of field or disposition, to ignore the racial events confronting them or to avoid at least some immersion in racial issues. For a discipline such as sociology, obviously, race relations is a topic of inherent interest. One never had to justify studying some facet of the dramatic events encountered as part of daily life in the area around the university and in the city as a whole. So here was a strong encouragement for its study.

Everett C. Hughes, one of the leading sociologists at Chicago during my student days there, was fond of encouraging students to skip his lectures and get out into the real world to study it. Being in the field, for Hughes, was the best way to learn. Of course, I do not think Hughes totally meant this, as he was himself very well read—and also served as editor of the *American Journal of Sociology* for many years. But he was serious about encouraging us to get out and know what the world was like, rather than experiencing it solely through books and articles. Ironically, because I was a disastrous student during part of my career at Chicago, I was able to do more of this than might have otherwise occurred. Although starting off very well at Chicago, I gradually deteriorated in succeeding years. I was making painfully slow progress and, as a consequence, was an undesirable student when research assistants were hired. Yet my need for food and shelter was no less than that of anyone else. As a consequence, I had to pick dead-end jobs, that is, jobs that did not provide me with training in sociology. For example, I worked in the admissions office of Billings Hospital and, in the summer, at a printing plant.

At one point during my career as a graduate student, I worked in the evenings as a part-time postal clerk in the main post office in downtown Chicago. I was assigned to the parcel-post section, which meant taking parcels off a moving conveyer belt and tossing them into one of perhaps 15 or 20 different chutes—for example, there might be one for Iowa, another for New York State, the Southwest, and so forth. It was not too difficult to pick up the necessary skills. There were a large number of men working "the battleship," as this area was called, and one could choose either to work silently or to talk with others while tossing parcels. And, as at a cocktail party, after a while one could move to another point on the platform and start a different conversation with someone new.

Almost everyone working the battleship was Black. There were perhaps 10 whites on my shift, and a few Asians, and I remember one Mexican American. Although I was often content to say very little, after a while I got to know a number of the people, and it was impossible, at that point, not to hear about being Black. The people were of diverse backgrounds, and I was often unable to figure them out and hence would be surprised. For example, there was Smitty, who appeared to be a little slow, seemed agreeable to virtually anything that I said, and was perpetually moving in a shuffle. He surprised me one day by pulling out a piece of chalk and writing equations on the conveyor belt while at the same, in a singsong way, reciting some algebraic rules. What was this all about? I found out that Smitty had attended college for two years and then became a teacher in a Black grade school in his home state of Mississippi. Some years later, he migrated to Chicago and a blue-collar job. Senator Bilbo from Mississippi was then nationally known for running on an anti-Black platform that was vehement even by the standards of that time—which of course was before Blacks were able to vote in any serious number in the South. Smitty described standing in the back of a crowd in the square of his hometown to hear his senator speak, and Bilbo's ranting and raving against Blacks. Teacher or not,

Smitty left for the sake of his large family. Smitty was deeply religious and saw no point in smoking, drinking, or swearing. In our conversations, I noticed that now his choice of words, his pronunciation, his pitch, and even his facial expressions were changed. He suddenly appeared more serious, was no longer a simpleton, and was stern when there was something serious to talk about. And there often was. Smitty was someone who had learned to survive in Mississippi by avoiding giving any hint to whites of an intelligence or purposefulness lurking below.

I got to know many of the people working on the battleship. Some were full-time postal workers. Many, however, were working part-time to supplement the income from their daytime jobs. More than a handful would show up still dressed in the suits, white shirts, and ties required for their full-time day jobs. I had many good conversations on the battleship, often about race relations. It was not that I was pushing my coworkers about the topic as much as it was something they wanted to talk about now that we knew each other. Indeed, much to my amazement, there were times when I got tired of hearing one more story. It was consuming many Blacks working in the post office, and sometimes their stories consumed me. I hope you understand that I did not view this as a sociological matter, or even an intellectual matter; rather, it was an eye-opening experience that I happened on in the course of looking for a job that could help me work my way through graduate school. As a matter of fact, I suspect that the people I talked with at work would have backed off immediately had I pushed the topic. Curiously, of the handful of whites working on the battleship, several were fairly open with me in expressing their dislike of Blacks. Although I saw no open conflict or expression of feelings at work, it was clear that the Blacks there were aware of their coworkers' antipathies.

I left the post office to take a full-time summer job at one of the steel mills then operating on the far South Side of Chicago. Most workers at the mill were white. For unskilled blue-collar workers, the steel mill offered well-paying work in this period, before there was competition from either foreign steel or foreign automobiles. All in the course of one summer, I started as a laborer, we then went on strike, and after I came back I was a third helper (briefly at one of the open hearth furnaces, but mainly in the tilting and electric department, where we made steel in furnaces with the electricity passing between among huge carbon electrodes). I also received more of an education than Hughes would have approved of.

It was the summer of a presidential election year. My fellow graduate students at the university were disappointed in the keynote speaker at the Democratic party's convention, whose speech seemed "corny." The only justification for it was that it probably played very well with the "masses," that is, working-class Americans who were a central part of the party's support base. In point of fact, as far as I could tell, the blue-collar workers around me at the mill had not heard the speech, had not read about it, and did not in the least care. The Democratic party at that point was more for the workers and that was the end of the discussion, pure and simple. My friends and acquaintances at the University of Chicago did not have the foggiest idea about my coworkers' indifference.

Blacks at the mill were a numerical minority, and not entirely first-class citizens. I never saw a Black foreman, for example, and there was a form of segregation in the locker-room assignments. Essentially, everyone showered after work. Some locker-room areas were assigned to Blacks and "DPs" (displaced persons, i.e., Europeans who had come to the United States after World War II because they had been displaced from their home countries by the war); other locker areas were occupied exclusively by American-born whites and some DPs, but no Blacks.

I did not get to know very many of the Blacks in the mill, but for the most part I thought there was a quiet confidence and certainty among the Blacks with whom I interacted. Their jobs were excellent ones for blue-collar work; the pay was high, it was *masculine* work, and it was relatively steady work. It was at times painfully hard work—at some points we had to be close to the furnaces, with heat that was so severe one could not endure it for more than a few minutes.

I learned about race and ethnic relations in the steel mill, particularly as they compared with those at the post office. For example, with the large numbers of whites present, all sorts of ethnic subdivisions among the whites now popped up: for example, Poles, Serbians, Slovenians, southern Whites, and Italians. There were not too many unpleasant moments for me at the mill, but there were a few. Mike appeared out of the blue one day and began yelling on and on at me in a foreign tongue (he was a displaced person from Serbia). In a literal sense I understood not one word, but I knew full well that he was cursing me and castigating me for every offense imaginable. As if there were any danger of my not grasping the message, in English he concluded with satisfaction that in Serbia they would string Jews up. I noticed that his use of the term *Jew* was for him simultaneously a description of what I was, an epithet, a condemnation, and an expression of total disgust. This was an entry for me into the world of what pre-World War II Eastern Europe must have been like. It was not, at least for the most part, the world of contemporary America. But it was, at least in that era before the civil rights movement, parallel to what the experience of Blacks was like. That someone was Black was, for many whites, all that one needed to know and all that one needed to say.

In the fall, after my summer as a steelworker, I was able to get a research assistantship at the Population Research Center. I was hired to work for Otis Dudley Duncan, with whom I had only a passing acquaintance from a previous stint at the Population Center (early in my career at Chicago, I had worked there under Evelyn Kitagawa). It was the beginning of a major turnaround in my fortunes as a graduate student, and I will always carry an enormous debt to Dudley—to say nothing of my appreciation of him as a brilliant scholar with extraordinary standards, integrity, and dedication.[6] I worked there for the rest of my graduate career, on a number of projects, one of which was a pleasing merger of my own interests in white ethnic groups with Dudley's interest in residential segregation. Dudley and Beverly Duncan (1957) had written a path-breaking study of racial residential segregation in Chicago. As a small offshoot of both Dudley's substantive interest in residential segregation and his pioneering developments in its measurement, we would take a look at the segregation of European immigrants and their American-born offspring. Under his wing, I was turned loose to work on this. The product was a nice paper (Duncan & Lieberson, 1959), and in turn Dudley suggested that I consider expanding the work on my own as a dissertation project, which I did and later published as a monograph (Lieberson, 1963). Included within it, at Dudley's suggestion, was a consideration of Black versus white ethnic residential segregation, which by the way came up with some very interesting and surprising results. In all but 1 of 10 cities studied, some European immigrant groups were more segregated than Blacks earlier in this century (Lieberson, 1963, Table 42). There is a certain irony here, as the term ghetto was first employed to describe the Jewish section of a city, and is probably derived from the Italian word for the cannon foundry located in that part of Venice where Jews were first located (Wirth, 1928, p. 2).

After Chicago

I maintained an interest in race and ethnic relations through the years, choosing to teach a course on the subject during my first year as an academic, at the University of Iowa in the spring of 1960. I still maintain this interest, with lapses every now and then as I recharge my batteries or get intensively focused on another topic. I often learn from my students, particularly undergraduates. I like to have discussions in class. Sometimes they are animated, sometimes disturbing, sometimes conflictual, and sometimes infuriating. Tending as I do toward mulling over hurts—real and imagined—such a course has often led me to think more and more about a particular topic or simply to try to make sense of what happened in class. I have learned a lot from Black students, sometimes in a pleasant way and sometimes not. For some weird reason, occurrences of Black hostility toward me—not always unjustified after I think about it—do not upset me as much as I might have expected. The interaction in class has always seemed of value for all of the students present, and for some reason I tend to take the unpleasant moments less personally than I am otherwise disposed to do. But I think the main reason is that I often feel that I can understand why the response is in the form that it is—or at least I think it through afterward.

For example, years ago I used to give a talk on race relations as part of the social science program at the Seattle Police Academy. At the end of one talk, a Black cadet was clearly angry with me, indicating that I did not know what I was talking about even if I was a professor. "Okay, I probably don't, but could you be more specific?" It turned out that I had said something about Black educational opportunities and schools being inferior to those available to whites—a fairly standard kind of viewpoint, I would say. And he felt that I was implying that his education was not as good as that of the other cadets. As he was the only Black in that class of cadets, I could see his problem. It was not so much what I was saying per se, but rather what its impact would be for him in dealing with whites in what was already a ticklish situation. This event, along with incidents in various of my courses, led me to think about how the groups were often fully aware of the stereotypes existing about them and, in turn, the consequences this had for behavior (Lieberson, 1982).

At any rate, I began to develop an interest in the differences between Blacks and European immigrant groups; the issue being why the latter were doing so much better than the former. Given that the immigrants suffered from many hardships, were initially very poor on the average, and were the objects of prejudice and extensive discrimination, how did it come about that they now seemed to be doing so well relative to Blacks? In one form or another, this question kept coming up. I could see that the issue was a sticky one for all concerned: There was a certain anxiousness among Blacks as I would respond, and I interpreted this as reflecting their own concern about the question, although it was nearly always whites who raised the issue. The white students were genuinely curious—they did not usually ask the question rhetorically or polemically, to make a point. Rather, they asked out of curiosity. As I point out in *A Piece of the Pie*:

> The origin of this book lies in a question that I often encounter when teaching undergraduate college courses on race and ethnic relations. My lectures on the "New" immigrant groups, those who began to migrate in sizable numbers from South, Central, and Eastern Europe after 1880, frequently lead to questions about why these groups fared so much better in the United States through the years than did blacks. I have always argued that the handicaps faced by blacks were more severe than those encountered by the new Europeans. The latter, notwithstanding their foreign tongues and broken English, their clothing, alien ways, non-Protestant religions, and the like, were after all White and a generation or two later it was possible for their descendants to shed as many of these markers as necessary. Blacks on the other hand were blacks no matter how anglicized their surnames, the absence of ties to distant lands, their language, their clothing, or their Protestantism. Besides the new Europeans got to the Northern cities in sizable numbers first, before the demand for unskilled workers declined. Anyway there were the unions and discrimination of all sorts in the North as well as in the South of a magnitude never experienced by the Europeans.
>
> This was a satisfactory answer, at least for classroom purposes. First, all of my statements were certainly true. Second, it seemed to be an acceptable response for both blacks and nonblacks in the class. If any students were not convinced, they were not inclined to say anything. But I had a nagging dissatisfaction with the answer. If what I said was true, was it all of the truth? Were the differences between South-Central-Eastern Europeans and blacks merely a question of differences in the opportunity structure? I did not know the answer.
>
> I discovered that I was not alone; among my sociologist friends there were others who had one answer for public purposes but privately were not at all

sure about it. There was the reluctant suspicion held by many that some unknown part of the gap between the new Europeans in America and blacks was a reflection of something else. I got to thinking about one of my colleagues at the time, who in his midsixties was completing an enormously successful career accompanied by virtually all of the highest honors possible in the scholarly path that he pursued. What would this American-born offspring of new immigrants, who faced poverty and other obstacles as a child, be doing if his skin pigmentation were different? I did not know the answer, but I was determined to find out as best as I could through whatever quantitative and qualitative clues were obtainable. This volume is the product. (Lieberson, 1980, pp. xi-xii)

The book took a painfully long time to do. In retrospect I can see why: In its own way it covered my own concerns and evolution as it developed into a broad set of comparisons between Blacks and a wide variety of white ethnic groups. It was not easy because I tried to develop as much systematic evidence as I could—both "soft" and "hard"—for all of the issues raised. I wanted it to be as rigorous a study as possible, rather than a statement of personal values or wishes. In the end, *A Piece of the Pie* was well received in the scholarly community, winning the 1982 Distinguished Contribution to Scholarship Award from the American Sociological Association.

Notes

1. See Lieberson (1992) for a discussion of this probabilistic perspective. A similar mix of background and chance factors operated in the development of a research program in sociolinguistics (Lieberson, 1981, pp. 378-382).

2. An important exception is the work of Anderson (1990).

3. The distinction between voluntary and involuntary is, however, often an artificial one. What leads us to chose aversion is often not independent of the fears and experiences based on integration.

4. At that time, it was possible to do so because the University of Chicago had a different undergraduate degree program, started under the Hutchins regime. After taking a variety of tests, I was admitted to the graduate school with the same status as if I had received a Chicago undergraduate degree.

5. The University of Chicago was my first introduction to the world of non-Jews as well. This is kind of ironic, I suppose, because I knew many non-Jews at Chicago who were amazed by the large number of Jews attending the university, but for me it was the opposite. So I suppose the University of Chicago was a learning experience for others as well.

6. By the time I left graduate school, my intellectual and personal debts to Beverly Duncan and Evelyn Kitagawa were also enormous. I was also greatly influenced by Hughes's way of thinking about racial and ethnic relations.

References

Anderson, E. (1990). *Streetwise: Race, class, and change in an urban community.* Chicago: University of Chicago Press.

Duncan, O. D., & Duncan, B. (1957). *The Negro population of Chicago: A study of residential succession.* Chicago: University of Chicago Press.

Duncan, O. D., & Lieberson, S. (1959). Ethnic segregation and assimilation. *American Journal of Sociology, 64,* 366-374.

Lieberson, S. (1958). Ethnic groups and the practice of medicine. *American Sociological Review, 23,* 542-549.

Lieberson, S. (1963). *Ethnic patterns in American cities.* New York: Free Press.

Lieberson, S. (1980). *A piece of the pie: Blacks and white immigrants since 1880.* Berkeley: University of California Press.

Lieberson, S. (1981). *Language diversity and language contact: Essays by Stanley Lieberson.* Stanford, CA: Stanford University Press.

Lieberson, S. (1982). Stereotypes: Their consequences for race and ethnic interaction. In R. M. Hauser, D. Mechanic, A. O. Haller, & T. S. Hauser (Eds.), *Social structure and behavior: Essays in honor of William H. Sewell* (pp. 47-68). New York: Academic Press.

Lieberson, S. (1992). Einstein, Renoir, and Greeley: Some thoughts about evidence in sociology. *American Sociological Review, 57,* 1-15.

Lieberson, S., & Silverman, A. (1965). The precipitants and underlying conditions of race riots. *American Sociological Review, 30,* 887-898.

Robinson, J., with Duckett, A. (1972). *I never had it made.* New York: Putnam.

Wirth, L. (1928). *The ghetto.* Chicago: University of Chicago Press.

8

How Events Shape
Theoretical Frames

A Personal Statement

THOMAS F. PETTIGREW

Starting Out

Calling your seventh-grade history teacher a bigot was not considered appropriate student behavior in 1943 at Albert Hill Junior High School in Richmond, Virginia. My only defense was that, given her use of derogatory names for Black Americans and praise of Hitler's anti-Semitism, the epithet was justified. The principal expelled me for the day, the first of several such incidents. These bruising encounters taught me early the power of southern norms in support of racial and religious intolerance. A tyranny on white as well as Black citizens was necessary to maintain the region's normative structure.

Growing up in the South of the 1930s and 1940s sensitized everyone to race as a primary social category. Many factors undoubtedly shaped how any southerner, Black or white, responded to racial injustice. A half century later, I hesitate to speculate on why I resisted the tyranny. One levels and sharpens old memories in reconstructing an explanation that

AUTHOR'S NOTE: The writing of this chapter was facilitated by a Rockefeller Foundation fellowship to the Bellagio Study and Conference Center, Bellagio, Italy.

159

links with later events. But two important influences were critical: my immigrant Scottish family and Miss Mildred Adams.

Most of my boyhood friends felt much the same as I about racial matters. They lacked, however, the support of a family that sanctioned, even encouraged, resistant behavior. My father was a Scottish-American, born and raised in the Virginia mountains. He conformed to the culture's dictates, but lacked the visceral racist feelings of the Black belt. My mother and grandmother were Scottish immigrants who harbored doubts about many aspects of American life. They would react to my school expulsions by appearing at once at the principal's office to defend my actions.

Just as important was the influence of the family housekeeper. I have dedicated several books to Miss Mildred Adams, for she fired me early with indignation over racial injustice. Gradually, gently, she allowed me to glimpse into Black life and sense how white supremacy limited the life chances and choices of Black Richmonders. I vividly recall sitting in the basement every Wednesday afternoon when she did the wash and ironing. She would tell me about her life—its harsh beginnings in rural Virginia, her disappointment with New York City, where she went to escape southern segregation, and the limitations of her present life. Repeatedly, I experienced with her small incidents that proved Mildred Adams was softening the cruel reality of racism for my young ears. Once a "white" movie theater refused us admission, although she had taken care to dress in an all-white uniform.[1] By the time I was 10 years old, the many psychological and cultural defenses that blind most white Americans to the racial injustice that surrounds them were no longer available to me.

It was not until 1951 that I learned I could pursue a career studying race relations. It occurred during a social psychology class at the University of Virginia. Until that point, I had thought of my concerns about race relations as strictly political, something you focused on outside your career. The idea that you could actually study, conduct research, even make a living specializing in race relations was an exciting revelation to me.

Once my instructor learned of my interest, he advised me to apply to Harvard University's Department of Social Relations for doctoral work. Somehow he knew that Gordon Allport was writing a book on the subject—the classic volume *The Nature of Prejudice* (Allport, 1954). I followed my instructor's advice. Unaware of how arrogant it appeared, I mentioned in my Harvard application that I wanted to work with

Allport on race relations, otherwise I was not interested in attending. Allport himself was in charge of graduate admissions, fortunately, and my naive impertinence did not prove fatal. The social psychology doctoral program accepted me, and gave me the special opportunity to work with Allport, a great teacher and social scientist (Pettigrew, 1969a, 1990). Thus began my 28-year association with Harvard University.

Harvard's Social Relations Department brought four disciplines together: sociology (led by Talcott Parsons and Samuel Stouffer), social psychology (led by Allport), personality psychology (led by Henry Murray and Robert White), and cultural anthropology (led by Clyde Kluckhohn). Graduate students took at least introductory work in all four fields. My training at the University of Virginia had prepared me for psychology, but nothing had prepared me for the sweepingly broad lectures of Parsons. Only years later, after repeatedly teaching a graduate course with him in the 1960s, did I grasp the principal features of Parsonian theory.

In 1952 and 1953, race relations was not a favored specialty. I was the object of concern among my fellow doctoral students. They advised me to choose another specialty, as there were few jobs, little status, and virtually no research funds in race relations. But my early experiences with racial injustice had fired my desire to be a social scientist, so such concerns seemed irrelevant. The scene changed in 1954, when the U.S. Supreme Court ruled against racial segregation in the public schools. Suddenly, my peers became extremely interested in the topic, and their concern for my future diminished.

Throughout this period, Allport and Stouffer, my principal mentors, encouraged my interests. It was an exciting time to be working with them. Not only was Allport writing his classic book on prejudice, but Stouffer was engaged in the research for his important work on attitudes about McCarthyism, *Communism, Conformity and Civil Liberties* (Stouffer, 1955). I did minor bibliographical work for Allport, who completed his book during the summer months of 1953. Instruction from him was formal and conceptual, though always fashioned to fit the student's interests. By contrast, instruction from Stouffer was invariably informal and empirical. Intensely engrossed in his work, Stouffer taught by example. You followed him around from office to computing room and back, absorbing as best you could his excitement, expertise, and "feel" for survey research and analysis. Whenever someone advanced an interesting idea in his graduate seminars, Stouffer would promptly march the entire class to the computing room. There he would wildly stuff the punch cards into the old IBM 101, and test the idea with his survey data on the spot.[2] To this day, I have never lost the sense of excitement and curiosity in analyzing survey data instilled by these memorable occasions.

A Door-to-Door Thesis

Both teachers shaped my doctoral thesis. I came to Harvard with my problem—that authoritarian personality theory (Adorno, Frenkel-Brunswick, Levinson, & Sanford, 1950), then in high vogue, did not explain the intensely anti-Black attitudes of white southerners. From Allport, I learned how to cast my contentions in sharper conceptual focus. From Stouffer, I learned how to test them on probability samples with survey methods.

In the summer of 1955, I set out with Charles Lamont, my undergraduate assistant and undaunted friend, to sample white racial opinions in small towns in the South and North. To deter trouble, I put Virginia license plates on my old Chevrolet, and Stouffer got official interviewer certification papers for me from a national survey agency. In the most deep-South community sampled—Moultrie, Georgia—the tension was palpable. In May 1955, the Supreme Court had followed up its historic desegregation ruling with a vague implementation órder for "all deliberate speed." The white South, quite deliberate but never speedy, interpreted this order as a signal of weakness. Resistance groups called White Citizens' Councils soon mobilized in such Black-belt towns as Moultrie.

So our survey schedule had to minimize recognition of its purpose. Employing a device from Stouffer's McCarthyism survey, we asked our white respondents what they considered the most important problem facing the nation. The school desegregation issue was so salient in the South that most subjects immediately named it as the most important. If they did not, we asked for the second most important problem—if need be, the third most important. By then, the entire sample had specified racial issues of some sort. Then we introduced our racial attitude questions as a subject they had raised themselves. This cover worked well for white respondents. Black citizens who overheard the interviews, however, easily determined our purpose and soon invited us to speak at the local NAACP![3]

Authoritarian personality theory was a major advance in the understanding of prejudice and related phenomena *at the individual level of analysis.* However, it failed completely to consider the social contexts of these phenomena. My doctoral thesis underscored this weakness by demonstrating that the mean levels of authoritarianism were not significantly different between the northern and southern samples. The F-Scale measure of the concept did predict individual differences in racial prejudice equally well in the two regions—showing its validity at that level of analysis (Pettigrew, 1958, 1959, 1961). These findings led me to embrace normative theory (Pettigrew, 1991b) and to emphasize the role of social conformity in racial prejudice among white southerners.

Lamont and I returned to Harvard, tired but smugly pleased over our accomplishment of having traveled 4,000 miles to conduct 366 personal interviews door to door in eight communities. Proudly, I took the first opportunity to tell Stouffer of our achievement. I caught up with him on the third floor of Emerson Hall, rushing between his office and the computing room. He was less than impressed. "How many interviews— 366? What can you analyze with so few cases?" I was crestfallen, though I did manage an analysis. As always, Stouffer had a point: I had not obtained full regional samples, and the small number of cases severely limited the analysis. Fortunately, Middleton (1976) followed up the work with better samples, and both replicated and extended the results.

Allport provided me with an opportunity to test my contentions cross-culturally. He had secured a Ford Foundation grant to visit a social research center at the University of Natal in Durban, South Africa. And he obtained a small grant for me to accompany him on the condition that I finish my thesis by January 1956. With such an incentive, I worked intensively to complete the analysis and writing. I left for South Africa in early March 1956 for a half year's stay in that troubled land.

This adventure proved a mind-shaping experience. It was my first opportunity to live and study in a foreign country—and I have taken every such opportunity afforded me since. In 1956, South African race relations were like what race relations must have been in my native South about a decade before my birth. Indeed, there is a 20- to 30-year lag in much of South African history compared with that of the American South.[4] I replicated my thesis work, though I could obtain only university student respondents (Pettigrew, 1958). There was one major difference, however: Afrikaners *were* more authoritarian than other white South Africans. Nonetheless, conformity to rigorously enforced racist norms remained critical.

Shifting Theoretical Frames

Although critical of authoritarian personality theory, my work of the 1950s was still largely conducted within the theoretical frame that dominated race relations research during the decade. That frame involved an emphasis on attitudes and stereotypes while paying scant attention to the macroinstitutional level of analysis—actual group relations, dominance structures, power, and so on. There was even little attention during this period to the situational level of face-to-face intergroup interaction. To be sure, there were exceptions (e.g., Barnard, 1951; Schermerhorn, 1956), but the dominant paradigm consisted of this micro frame of analysis.

This restricted frame was almost as true of work done in sociology as it was in social psychology. Indeed, Kurt Back and I argued that this too-micro-oriented frame was a major reason sociology was so unprepared for the civil rights movement when it burst upon the national scene in the 1960s (Pettigrew & Back, 1967).

It was the civil rights movement that shook the race relations field out of its micro-oriented preoccupations. Both social psychology and sociology had the ideas and conceptual tools to begin to understand the momentous events, but these ideas and tools had not been part of the 1950s emphasis on attitudes and personality types. The events of the 1960s shaped a new theoretical frame, one that not only highlighted existing situational and structural ideas but gave inspiration for new approaches. The greater inclusion of Black social scientists in the controversies of the period was critical to this process. Kenneth C. Clark (1965) was an especially prominent example of this trend, and through our friendship, he has had a lasting influence on my thought and work.

Although the new frame reinstated the central importance of macro considerations, its broad sweep included revisionist thinking at the micro level as well. In particular, it questioned the older view of Black Americans as mere passive victims. This image had been useful in earlier popular efforts to prove the evils of racial segregation. But now proactive images received a hearing. From recalling slave revolts to starting voter registration campaigns, a fresh image of Black citizens taking their fates into their own hands gained prominence. Like many corrections, this shift sometimes went too far, on occasion virtually denying that three and a half centuries of slavery, segregation, and racism had had negative effects on Black America (e.g., Adam, 1978;

Pettigrew, 1978a). On balance, however, this micro aspect of the new analytic frame was a healthy corrective to earlier, exclusively reactive views of Black Americans.

The particular events that made these lessons salient for me occurred in the late winter and spring of 1960. I received a small research grant to spend a sabbatical semester in the South, interviewing white southern liberals. But just as I arrived, the student sit-in movement began at a Woolworth's lunch counter in Greensboro, North Carolina, and spread rapidly across the region. I abandoned my planned research and immediately started studying the sit-in movement. I was in the right place at the right time to observe a striking phenomenon. Soon it was possible to predict where the next sit-in campaigns would occur. The students from North Carolina Agricultural and Technical University had sparked the process, and the school's athletic teams carried the word about how to conduct sit-in campaigns as they traveled to games at other predominantly Black colleges. By following the schedules of these teams, it was often possible to be where the lunch counter revolution was next to strike.

The most vivid occasion for me occurred in Sumter, deep within the black belt of South Carolina. The student body of a modest Black Baptist institution, Morris College, demonstrated for equal rights and the police promptly herded them into the town jail. As they marched into prison, dressed in their "Sunday best," carrying American flags and singing hymns and the national anthem, a crowd of local whites gathered to watch. The whites' reactions were startling. In contrast to the confident, determined, if frightened students, the white onlookers were sullen and silent. There were no angry jeers or name-calling. It was clear that the national and religious symbols invoked by the students hit their target. There was an unhappy acceptance by the white crowd that the racial segregation era was dying; Black citizens were burying it.

The four young men who began the sit-in process in 1960 were freshmen. None had taken a course yet at North Carolina A&T in either sociology or social psychology. And it was better that they had not done so, for the social science of the time, ensnared in its micro frame of analysis, would have provided the students with reasons that direct-action protest would have little chance of success. The white South "was not ready yet"; such actions only trigger counteractions that make matters worse. White southern attitudes, even in comparatively liberal Greensboro, needed to "come around" a bit more. Bottom-up causal paths predominated in the thinking of the time; attitude change was thought to be essential before institutional change was possible.

Happily, such reasoning did not impede the young men. Inspired by the success of the Montgomery bus boycott a few years before and angry over how several female students had been treated earlier at the Woolworth's counter, they acted on a top-down model of change. Attract bad publicity to Woolworth's, cost the store lost profits, and then the store's management would alter its racial policies for business reasons. White attitudes would have to adjust to the top-down change, rather than serve as the all-powerful obstacle to be overcome first.

The resigned faces in the white crowd that dramatic day in Sumter were the occasion for my complete conversion to the new analytic frame. To be sure, as a critic of the authoritarian personality model, I saw this new frame as a logical extension of my earlier contentions. Moreover, there was an extensive literature in both sociology and social psychology available to develop this reasoning. The point here is that the new perspective that emerged during the 1960s did not represent a total break with the past. As Kuhn (1970) argues for paradigm shifts in science generally, the old perspective was already challenged and undermined before its dethronement (e.g., Schermerhorn, 1956). But the dramatic events that paced across the American stage during the 1960s both extended and legitimated the changed mode of thinking. The old frame of analysis had neither anticipated nor explained the new events.

The Influence of Later Events

The heady early success of the civil rights movement led social science to overemphasize the possibilities for social change that had been so underestimated previously. Soon correctives were triggered by the sobering events that followed—the Vietnam War, internal conflicts within the movement, and the Nixon era, with its racist messages encased in such symbols as "antibusing." These events signaled the close of the civil rights era, a brief window in U.S. history when the nation began to live up to its promises of equal rights for its Black citizens.

For the field of race relations, 1965 to 1975 was a time of theoretical consolidation. Excesses of the new analytic frame were rolled back, and more attention was paid to the problem of the links among levels of analysis—the individual, the situational, and the institutional and societal. Blalock's (1967) thoughtful volume *Toward a Theory of Minority-Group Relations* is a prime illustration.

Two types of activity influenced my work during this period. At the national level, my work focused on broad public school desegregation policy. I served as a consultant to the U.S. Commission on Civil Rights, to the U.S. Commissioner of Education, and to Senator Walter Mondale. I was also a member of the advisory board for the Coleman Report (U.S. Office of Education, 1966) and a member of the White House Task Force on Education in 1967. At the local level, I consulted for many state and urban school systems and served as an expert witness in public school desegregation litigation. These national and local experiences reinforced my conviction that institutional change could be designed to optimize positive outcomes for individuals. Especially impressive were the broad similarities in issues and problems found in the cities in whose desegregation cases I participated—from Springfield, Massachusetts, and Los Angeles, California, to Norfolk and Richmond, Virginia.[5]

One such similarity was the geographic barrier created by intense residential racial segregation. Before we could fashion optimally integrated interracial schools in these urban areas, we had to overcome this barrier. Even by 1960, it was clear only metropolitan approaches to school desegregation could have lasting value in many major urban centers. It was a time to give public speeches, write popular and technical articles, and provide federal court and congressional testimony on the subject (e.g., Pettigrew, 1965a, 1965b, 1967, 1968, 1969b, 1970a, 1970b, 1970c, 1970d, 1971, 1975a, 1975b, 1978b, 1979a, 1980b, 1981a).

In 1972, Congress passed a bill sponsored by Senator Mondale to fund several demonstration "metropolitan educational parks"—a major means of overcoming urban segregation patterns.[6] Predictably, President Nixon refused to sign the appropriations for it. Though allowing them in Nashville, Charlotte, Louisville, and Wilmington, the U.S. Supreme Court narrowly rejected metropolitan desegregation plans for Detroit and my native Richmond.[7] The necessary means to make good on the promises of the 1960s were rejected in the 1970s.

Resistance to metropolitan approaches exploited the racial barriers established by residential segregation. "Busing" was the rallying cry against such plans, though the metropolitan plan for the Richmond area public schools would have *reduced* the transportation of children. Soon even a leading sociologist joined the debate, ignored metropolitan possibilities, and argued that the effort to desegregate public schools in central cities should be abandoned because it caused "white flight" (Coleman, Kelly, & Moore, 1975). Apart from serious problems with the supporting data for this argument (Pettigrew & Green, 1976), the "white flight" thesis was yet another attempt to use white reactions and existing segregation to argue for the maintenance of racial segregation. Black Americans have heard such reasoning throughout their history. It is analogous to the white South's arguments in the early 1950s that public school desegregation would ignite white violence. Repeatedly throughout American history, the constitutional rights of Black citizens have been undermined because of the fear of white reaction. The rejection of metropolitan approaches to urban school desegregation in the 1970-1975 period was yet another instance of this tragic history. However, if and when the nation again addresses its racial problems and genuinely attempts to desegregate its urban schools, we will have to return to metropolitan approaches.

Summing Up: Seven General Propositions

Science is a social process. No one social scientist makes a contribution independent of the efforts of others. At best, we are all "workers in the vineyard." We can only influence in small ways the far-flung "disciplinary dialogue" that transpires during our careers. Within this limited context (and prodded by the editor), I advance seven general propositions that arise from my work in race relations over the past four decades. These propositions may at first seem self-evident truisms, but each directly counters widely voiced contentions that others regard to be just as self-evident.

Racial norms are a major determinant of race relations. Throughout my experiences in the American South, South Africa, and the Netherlands, the persistence and power of racial norms have singularly impressed me.[8] Indeed, my decision to spend four years in the Netherlands was motivated by my interest in studying a nation that has evolved over the centuries strong antiracism norms unique in the Western world (Pettigrew & Meertens, 1992, 1993). Sociology overpredicts intergroup conflict, for we have given scant attention to situations of relative harmony among groups.

Normative theory has both advantages and disadvantages (Pettigrew, 1991b). A major asset is that it allows, indeed requires, a broad interdisciplinary approach. Thus normative theory has the potential of uniting the contributions from all the social sciences into a broad understanding of race relations. Yet the theory has potential weaknesses that make "norms" one of the most misused concepts in social science. First, there is the danger of circular reasoning. Sometimes intergroup behavior is "explained" by group norms, then these assumed norms are "proven" to exist by reference back to the original behavior. Obviously, independent evidence of intergroup norms is necessary. Second, needed specification is often lacking. Normative analyses typically describe norms without tracing them to their origins. But basing an explanation upon a normative argument begs the question as to how these norms were established, have evolved, and are now maintained. Finally, normative analyses of intergroup relations often overlook the central issue of differential power and dominance, for one group usually has the power to set and defend the dominant norms. These problems are not intrinsic to normative analyses, however, and with care they can be avoided.

Norms are changed more from top-down structural alterations than from bottom-up attitude changes—with face-to-face situations serving as a critical intermediate link. Without denying bottom-up causal paths in which accumulated attitude changes lead to normative shifts, all my American, South African, and Dutch work points to the primary causal significance of structural change.

This is a proposition on which both structuralists and social psychologists can agree. The latter have established through consistency theory and its vast research literature that behavioral change can set off major shifts in individual opinions. How, then, is behavioral change typically achieved? In intergroup relations, behavior changes when intergroup situational norms are changed—in schools, neighborhoods, and on the job. And intergroup situational alterations typically require top-down institutional change. The old saw that "laws cannot change the hearts and minds of men" is in error. It ignores the critical intermediary role of changed situational norms brought about by effectively enforced laws that in turn lead to altered attitudes.

This trilevel contention, combining structural and social psychological theory, has been central to my applied work on integrated schools and affirmative action. And it has received strong support from events in my native South over the past generation (Pettigrew, 1991a). It is the region that has experienced the greatest structural change, and it is also the region where the greatest change in white racial attitudes has been recorded. These attitude changes have also typically occurred *after,* not before, the institutional changes. Furthermore, when federal pressure on the region evaporated in the 1980s, both the institutional and attitude improvements abated. To be sure, the South still has a long road to travel before it attains anything resembling racial equality, but its record to date supports the importance of top-down normative alterations.

Race-class interactions have become predominantly important in American race relations. The expansion of the Black middle class and its initial entry into the broader society were major achievements of the civil rights movement of the 1960s. These gains led to social stratification changes in American race relations, changes that made Black-white relations more conditioned by social class factors.

Wilson's (1978) claim that these changes signaled "the declining significance of race" represents a serious misreading of this complex situation (Pettigrew, 1980a). The rising role of social class definitely *changed* the "significance of race," but, unfortunately, this does not necessarily entail any "decline" in the importance of race per se. In analysis of variance terms, the main effect of race remains important, but there has been a sharp rise in the significance of the interaction between race and class (Pettigrew, 1981b). Hence social class now importantly shapes the meaning and significance of race in the United States. Upper-status Black Americans still face *racial* discrimination, for example, but the forms of these restrictions on their life chances and choices are typically more subtle and indirect than those faced by lower-status Black Americans.

Modern prejudice and discrimination are becoming increasingly more subtle, indirect, and difficult to combat. The David Dukeses of the nation and the videotaped police beating of Rodney King show that blatant forms of racism still thrive in the United States, but the greater race-class interaction has led to gains in importance for subtler forms of racism. Compared with the open bigotry and explicit color lines of old, these subtler forms of prejudice and discrimination are far more difficult to detect and remedy (Pettigrew, 1985b, 1985c, 1989; Pettigrew & Taylor, 1992). Nor are these modern forms limited to American race relations. Recent work has uncovered similar patterns throughout Western Europe (Pettigrew & Meertens, 1992).

Minorities respond to oppression both reactively and proactively. As noted, my career began in the pre-1960s, when a reactive model of Black American behavior predominated. Then, from 1961 to 1975, a proactive model gained prominence. The field pushed each model to extremes. Black Americans have reacted to oppression *and* have proactively combated racism. Both aspects of social reality are necessary for robust theory.

Two final propositions concern social science broadly; although highly relevant for the race relations area, neither is limited to it.

Science is not and cannot be value free. As an undergraduate, I read Gunnar Myrdal's (1944) famous Appendix 2 of his classic, *An American Dilemma.* In "A Methodological Note on Facts and Valuations in Social Science," the blunt Swedish economist argues that values are inherent in social science. Better to be aware of your values, struggle against their biasing effects, and alert your readers to them, he maintains, than to fool yourself and others that you can be coldly "objective." "There is no other device for excluding biases in [the] social sciences," he writes, "than to face the valuations and to introduce them as explicitly stated, specific, and sufficiently concretized value premises" (p. 1043). I found Myrdal's argument persuasive, and nothing during the ensuing four decades has dissuaded me. Indeed, I am repeatedly amazed by sociologists who regard their work as totally "objective" even as they damn the rival work of others as obviously biased—especially when it comes from those of us who, like Myrdal, openly state our values. Objectivity is a never fully attained goal in science, not an assumed state from which to deny bias. Such a self-serving "pseudo-objective" stance is a disservice to the discipline, the researchers, their work, and the consumers of their work.

Candor requires that I also admit having experienced equal impatience with those who substitute strident ideology for serious scholarship. Often these "ideologists" perceive social science as simply a power game, one won or lost by political means. Theory becomes dogma; research becomes mere demonstration of ideological assertions.

On occasion, both the pseudo-objectivists and the ideologists have not too politely attacked my work as representing the opposite extreme. In turn, the similarities of the two camps impress me. Each justifies its position in part by its opposition to the other. Both are serenely secure in the rectitude of their presumed objectivity or ideologically revealed truth. As such, both camps deny the vast complexity of the social world and the essential tentativeness of science.

More fundamentally, the two positions hold that science and values necessarily conflict. Donald Campbell (1959) forcefully counters such a view.[9] While joining Myrdal in doubting the possibility of a value-free social science, he argues that strong goal motivation creates greater, not less, investment in tracing an accurate map of reality. He points to rats in mazes: High hunger motivates rapid and accurate, not slow and error-prone, learning of the maze. Thus goal commitment, Campbell argues, leads to good science. The problem comes with means commitment, that is, letting the desired ends distort the means. This travesty results in both poor science and poor support and implementation of one's values. It is here that the Myrdalian struggle against the biasing effects of our values is relevant.

Social science in general, and sociology in particular, is not well structured to influence social policy effectively and competently. In a series of papers over the years, I have questioned the problematic fit between social science and public policy (Archer, Aronson, & Pettigrew, 1992; Haney & Pettigrew, 1986; Pettigrew, 1979a, 1985a, 1988; Pettigrew & Green, 1976). In particular, sociology has rarely addressed the thorny ethical issues involved. Nor are we well equipped to deal competently with the mass media and the legal system—two major mediators of sociological influence on social policy. Often our findings and models, unlike much of economics, are ill fitted for effective and timely use in policy decisions. Responsible input from the sociological study of race relations is particularly needed, given the distorted data and perspectives typically provided by the mass media to policymakers.

A Cautionary Final Note

The dramatic racial events of recent American history shaped the study of race relations. This chapter relates how these events impinged on me and shaped my perspective on the field. Now, having described this process "up close," I must make some qualifications. First, dramatic events are not the only influences on theoretical frames in the field. Second, there are distinct dangers, as well as advantages, to having events influence social science. These qualifications deserve discussion.

Multiple Influences

Dramatic racial events were simply one of many factors shaping the development of the race relations field during these decades. Obviously, sociology and social psychology were also changing. Both disciplines grew rapidly in personnel and research funds. Indeed, by 1970 there were far more post- than pre-World War II Ph.D.s in both disciplines and among those specializing in race relations. These new Ph.D.s were less committed to the older, micro-level theoretical frame, and ready for new approaches.

The field was also growing in sophistication. One review of race relations research in major sociological journals from the 1890s to 1980 illustrates this enormous development (Pettigrew, 1980c). As events unfolded, the race relations field brought new tools, particularly new empirical tools, to bear on the analysis of the events. For instance, structural modeling techniques have furthered our ability to link the micro and macro levels of analysis.

On a personal note, a major influence for me throughout my career has been my doctoral students. The best-kept secret of academia is how much teachers learn from their students. At Harvard and more recently at the University of Amsterdam and the University of California, Santa Cruz, I have benefited from a continuous stream of superb doctoral students—from the first (M. Richard Cramer) to the most recent (Heather Smith and Sjiera de Vries).[10]

The Dangers of Events Shaping Theory

The older micro-centered theoretical frame that dominated race relations work through the 1950s was ripe for change by 1960. The shift in dominant frame, hastened by the civil rights movement, was needed, even overdue. Social science must always be learning from the events of the "real world." And the race relations field did learn significant lessons during this period that served as helpful correctives.

Yet social science cannot be largely swayed by events, no matter how dramatic. Social science should learn from events, but not—as is often the case in journalism—be myopically entranced by them. The goal of generalization requires that social scientists not stay too close to the immediate. Rather, they must view events as the latest instances within lengthy time series. American social science was too impressed with the solidity of the South's racial segregation system, not unlike the mistake made by specialists about the solidity of the totalitarian regimes of the Soviet Union and Eastern Europe.

When these systems collapse, theoretical shifts frequently overinterpret the unexpected. The many informal ways the segregation system maintains itself today, such as with the continuation of intense residential segregation, are too often ignored. By the 1970s, many exaggerated the ease of social change. And currently the nation's racist reentrenchment is being overgeneralized as proof that the civil rights movement accomplished nothing and the United States is fundamentally incapable of racial change toward greater equality.

In social psychology there has been a roughly 30-year cycle between emphases on situational and personality causation of behavior. There is a related cycle in the intergroup relations field between emphases on bottom-up and top-down causal patterns of social change, between a primary focus at the micro level of attitudes and stereotypes and at the macro level of institutions and societies. The mass media, focused on dramatizing the present, amplify such swings of the pendulum—as, for example, between the apparent idealism of the 1960s and the cynicism of the 1990s. The hope is that social science can achieve the opposite—a balance that narrows the pendulum swings of interpretation by locating relevant events in their larger contexts.

Notes

1. On another occasion, while visiting Adams's home, I heard screaming emanating from a window across the street. She explained that these were the recurrent cries of a mentally ill neighbor. Though the screams regularly pierced the air, even in the middle of the night, the neighbors tolerated the interruptions. Not to do so meant that she would be institutionalized at the segregated state facility for the Black insane in Petersburg. "That's a snake pit," commented Adams, "the neighborhood couldn't do that to her."

2. The IBM 101 was a much-beloved precomputer machine of that period. It combined the sorting, counting, and printing functions of earlier machines, but it contained no memory.

3. Many white respondents assured us there was no local branch of the National Association for the Advancement of Colored People. This misbelief was essential to their maintaining the fiction that "their colored people" were content and unaffected by the racial storm brewing.

4. Thus the first English settlement in North America, Jamestown, was settled in 1607, and Van Riebeck brought Dutch settlement to the Cape in 1652. The South's Civil War erupted in 1861, the Anglo-Boer War in 1898. And the formal end of legal racial segregation came to the South in the 1950s and 1960s, whereas, one can hope, the formal end of *apartheid* will arrive during the 1990s.

5. The four principal cases in which I was involved were *Barksdale v. School Board of Springfield, Massachusetts* (1965), *Brewer v. School Board of Norfolk, Virginia* (1969), *Bradley et al. v. School Board of Richmond, Virginia* (1971), and *Crawford et al. v. Los Angeles Unified School District* (1978-1980). I have described elsewhere my experiences in these cases (Pettigrew, 1979b).

6. Such metropolitan educational parks would be optimally placed near the suburban and central-city boundaries and would provide education from kindergarten through high school. Properly designed, such parks have numerous advantages: They maximize equity, choice, stability, and cost-efficiency as well as deter resegregation (Pettigrew, 1981a).

7. The Detroit metropolitan case (*Milliken v. Bradley*, 418 U.S. 717, 1974) was lost, 5 to 4. The Richmond metropolitan case won in the district court, lost in the U.S. Fourth Circuit of Appeals, and was turned down by the U.S. Supreme Court for an appeal hearing by a vote of 4 to 4. Incredibly, from a social science perspective, Associate Justice Potter Stewart declared in his concurring opinion in the Detroit case that metropolitan housing segregation by race had been "caused by unknown and perhaps unknowable factors." Time has proven Associate Justice Thurgood Marshall's dissenting view correct when he described the Detroit decision as "a giant step backward" (Pettigrew, 1975b).

8. Key (1949) demonstrated that Tennessee's vote by county on secession in 1861 continues to correlate with racial voting in the twentieth century—suggesting the remarkable persistence of racial norms. More recently, I have noted the same phenomenon for racial political voting in California counties throughout this century in spite of the massive immigration and change experienced by the state.

9. I am indebted to Professor Marylee C. Taylor for her critique of this section.

10. To be specific, Eliot Smith and Marylee Taylor reawakened my interest in methodology, Judith Porter recast my thinking about racial identity, and Robert Riley involved me in political surveys. I was introduced to ethnic perspectives by Pat Pajonis Gabon, to organizational theory by Joanne Martin, to medical social psychology by John Jemmott, to working-class feminist issues by Myra Ferree, to clarity in survey analysis by Reeve Vanneman, and to network theory by Mark Granovetter. The list could be easily extended. Their diversity and independence of thought have made university teaching a most satisfying life; indeed, I cannot imagine another career. Taken collectively, graduate students have had far more influence on my work than have current events.

References

Adam, B. D. (1978). Inferiorization and "self-esteem." *Social Psychology, 41,* 47-53.

Adorno, T. W., Frenkel-Brunswick, E., Levinson, D., & Sanford, N. (1950). *The authoritarian personality.* New York: Harper & Row.

Allport, G. W. (1954). *The nature of prejudice.* Reading, MA: Addison-Wesley.

Archer, D., Aronson, E., & Pettigrew, T. F. (1992). Making research apply: High stakes public policy in a regulatory environment. *American Psychologist, 47,* 1233-1236.

Bernard, J. (1951). The conceptualization of intergroup relations with special reference to conflict. *Social Forces, 30,* 243-251.

Blalock, H. M., Jr. (1967). *Toward a theory of minority-group relations.* New York: John Wiley.

Campbell, D. T. (1959). *Systematic errors to be expected of the social scientist on the basis of a general psychology of cognitive bias.* Symposium presentation at the annual meeting of the American Psychological Association, Cincinnati, OH.

Coleman, J., Kelly, S. D., & Moore, J. (1975). *Trends in school segregation: 1968-1973.* Washington, DC: Urban Institute.

Clark, K. C. (1965). *Dark ghetto: Dilemmas of social power.* New York: Harper & Row.

Haney, C., & Pettigrew, T. F. (1986). Civil rights and institutional law: The role of social psychology in judicial implementation. *Journal of Community Psychology, 14,* 267-277.

Key, V. O. (1949). *Southern politics in state and nation.* New York: Alfred A. Knopf.

Kuhn, T. S. (1970). *The structure of scientific revolutions* (2nd ed.). Chicago: University of Chicago Press.

Middleton, R. (1976). Regional differences in prejudice. *American Sociological Review, 41,* 94-117.

Myrdal, G., with Sterner, R., & Rose, A. (1944). *An American dilemma: The Negro problem and modern democracy.* New York: Harper & Row.

Pettigrew, T. F. (1958). Personality and socio-cultural factors in intergroup attitudes: A cross-national comparison. *Journal of Conflict Resolution, 2,* 29-42.

Pettigrew, T. F. (1959). Regional differences in anti-Negro prejudice. *Journal of Abnormal and Social Psychology, 59,* 28-36.

Pettigrew, T. F. (1961). Social psychology and desegregation research. *American Psychologist, 16,* 105-112.

Pettigrew, T. F. (1965a). Extending educational opportunities: School desegregation. In *Proceedings of the 1965 White House Conference on Education.* Washington, DC: Government Printing Office.

Pettigrew, T. F. (1965b). Metropolitan Boston's race problem in perspective. In *Social structure and human problems in the Boston metropolitan area* (pp. 33-51). Cambridge: Joint Center for Urban Studies of MIT and Harvard University.

Pettigrew, T. F. (1967). Urban and metropolitan considerations: With special focus on civil rights. In U.S. Senate Committee on Labor and Public Welfare, *Notes and working papers concerning the administration of programs authorized under Title III of Public Law 89-10, the Elementary and Secondary Education Act of 1965 as amended by Public Law 89-750* (pp. 152-163). Washington, DC: Government Printing Office.

Pettigrew, T. F. (1968). Model cities and race relations. In *Shaping model cities* (pp. 28-37). Cambridge, MA: A. D. Little.

Pettigrew, T. F. (1969a). Gordon Willard Allport, 1897-1967. *Journal of Personality and Social Psychology, 12,* 1-5.

Pettigrew, T. F. (1969b). Racial issues in urban America. In B. J. Frieden & W. W. Nash, Jr. (Eds.), *Shaping the urban future* (pp. 47-94). Cambridge: MIT Press.

Pettigrew, T. F. (1970a). The metropolitan educational park. In F. F. Korten, S. W. Cook, & J. I. Lacey (Eds.), *Psychology and the problems of society* (pp. 133-139). Washington, DC: American Psychological Association.

Pettigrew, T. F. (1970b). Racial segregation and Negro education. In D. P. Moynihan (Ed.), *Toward a national urban policy* (pp. 166-177). New York: Basic Books.

Pettigrew, T. F. (1970c). Statement to the Select Committee on Equal Educational Opportunity of the U.S. Senate. In *Hearings of May 13, 1970* (pp. 744-801). Washington, DC: Government Printing Office.

Pettigrew, T. F. (1970d). Urban integration: The metropolitan educational park concept. In A. M. Kroll (Ed.), *Issues in American education* (pp. 118-138). New York: Oxford University Press.

Pettigrew, T. F. (1971). A return to the common school: School composition, achievement, and the metropolitan education park. In J. W. Guthrie & E. Wynne (Eds.), *New models for American education* (pp. 164-193). Englewood Cliffs, NJ: Prentice-Hall.

Pettigrew, T. F. (1975a). The cold structural inducements to integration. *Urban Review, 8,* 137-144.

Pettigrew, T. F. (1975b). A sociological view of the post-Bradley era. *Wayne Law Review, 21,* 813-832.

Pettigrew, T. F. (1978a). Placing Adam's argument in a broader perspective: Comment on the Adam paper. *Social Psychology, 41*, 58-61.

Pettigrew, T. F. (1978b). *Report to the Honorable Judge Egly.* Pomona, CA: County of Los Angeles Superior Court.

Pettigrew, T. F. (1979a). Racial change and social policy. *Annals of the Academy of Political and Social Science, 441*, 114-131.

Pettigrew, T. F. (1979b). Tensions between the law and social science: An expert witness view. In *Schools and the courts: Desegregation* (Vol. 1). Eugene: University of Oregon, ERIC Clearinghouse for Educational Management.

Pettigrew, T. F. (1980a). The changing—not declining—significance of race: Essay review of W. Wilson's *The declining significance of race. Contemporary Sociology, 9*, 19-21.

Pettigrew, T. F. (1980b). Racial change and the intrametropolitan distribution of Black Americans. In A. P. Solomon (Ed.), *The prospective city* (pp. 52-79). Cambridge: MIT Press.

Pettigrew, T. F. (Ed.) (1980c). *The sociology of race relations: Reflection and reform.* New York: Free Press.

Pettigrew, T. F. (1981a). The case for metropolitan approaches to public school desegregation. In A. Yarmolinsky, L. Liebman, & C. S. Schelling (Eds.), *Race and schooling in the city* (pp. 163-181). Cambridge, MA: Harvard University Press.

Pettigrew, T. F. (1981b). Race and class in the 1980s: An interactive view. *Daedalus, 110*, 233-255.

Pettigrew, T. F. (1985a). Can social scientists be effective actors in the policy arena? In R. L. Shotland & M. M. Marks (Eds.), *Social science and social policy* (pp. 121-134). Beverly Hills, CA: Sage.

Pettigrew, T. F. (1985b). New Black-white patterns: How best to conceptualize them? In R. Turner (Ed.), *Annual review of sociology, 1985* (pp. 329-346). Palo Alto, CA: Annual Reviews.

Pettigrew, T. F. (1985c). New patterns of racism: The different worlds of 1984 and 1964. *Rutgers Law Review, 37*, 673-706.

Pettigrew, T. F. (1988). Influencing policy with social psychology (1987 Kurt Lewin Memorial Address). *Journal of Social Issues, 44* (2), 205-219.

Pettigrew, T. F. (1989). The nature of modern racism in the U.S. *Revue Internationale de Psychologie Sociale, 2*, 291-303.

Pettigrew, T. F. (1990). A bold stroke for personality a half-century ago: A retrospective review of Gordon W. Allport's *Personality: A psychological interpretation. Contemporary Psychology, 35*, 533-536.

Pettigrew, T. F. (1991a). Advancing racial justice: Past lessons for future use. In H. J. Knopke, R. J. Norrell, & R. W. Rogers (Eds.), *Opening doors: Perspectives on race relations in contemporary America.* Tuscaloosa: University of Alabama Press.

Pettigrew, T. F. (1991b). Normative theory in intergroup relations: Explaining both harmony and conflict. *Psychology and Developing Societies, 3*, 3-16.

Pettigrew, T. F., & Back, K. W. (1967). Sociology in the desegregation process: Its use and disuse. In P. F. Lazarsfeld, W. H. Sewell, & H. Wilensky (Eds.), *The uses of sociology* (pp. 692-722). New York: Basic Books.

Pettigrew, T. F., & Green, R. L. (1976). School desegregation in large cities: A critique of the Coleman "white flight" thesis. *Harvard Educational Review, 46*, 1-53.

Pettigrew, T. F., & Meertens, R. (1992). *Subtle racism: Its components and measurement.* Manuscript submitted for publication.

Pettigrew, T. F., & Meertens, R. (1993). *The* verzuiling *puzzle: Understanding Dutch intergroup relations.* Manuscript submitted for publication.

Pettigrew, T. F., Schwartz, R., & Smith, M. (1968, January 6). Is desegregation impractical? *New Republic, 157,* 27-29.

Pettigrew, T. F., & Taylor, M. (1992). Discrimination. In E. F. Borgatta & M. L. Borgatta (Eds.), *The encyclopedia of sociology* (Vol. 1, pp. 498-503). New York: Macmillan.

Schermerhorn, R. A. (1956). Power as a primary concept in the study of minorities. *Social Forces, 35,* 53-56.

Stouffer, S. A. (1955). *Communism, conformity and civil liberties.* Garden City, NY: Doubleday.

U.S. Office of Education. (1966). *Equal educational opportunity.* Washington, DC: Government Printing Office.

Wilson, W. J. (1978). *The declining significance of race: Blacks and changing American institutions.* Chicago: University of Chicago Press.

9

From Home to HBCUs

A Sociologist's Reflections on Change and Transition in the Historically Black Colleges and Universities

RICHARD ROBBINS

Finding the South:
Via Brooklyn, Harlem, Paris

The sociological imagination is fired, C. Wright Mills has observed, by recognition of the nexus between private problems and public issues, between my being out of work and our understanding of unemployment. That is true in my life. Socialization in the midst of the ethnic mosaic was not only the point of departure for my later interest in sociology in general but, within that, for my focus on racial and ethnic relations in particular. Growing up in New York City, native-born of foreign-born Russian stock, the then-governing metaphor of the melting pot was not an abstraction but a personal down-the-street reality. In Brooklyn I looked out on a neighborhood of ethnic diversity—Irish and Italian Catholic, Norwegian Lutheran, East European Jewish. In the stores the women behind me spoke Italian; on the trolley the man across the way read his Yiddish newspaper.

Bigotry as well as diversity flourished on Gelston Avenue. In the 1930s, in the grim years of the Great Depression, it took a mean and primitive form. We Jewish boys were taunted as "Christ killers"; our high school, New Utrecht, was derided as "Jew Utrecht." We struck back with epithets of our own. Yet, without minimizing that primitive anti-Semitism and the far more pervasive color racism, and remembering that then no significant civil rights movement or law existed as counterforce, there remained all the same a rough-hewn live-and-let-live tolerance that held in bounds the worst forms of prejudice. Moreover, each ethnic group could fall back upon the security of its subculture and subcommunity. The web of kinship, the network of collective institutions, meant for us, in terms of Georg Simmel's sense of forms of sociation, solidarity within to confront conflict without. The great suburbanization of America, diminishing central-city diversity, segregating city and suburb by race and class, still lay two decades ahead. Even further ahead lay the remarkable resurgence of immigrant ethnicity in the largest cities, a new multiethnic mosaic, only with different countries of origin—South Korea, Haiti, Vietnam, the Dominican Republic.

If immigration and ethnicity were the facts of life and not the facts of the textbook, color presented a different, more distant reality. It was as much isolation as discrimination that defined Black-white relations. Harlem was measured as far from Little Italy and the Jewish Lower East Side in more ways than subway stops. It was largely, but not yet entirely, Black. There were the white-owned stores, many of them Jewish owned. Small but still viable predominantly white areas still existed. But clearly by the 1930s Harlem had already become the national Black capital; it meant more to Black people in the South than to white near neighbors in New York. Negroes—that was the modal term—going to meet the man for work downtown returned on the subway at night to Harlem, sometimes carrying supplies, as prices were cheaper downtown. Their Harlem, seen from inside, was certainly a place of problems and poverty, but it was a vibrant community as well, working-class and middle-class, secular and religious, defined by busy 125th Street and by bourgeois Sugar Hill, a community as striking and complex as our enclaves in Brooklyn and the Bronx (Osofsky, 1968; see also Anderson, 1983; Robbins, 1949). Whites perceived Harlem from the outside; Negroes worked for whites throughout the city and, then, after 5:00, it was home to Harlem. It was a white youngster who explained to me the "slave market" in the Bronx—Negro women lined up along the street in the early morning to be selected at the lowest wages for domestic work. Thus did southern history come forward from the books to the Bronx.

Yet for a small number of white Jewish families this isolation from Harlem did not govern entirely. I refer to the tradition of Jewish liberalism in general, and to liberal Jewish activism in particular. Jewish segments in the labor movement, in the universities, on the democratic Left, in businesses, and in the law and other professions (minorities to be sure in each of these categories) argued for a bond with Black Americans whose root is the sense that a common force has perpetrated injustices against both groups. It follows that a coalition is required to combat racial and ethnic prejudice. That alliance was important from the 1930s through the 1960s, especially in advancing civil rights through the instruments of courts and Congress. Today, for various complex reasons that need not detain us here, that alliance is severely strained. On the white side, it is sometimes said that too many Jews, in opting for the suburbs, have opted out of the struggle, that the very term *Jewish liberalism* has become an oxymoron. But Jews can retort that it was the Black side, Black nationalism of the 1970s, that rejected Jewish coalition support. And Jews were rightly affronted by an ugly anti-Semitism among the most fiercely militant groups in the Black community, as Blacks were by a persistent, even if declining, anti-Black prejudice in the Jewish community. For those of us for whom the coalition was a most important article of faith, this has been a dismaying trend. But I believe there are signs that the alliance may someday be forged again.[1]

In the 1930s, at least, to return from now to then, the coalition was a force. Jewish participation in interracial protest movements and organizations was extensive; confronting the racial barrier as well as anti-Semitism was a priority for the Jewish Anti-Defamation League. Jewish philanthropy, expressed, for example, in the Rosenwald schools in the South and in the Rosenwald fellowships (it is still instructive to see the list of young Black writers who held them), made a difference. It should not be discounted because sometimes accompanied by a calculated paternalism and condescension. The majority of white southern Jews, right up to the 1950s, remained safely placed within the system of racial segregation. Even if they wanted to challenge the system they could not, for fear of anti-Semitic backlash: They were white, but they were Jews. Even so, there *were* southern white liberal Jews and they played a part in human relations activism from the antilynching campaign of the 1930s through the triumph of *Brown* in the 1950s, to the civil rights movement of the 1960s.

In my own case, in New York, there was a little more. In the context of the general Jewish-Negro alliance, democratic socialist Jewish families required more. Socialist young people were taught specifically that the battle against racial discrimination could be understood only in terms of working-class and trade union mobilization against those who exploited workers, white or Black. Thus we knew early on who A. Philip Randolph was—a union leader, a democratic socialist, who was Black—and we went to hear him speak. A small line of friendship in the peace and socialist movements extended from Brooklyn to Harlem. (It is sometimes forgotten that both Bayard Rustin and Martin Luther King drew on this movement in shaping the nonviolent direct-action strategy and then applied it to civil rights.) We took the subway to visit the Schomburg Library. We read Du Bois's *The Souls of Black Folk* (1903/ 1961); it made a deep impact. Later on, in the forties, several years before the great test of nonviolent direct action, the Montgomery bus boycott, we worked in CORE (the Congress of Racial Equality), making use of nonviolent direct action. In no way did we define this activity as providing us, white and Jewish, with a dispensation from general Black anger at general white racism. Much more simply, socialization in New York, in the setting of Jewish liberalism and democratic socialism, steered us, as ordinary persons, in a less than ordinary direction.

I would suggest that such a socialization within the multiethnic, multiracial city leads an individual by late adolescence to a desire to know more about racial-ethnic problems. Later on one is led to that discipline, sociology, that is centrally concerned with this subject. (The "overproportion" of Jewish sociologists in the special field of racial-ethnic relations is probably a result of this pattern.) In terms of immigrant ethnicity, we thought to know more about that Europe from which our folk had come. In terms of race within American society, we thought to know more about the South, real to us so far only in books. Of course, we read avidly about the sentimental South, the South of *Gone With the Wind,* but we knew about the "other South" as well, the South of the Scottsboro case and rural poverty, white and Black, the South with its "darker history" of loss and defeat in the midst of the American celebration, the South with its latter-day "peculiar institution" of racial segregation. As Faulkner knew so well, we keep asking still: Tell me about the South. So we imagined then not only "returning" to Europe, which we knew indirectly through our ethnic neighborhoods, but taking the train to Atlanta and Nashville, cities in a region we knew not at all.

What we could *not* imagine, we young ethnics of New York, was the enormous impact of World War II—its global scope, its mobilization of our industrial economy, and, above all, its impingement on our personal lives. Suddenly, "the system" reached into our circumscribed neighborhoods, drafted us into the military, dispatched us to sprawling, dusty encampments in the Deep South, then sent us to the far corners of the earth. So war, rather than further education, got me both out of the country and into the South. As a military trainee in a segregated army in a segregated region, I came to terms with southern race relations for the first time in a direct way, on and off the post. Young Black men from Harlem, also shipped to the Deep South, came face to face with rigid racial segregation; they lived with it, on the post and off, in the town. We young white men, Jewish, from Brooklyn, met our new white "buddies" from Georgia and Alabama. Race always came up, and the little dialogue would almost always end fruitlessly: "Can I ask you not to say 'nigger'?" "Don't tell me what to do Yankee! But, okay, N-e-e-e-egrah!"

As for "returning," via the military, to ethnic roots in Europe, the opposite occurred. Trained as French-language interpreters at the Georgetown University School of Foreign Service, in a military program aimed at deploying us in the invasion of France, we were then sent out to the far Pacific, oversized diplomas in hand, to Saipan, Iwo Jima, and other places where no French were in sight. Welcome to the sociology of military bureaucracy! Only years later did a Fulbright grant enable me to reach France finally, as well as other countries from which our immigrant grandparents set off.

I set out this minimemoir as prologue to my proper subject, change and transition in the historically Black colleges and universities, the HBCUs, in the South, with this purpose in mind. I believe that the larger-than-expected proportion of sociologists specializing in racial and ethnic relations who are themselves from racial or ethnic family backgrounds can very frequently be traced to the socialization pattern of this group from childhood to early adulthood. I anticipate the immediate objection. I do *not* mean that Black sociologists must come inevitably to specialize in race, Jewish sociologists in anti-Semitism, women sociologists in gender studies, and so on. On the contrary, a sociologist's choice to enter a specialized field totally unrelated to his or her socialization has the same standing as the choice to pursue X subject because one happens to be an X. I *do* mean that membership in an ethnic or racial minority, with all the burdens and joys attendant on that status in the growing years, carries one eventually from subjective experience in the ethnic neighborhood to professional career focused on objective study of ethnic relations. At least so it was in my own case, in entering sociology and in becoming, as James Baldwin used to describe me with a smile, "a big race man." This minimemoir is my illustration.

Finding the Southern HBCUs: The 1950s, Brown, and After

The great watershed date is May 1954. The U.S. Supreme Court, unanimously, struck down as unconstitutional, in *Brown v. Topeka Board of Education et al.,* racial segregation in the public schools. *Brown* did far more than reverse *Plessy v. Ferguson* (1896), which held that equal protection of the law was not invalidated by segregation. It made possible long overdue changes in all institutional spheres, in employment, housing, voting—wherever the wedge of law could pry open the door of racial discrimination. We know now, 40 years later, that *Brown,* and the civil rights revolution that followed, was prelude, not final solution; that racial inequities would continue in everything from infant mortality to wage and salary levels in adulthood, to length of life in old age. It became clear by the 1970s that affirmative action policies would have to reinforce equal opportunity under the law if minorities were actually to make use of the opened door—and clear by the 1980s that conservative misinterpretation of affirmative action ("It's quotas") and growing resistance to it would slow inexorably further progress in civil rights. So, too, in the political sphere, the astonishing increase in Black voting throughout the South in the 1960s would have to be followed by the more difficult and complex process of achieving access to power in the state houses and the Congress. Nonetheless, it cannot be denied that *Brown,* the collapse of de jure segregation in the South, and the passage of the civil rights and voting legislation of 1964 and 1965 initiated the most decisive change in race relations in American history and opened the way to the even more complex economic, social, and educational problems in race relations with which we wrestle now. No conservative counterreaction can ever change that fact.

In 1954 I arrived at Wellesley College in Massachusetts as a young instructor in sociology and anthropology. I had marked out a career research path: race and ethnicity, urban community, and sociology of education in sociology; regionalism, especially southern regionalism, in American studies. My M.A. from Washington State University, doctorate from the University of Illinois, and book and articles were focused on such matters as American immigration policy, the Black press in New York, the politics of Italian Americans, and international migrations in Europe and Asia. In the early 1950s I lived in France, and there, and elsewhere in Europe, I learned what I should have known before: Comparative, cross-cultural, historical analysis is the indispensable key to full sociological understanding of race and ethnicity. Until fairly recently, American sociological research has been far too parochial, perhaps because "the Negro problem" at home presented such an overwhelming challenge. (But Du Bois knew, at the turn of the century. For him the color line spanned the world.)

Europe taught me as well a certain skepticism toward European conceptions of race in America, and toward our conception of race there. France did indeed deserve its reputation as a haven for American Black exiles, as a milieu where person counted more than color. Two cheers for that French indifference—better than either prejudice or patronization—to interracial couples strolling Paris. But close Black friends, American and French colonial, sketched a different story when it came to mundane problems of jobs and housing at home, French colonial control in a Madagascar or Senegal *outre mer* (on being Black and American in Paris, see Baldwin, 1955). And it was a shock to discover that even after the Holocaust, anti-Semitism could reemerge. (At the Sorbonne on my first day in Paris, I encountered the fresh graffito *au four encore les juifs!*)

I began to study the interesting European approach to ethnic diversity, ethnonational pluralism in Belgium, France, Spain, and Yugoslavia, concluding that the effectiveness of the formula, from loose confederation to tightly integrated union, depended on two essential conditions: The center and its subnational entities could not be too unequal economically, and the varying degrees of political autonomy to the entities would have to be worked out through democratic processes.[2] On both these counts the Soviet Union was sham, not authentic ethnonational pluralism. Above all, in those years, I came to understand the European use of the double standard on racial questions. Deeply critical of our abysmal failure to make real progress on race, they were highly resistant to accepting the obvious parallels—French treatment of Algerians, British of West Indians, Swiss of Italians, and German of Turkish "guestworkers."

Returning to the United States, I recognized, as did every sociologist, that after *Brown* school desegregation would become a paramount focus of our research on race, in northern cities as well as in the South. But most of us did not think about *higher* education. The process would be played out basically in elementary and secondary education. So we came to college-level analysis only later. But even in the fifties closer attention should have been paid to higher education, beyond recording the rising proportion of Black enrollment in mainstream "white" institutions, for it was obvious that, contrary to expectations about integration, the great majority of more than 100 HBCUs would, indeed *should,* continue. Yet under what changed conditions and with what prospects for the future?

So, while going to the South to study race and higher education remained the ultimate goal, I, like so many sociological colleagues, worked primarily on the question of racial balance, "forced busing," and equal educational opportunity in the urban North—in my case, in Boston.

It was clear in these inner cities that white rhetoric about "forced busing" and "preserving the neighborhood school" concealed the real problem, hostility to Black children coming to "our school." (Thousands of children were being bused great distances to schools all over the country without resistance so long as color was not involved.) As a citizen I strongly supported busing, together with such policies as redistricting, to achieve racial balance. As sociologists of education, however, many of us questioned whether school achievement and quality of education were being sufficiently advanced once the bus alighted at the school door. In any case, as an activist I wanted to do more, and so became part of ACC, Another Course to College. In response to the after-busing-what question the Boston school system established a network of magnet schools. They would draw students citywide in racial balance but, additionally, would promise challenging curricula and improved quality of schooling. Each school was linked to an urban university. Twice a week, on time release from the University of Massachusetts, Boston, I became a regular high school teacher of French and history at the Faneuil High School on the lower side of Beacon Hill. ACC could not, of course, resolve the fundamental sociological dilemma of inner-city public education. Nor could any other magnet or "enrichment" program bring about basic change, whatever the remarkable success in a few urban schools, almost always the result of the impact of an extremely dedicated principal. The deterioration of inner-city schools, with tragic consequences for minority children in ever-larger proportion in them, was but one more index of the deep urban crisis and the complex interplay of class, race, and poverty.

Nonetheless, ACC succeeded within these limits. We sent a striking proportion of our students, all from working-class and/or minority backgrounds, on to college. In the end I came to see that the "great busing controversy" would recede not when one side or another would triumph politically but when different strategies, beyond busing, would commence to take hold. Magnet schools, controlled parental choice of school within racial guidelines, recruitment of more minority teachers and administrators through affirmative action, court decisions to compel more equity in allocation of school resources by the state to urban districts—these and other strategies would eventually replace the contentious busing and "white flight" issues.

In the midst of all this I had moved from Wellesley College to another women's college, Wheaton, in Massachusetts, and on to the University of Massachusetts in Boston in the late 1960s, where I founded and chaired a department of sociology and anthropology, and where I taught courses in urban and educational sociology and (in American studies) a seminar on "the New South." But I was increasingly drawn to concentrate on the sociology of *higher* education. The rising proportion of students going on to college, the linkage of higher education with a service economy in a postindustrial society, the dramatic expansion of the community colleges in preparing students for the paraprofessions, all pointed to profound changes that Christopher Jencks and David Riesman (1969) were bold enough to call a "revolution." In 1965, while I was still at Wheaton, the opportunity finally arrived for me to combine these interests—sociology of higher education, race relations, southern regionalism. Hugh Gloster, dean of Hampton Institute in Virginia (now Hampton University) invited me to be visiting professor there. At the same time I was funded for research on the impact of desegregation on aspects of the HBCU system. (Our friendship had developed after Gloster's daughter had been a student of mine.) So I went south to Hampton, to live just off campus in an all-Black neighborhood, to send my children to the Hampton lab school, to extend the journey from home to HBCUs.

Finding the Direction of
the Black Colleges in the South

Other sociologists were occupied, quite rightly, with the end of racial exclusion in mainstream higher education in the South, with the social consequences of increased numbers of Black students in the Vanderbilts and North Carolinas. (There were *unanticipated* consequences in the transit from desegregation to integration, such as persistent white student racism on some campuses and the politicization of Black students on others, but that is another story.) I wanted to raise a no less important issue: What would happen now to the historically Black institutions originally formed because of imposed segregation by whites by race? Over nearly a century of struggle, against great odds, these schools had carried the major share of educating Black students, and they had done so heroically, granted all their limitations and inadequacies, with severely limited resources and in the face of very pinched support from the white world outside. How would desegregation now affect their mission? What could the public institutions expect from structural integration into state systems that had previously grievously underfunded and marginalized them? How could the private Black institutions now compete directly with white counterparts as voluntarism rather than race would increasingly define where young Black men and women would like to go to college?

Within this framework, if the still-called Negro colleges were to continue—and, to repeat, many of us argued that they should and would—then the primary charge to them would have to be the provision of an education roughly equivalent to that of the now desegregated, comparable-level, predominantly white institutions. The most fundamental index of that equivalency would have to be faculty and curriculum strength in depth in the basic academic disciplines. And for that universalist criterion to have a chance to be applied, the public institutions in particular would require state resource funding ("enhancement") far beyond the percentage of total enrollment carried by the HBCUs. Simple justice mandated such a compensatory strategy to achieve a level playing field after a century of grossly inequitable division of public funding under segregation.

At the same time, it was clear in the 1960s as it still is now that there remained another function of great importance for the Black college and, indeed, for the nation as a whole, if we are seriously committed to pluralism in higher education—the Catholic college system, the women's college system, the Black college system, and so on. (One says "Black college system" but it is important to note the great diversity and unevenness *within* it; it is unfair to compare Black and white as a whole, for both have wide ranges of educational quality.) College in this country is a social experience, a way of experiencing a sense of community "in a home away from home," where a social bond is formed with peers. We can satirize or sentimentalize college as *Gemeinschaft*; it still expresses community. That the basis for this Durkheimian social cohesion was initially artificially imposed by segregation does not diminish its importance or imply that it should now disappear. It follows that some Black students would want to continue to go to Black colleges in terms of social solidarity even if "the white school" in the same area were superior in quality. Moreover, the attachment to college as community is a powerful tradition that has carried over after graduation. The networks of national Black fraternities and sororities and alumni clubs have had the same functions as their white counterparts, but, additionally, in the Chicagos and Bostons and St. Louises they have provided opportunities for continuing social cohesion where, until recently, the general communities were closed off. All this has been reinforced in family and kinship: "For three generations we have gone off to Fisk." Whites are now beginning to see why Southern versus Grambling in football has the same resonance in the Black community in Louisiana as Auburn versus Alabama in the white community in Alabama. The poorer as well as the excellent Black institutions share in this communal tradition and contribute to our national pluralism. Charles Willie exaggerates in saying that in saving the Black colleges we are saving the nation, but there is a core of truth in the assertion that the larger society benefits when different communities with similar functions coexist. In the case of the Black colleges they have not only educated young people of limited income at lower cost, young people often requiring intensive remedial work, they have provided a strong example of community at work among many, in a society built on quest for community.

It was with these thoughts that I set out for Hampton in 1965, to teach sociology, to research the problem of faculty strength in the Black colleges under desegregation, to join a Black community (a third of whose faculty was white) of purpose and cohesion. Since then I have taught at Hampton, North Carolina Central, and Maryland Eastern Shore (formerly Maryland State), with shorter research times at Fisk and the Atlanta University complex. I have participated in numerous conferences and presented papers on Black campuses from Mississippi to Maryland.[3] I remember in particular from the 1960s the Thirteen College Program, a long-term effort on the part of we specialists to work with younger faculty in 13 Black colleges to produce new, innovative curricula. Two studies, in 1966 and 1988, sought to analyze the condition of the Black college system, principally through an assessment of Black faculty in the social sciences (see Robbins, 1966).[4] I have watched and recorded the endless legal challenges and court orders in public higher education in the South as the states variously confronted the issue of how to integrate structurally two separate systems. And I have gained a sense of both commonality and diversity on so many campuses, well known and not well known: Hampton, Spelman, Shaw, Fisk, Norfolk State, St. Paul's, Johnson C. Smith, Howard, Tougaloo, Virginia Union, Morehouse, Morris. What follows are reflections on the present place of the Black college system in American higher education, the historical context within which the system must be set, and the challenges posed for the future.

Finding the Dimensions
of the Black Colleges in the South

Today, there are approximately 100 statistically Black colleges and universities in the United States. *Approximately* is necessary because the term *predominantly Black* requires qualification. A number of inner-city colleges, especially in the urban North, are heavily Black and Hispanic, and are even named for racial leaders, but do not share the historical tradition of the HBCUs. Also, a small number of historically Black schools have become statistically white majority—schools such as Kentucky State and West Virginia State. In 1985, 43 Black colleges were public, taking some two-thirds of total Black college enrollment; the 50 private institutions—41 of them receiving some support from the United Negro College Fund—were mostly denominational. Desegregation of the mainstream system has accelerated the decline in Black college enrollment as a proportion of all Black students in college in the United States—it is now at about 22%, compared with 50% at the end of the 1950s and 35% in the 1970s.[5] Yet, very recently, enrollments have risen modestly in the Black colleges, perhaps a result, in part, of the "pull" of social community in the HBCUs and the "push" of continuing racial incidents on mainstream campuses. Race apart, a critical factor is, as always, financial stability. Among the 40% constituting the public schools, survival is of course guaranteed by state funding, whatever the intense legal battles over proportional shares to Black and white schools. The private institutions, a majority still affiliated with the Baptist or African Methodist Episcopal churches, are less secure, with relatively thin endowments and Black philanthropic support, although, finally, they are commencing to benefit from younger alumni, increasingly upwardly mobile in business and the professions, and thus able to give more. In the 1960s and 1970s both federal support and foundation assistance increased to a significant degree in the form of loans, grants to institutions, and financial aid to Black students. Much of this has now fallen away, even the substantial aid promised to the private sector colleges by the Reagan and Bush administrations.

In terms of "reverse integration," the traditional single-race pattern continues. Whites at majority-Black colleges now constitute about 15% (three-quarters of them *American* whites), a proportion that is not likely to change dramatically in the future. What *has* changed, especially in the public colleges, is the transformation of the physical plant, long overdue, after decades of "malign neglect" by state legislatures. New libraries, residences, theater-art complexes, science centers, student unions—these are now found on virtually all the state campuses and the largest private ones, and even the small private schools have been able to construct some new buildings and rehabilitate a few old ones.

All of the above are quantitative measures. The fundamental qualitative question, the prospective change in the quality of education offered and in the strength of the faculty offering it, cannot be fully answered even now, nearly four decades after *Brown* and 20 years after *Adams* (the first of a series of cases brought in federal courts under which the southern state systems of higher education are directed by court order to accelerate progress both in Black integration into the mainstream institutions and in significant expansion of resources and funding to the Black institutions). Plainly, in the public state sector the Black colleges still lag behind comparable regional area white counterparts—although by narrower margins than in the past—as measured by such familiar indices as faculty distinction and proportion of doctorates, library strength, faculty salaries, average SAT scores of entering students, and depth of academic programs. Roughly the same could be said in the private sector, the lagging perhaps more so because these schools are not in the arena of federal court-ordered remedial action and do not share in the significant expansion of resources by state legislatures. It says nothing against the continuing important, indeed vital, educational mission of the Black colleges to conclude that near parity in educational quality—"near" is all that is required—in Black-white regional area educational comparison cannot be fully achieved in this century.

It is the burden of southern history that explains much of why equity and justice are still not fully served in southern higher education. A drastically compressed discussion of three time periods is needed here to anchor the present situation. Overall, the driving force has been, until very recently, a systematic and pervasive white racism, a corrupt structure of racial segregation. Black response to that corrupt system, remarkable and quietly heroic in the main, also generated in the nature of the case corruption and self-serving on the Black side as well. Thus the many books—most notably Ralph Ellison's powerful novel *Invisible Man*—with their sardonic accounts of those authoritarian and paternalistic founders and presidents whose dependence on the white world outside only intensified their iron rule within their own campuses.[6]

The first and longest period can be roughly dated from the end of Reconstruction and the withdrawal of federal troops to World War II, a time for Negroes rightly described in its first half by the historian Rayford Logan as "the Nadir."[7] The New South was only beginning to emulate northern urban-industrial development, so its economic resources were still too limited and too tightly anchored to an agrarian-commercial small city base. Thus general education, lower and higher, remained behind the rest of the country. Racial segregation compounded regional differentiation; the Negro tenant farmer, the Negro city artisan or college student, lived behind a double wall.

Into the twentieth century white state legislatures established but gave only minimal support to Negro colleges, some of which for many years were actually high schools or vocational schools. Private schools and colleges were frequently founded by missionary associations from the North, drawing on white business philanthropy. The white teachers and administrators went south and made an admirable commitment to education and racial amity in the face of implacable hostility from the white community just beyond the campus. Between them, the government's Freedman's Bureau and the private American Missionary Association established more than 200 "colleges" during this period.

Thin finances, whether legislature or church based, meant that it was extremely difficult to recruit and hold faculty of standing. But, ironically, segregation contributed to counterbalance. A significant number of outstanding Negro scholars and teachers, excluded by definition from the mainstream system, remained for their entire careers in the Negro colleges, especially at Howard, Fisk, and the Atlanta complex. (Today, in all the major disciplines, including my own, sociology, the situation is reversed; the best Black scholars go to the mainstream schools.)

The superior, average, and weak Negro colleges, in sum, existed in dependency to white financing and white control. White presidents were not uncommon—Fisk did not have a Negro president, the sociologist Charles S. Johnson, until 1946! The deficiencies of the modal number of the schools derived from the external society. The extraordinary thing, given these circumstances, is not what they failed to do, but what they accomplished. The doctors from Meharry, the social workers from Howard, the teachers of history trained at Fisk, the ministers and educators who came out of Lincoln and Wilberforce, and the science graduates from Tuskegee were sent out into the world. The ratio of Negro college graduates to white graduates, even by the 1930s, was incredibly small. Their preparation was uneven—but they were sent out.

This basic pattern changed only very slowly and within the framework of segregation. It was not until the second period, from the mid-1950s to the mid-1970s, that a time finally arrived in the South of great transition and high drama. There is no need to recount here what occurred in the civil rights revolution—the nonviolent direct-action movement that finally cracked open the carapace of formal racial segregation in public accommodation; the great surge in registration of Black voters previously excluded; the civil rights and voting rights acts of 1964 and 1965; the train of major federal court decisions and executive orders. Students were at the center of many of the sit-ins and voter registration drives.[8] Four of them from North Carolina A&T, sitting-in at a lunch counter in Greensboro, touched off a wave of similar protests in the South. Resistance to change from the white community, defending the last ramparts of segregation, was also powerful. Any sociology of social movements must be focused to some degree on the counterpower of groups with the will and power to hold off change or at least to delay the inevitable. If we consider Alabama and the bus boycott led by Martin Luther King ("He's a Morehouse man," my students were quick to say), we must also summon from memory Alabama in 1963, when Governor Wallace stood in the doorway of the administration building at the University of Alabama, barring the way of two Black students seeking admission under federal court order: "Segregation now, segregation forever!" he said. And we need to acknowledge the conservatism on some of the Black campuses, those administrators and faculty members who were exceedingly reluctant to support the civil rights activists. All the same, it is undeniable that the civil rights movement was of the greatest significance in breaking open the wall of isolation between the Black campuses and the white community.

At the same time, this period saw a new determination on the part of mainstream academia to work with the Black colleges on quality of education while undertaking initiatives, under affirmative action guidelines, to increase the numbers of Black students and faculty on their own campuses. This rush of activity—pairing of Black and white schools, striking increase in financial support for Black colleges by state legislatures and private foundations, the multitude of support programs for Black students in both systems—was belated, sometimes misdirected, and not always sustainable for the long term. ("Here come the missionaries again," a professor at Tuskegee put the matter to me.) Moreover, this large-scale effort, valuable as it was for both sides, began to wear out by the end of the 1970s, in part because of the ascendancy of political conservatism nationally, in part because of the ascendancy, for a time, of Black militant strategy to redefine Black campuses ideologically as centers of Black power, Black curriculum, Black identity. This movement, in the colleges and beyond, produced, and is still producing, a remarkable affirmation of cultural identity and achievement, in literature and the arts in particular. But in terms of real power and real structural change it represented an unrealistic and naive political strategy, bound to fail, of replacing coalition alliances with Black power exclusiveness.

At Hampton in those years this extraordinary ferment was faithfully reflected on our campus. We marched downtown to Queen Street in behalf of desegregating those places still holding out. Hampton and Cornell created an ambitious exchange program. Ford Foundation and other substantial grants introduced useful changes in curriculum and teaching practices. African and Afro-American studies, very limited as separate and distinctive educational enterprises at Hampton—as at many other Black colleges—now came solidly into their own. Eventually, as elsewhere, the students directed their attention to their own administration, sitting-in at the president's office, demanding changes in archaic rules and policies. The president, former all-American, doctorate in sociology, practitioner of old-school high-handed administration, did not care for the application of civil rights tactics in his own domain! Relatively conservative Hampton, with its solid endowment and its ethos of "making it" in the white world despite discrimination, also had its share of the new Black militancy. I was the adviser to our student activist group, grandly named Society for the Progress of Thought, SPOT, principally devoted to sponsoring a full range of outside speakers in the Voltairean spirit, from white establishment to Black Muslims, but organized as well to combat segregation downtown and administrative paternalism on campus. The administration differed with us over our inviting Stokely Carmichael to speak on Black power, but finally agreed he could speak if he would wear a suit. He would, and he did.[9]

The sixties—that was a time, as the song went, in the Black colleges and in the society as a whole. Some of the schools emerged from it little changed, still insular, and too tradition bound. But many others changed in interesting and sometimes far-reaching ways.

The third period, joining recent past in the eighties to present and future projections, is characterized by the institutionalization and relative stabilization of a changed dual system. It is "segregated" still in a technical sense, particularly on the Black side, where the proportion of white students is likely to remain small. Yet it is not any longer a segregation imposed arbitrarily from without (though desegregation problems still abound, as we shall see). Today's Black colleges, women's colleges, Catholic and Protestant denominational colleges, multiversities, community colleges, and so on represent a pluralism in American higher education.

In the mainstream system the basic trend continues in the South, slowly increasing proportions of Black students and faculty, with more attention directed to the problem of fostering integration beyond the statistical percentages so that both Black and white students are part of an integral, multiracial community.[10] It should have been readily foreseen that this process would be accompanied by persistent white racism, white-initiated racial incidents, and defensive Black counterassertion (seen by whites as counterracism). This turmoil, sometimes linked to sexist and antigay attitudes, should not have surprised at all, for there is abundant evidence that middle-class racial bigotry differs only in degree, not in kind, from that in the blue-collar and general populations. But perspective is needed; the problem of racial tension on mainstream campuses is relatively modest.

It is indeed *very* modest when we recognize that mainstream college campus racial conflict is but one symptom of the deep and enduring racial question in the national society: that white America still imposes and institutionalizes social, economic, and political inequality on Black America, and that this system of racial injustice is receding, even now, very slowly. The basic indices, from womb to tomb, as Lord Beveridge used to say, are familiar—Black underrepresentation in personal distributive income, middle- to upper-level occupations, access to adequate health care; Black overrepresentation in unemployment, unskilled occupations, childhood percentages below the poverty line, and much, much more. A rising Black college population, of course, makes a difference—even if at present there is a plateau owing to economic recession. But even on that indicator the gap remains; Black males with four years of college earn about 80% of income of comparable white males with the same level of education. In 1960, 24% of white high school graduates and 19% of Blacks enrolled in college. Thirty years later, in 1990, 34% of whites did, but only 31% of Blacks. College reflects the larger pattern (Hacker, 1992).[11]

Turning from the persistence of racial inequality and the mainstream college structure to the Black colleges once again, we can say that the long transition from a racially imposed system of separate and unequal to a pluralistic, voluntaristic system of separate schools of relative parity in quality at comparable levels of excellence, state by state, region by region, is still a considerable distance away. In the public sector, structural organizational integration of predominantly white and Black institutions (in boards of trustees or boards of governors, for example) may be somewhat closer to realization. If we concentrate on past to present in the three periods noted above, rather than on present to future, I think it can be said finally with some confidence that the Black colleges in the majority are better than they were and that even the weaker schools, like the counterpart weaker white schools, are still serving the community function, offering experience in social cohesion and solidarity.

Given the general condition of racial inequality in American society, which I have all too inadequately sketched above, this social function is even more important for Black life than for white. That young Black men and women are now free, if properly qualified, to select the mainstream colleges and universities does not cancel out their choosing predominantly Black schools for academic reasons or social community reasons or both—even if the predominantly white school in the same region offers a better biology or superior sociology department. It may well be that at some future time the distinction of mainstream and Black system will fade away in the public and private sectors. Then the entering Black freshman living in a given region will see that college

A and college B are comparable choices with respect to academic program and communal life, although A is statistically majority white and B is statistically majority Black, with A offering the better biology and B the superior sociology. In the South, however, that time is not yet at hand—nor will it be for some time to come.

Meanwhile, the vital question for present and future is how the HBCUs shall be maintained and further developed within the framework of pluralism in American higher education. For the private sector the answer is relatively straightforward. If it is important to reinforce the community function and heritage (and, of course, to continue the historic mission of educating young men or women who, otherwise, would never have gone to college at all), then the private colleges must continue to do what they have done for decades and what other private groups do as well to sustain "our own" hospitals, schools, social services. The private Black schools will continue to call on "our own" community resources primarily, with some help from friends, as in the UNCF national fund-raising.

But in the case of the public HBCUs the answer is much more complex, contentious, and still anchored in law, to *Brown* and *Adams*.[12] Here the issues remain centered on courts and state legislatures, and rightly so, for courts and southern state legislatures in the first place laid the foundation for separated and unequal educational institutions for Blacks. Now, as equity and justice have still not been achieved, southern state governments are still required to provide disproportionally larger resources to the Black public colleges in compensation for the past. The courts will see to that, with varying remedial proposals.

Recent federal cases demonstrate this complexity and contentiousness. In Louisiana in 1990, a special federal court panel of judges found the system of 22 public colleges and universities not in compliance with the *Adams* mandate for further desegregation, structural integration of higher education governance, and strengthening ("enhancement") of the Black schools. They recommended a unitary board of governors, designation of Louisiana State University as the flagship institution, integration of the predominantly white LSU and predominantly Black Southern University law schools, and that Grambling University be strengthened and made more racially diverse. The former governor, John McKeithin, observed, "I don't know any way to make a white go to Grambling or a Black go to Louisiana Tech." This misses the point. You cannot "make" students attend a specific school in higher education. You can mandate fairness to establish a more level playing field, so that students, Black and white, can exercise the option to attend one institution or another.

In 1991, in a second important federal case, Judge Harold Murphy of the southeast federal district concluded that racial discrimination still remained firmly entrenched in Alabama's higher education system. Alabama was directed to bring more Black faculty and students into the mainstream system and, additionally, to appropriate millions of dollars to enhance the two historically Black schools, Alabama State and Alabama A & M. The federal government filed the suit initially in 1983. By 1991 the Alabama Commission on Higher Education noted in its defense that 60% of Black students in the state were attending predominantly white institutions, even if the proportions of Blacks for the two flagship institutions, Alabama and Auburn, were only 9% and 4%, respectively. More broadly the court found that Alabama had never seriously undertaken a plan to make the two Black institutions competitive with nearby white institutions of the same type in the same regional area.

Then, in June 1992, the U.S. Supreme Court, in a landmark decision, perhaps as important for public higher education as *Brown* for the lower levels, ruled that the state of Mississippi had failed to implement sufficiently the desegregation of its state colleges and universities and thus was, in effect, perpetuating the legacy of segregation in its five historically white and three historically Black public institutions. In its 8-to-1 ruling (only Justice Scalia dissenting) the Court held in *United States v. Fordice* that a state did not discharge its constitutional obligations simply by opening its college doors to all, irrespective of race. Some 30 years after *Brown* and some 20 years after Title VI of the Civil Rights Act, the "white" system was still 98% white, the "Black" 93% Black. The Black plaintiffs who initiated the case in 1975 (the United States entered later) contended that Mississippi had not only failed to accelerate integration but had continued to fund the two systems inequitably; per capita student expenditure, for example, was $8,516 for the white system, $6,038 for the Black. Hence their contention that "*apartheid* still exists in Mississippi." But the federal court of appeals upheld the district court's contention that the state was complying with its affirmative duty simply by following a race-neutral policy and not restricting choice. Now the Supreme Court held that a race-neutral admissions policy was not enough and left to the lower courts recommendations as to both accelerating integration and strengthening the Black institutions so as to provide de facto as well as de jure freedom of choice. While all this could mean that, in theory, some public historically Black institutions could be "merged" out of existence as part of a comprehensive integration plan, it is much more likely to mean that in practical terms they will all remain while the 16 states involved make a more determined effort to enhance their status and provide them with resources comparable to those of similar "white" institutions.

The legal battles continue, after nearly 40 years of the desegregation process. Beyond the legal dimension, however, we need to consider in broader sociological context the proximate future of the historically Black colleges and universities.

Finding the Future of the HBCUs in the South

If we grant that there are good and sufficient reasons for maintaining the HBCUs as centers of learning and as centers of social solidarity into the next century, then we must also grant that it is unrealistic to expect them to achieve in the very near future a level of excellence in quality in parity with comparable white institutions. (Again, diversity is the qualifying factor. Average and mediocre white institutions should be measured against the same standards. And *within* the Black system itself, even within a single state, there is further variation. A Virginia State is a step below a Norfolk State, for instance.)

What has been achieved is considerable improvement in educational quality in perhaps a third of the schools and modest improvement in the rest, with a very few, the smallest and weakest, virtually unchanged. This present portrait differs from that drawn 25 years ago by Christopher Jencks and David Riesman (1969) in their splendid study of the entire pluralistic structure, *The Academic Revolution*: "Like the poorer private Negro colleges, then, public Negro colleges are for the most part likely to remain fourth-rate institutions at the tail end of the academic procession" (p. 473). Quoted in *Time,* this sentence set off a storm of anger in the Black college community, though several distinguished Black social scientists arriving at similar conclusions were not subjected to the criticism Jencks and Riesman received.[13] In any event, 25 years later, we may say that although they overstated the case to a degree and did not give sufficient emphasis to the best schools, the Fisks and Morehouses, whose graduates have contributed so much to American life, they were essentially correct in defining the enormous obstacles in the way of transforming educationally these inadequate schools—if it could be done at all.

What has been demonstrated in the last years of the second period and throughout much of the third is the immense difficulty in reconciling the different but related goals of integrating the mainstream structure and, at the same time, dramatically improving the historically Black system in the South through a truly significant deployment of resources so as to make the Black schools equal regional alternatives to the white. The Louisiana, Alabama, and Mississippi cases declare that the courts want the dual mandate implemented and more rapidly. Yet court-ordered change, coupled with expanded state funding for the public Black colleges, may still not produce the desired result in what remains of this century.

Consider, for example, the critical question of faculty excellence. The Black colleges would have to recruit outstanding scholars, the best Ph.D.s, Black or white, in the present younger generation. How can this be done when the larger predominantly white institutions, searching intensively, especially for young Black scholars, have all the advantages in terms of salary, research facilities, and course loads? This uneven competition becomes more so as the production of young Black Ph.D.s has now leveled off. (Of 36,000 Ph.D.s granted in 1990, 320 were awarded to Black men and 300 to Black women, a 2% ratio.) Moreover, in many northern and some southern urban mainstream universities, young Black scholars will now find a significant, even if still underrepresented, Black constituency of students and faculty to meet the criterion of social community cohesion that the HBCUs have claimed as their distinctiveness.

Or consider how, in the public sector in the South, state legislatures in virtually every state established in the 1960s and 1970s new colleges and universities in the very same metropolitan or regional areas where the HBCUs could have been designated to play this role. These schools have flourished and grown, often outpacing the nearby predominantly Black institutions. Technically open to all, these schools were put in place to extend the reach of the white system, so that in such cities as Montgomery, Nashville, Baltimore, and Greensboro, the Black public colleges did *not* become by redefinition *the* regional area institutions. To my knowledge this happened only in Nashville, where after years of litigation the new University of Tennessee Nashville was finally folded into the historically Black Tennessee State. All this concerns mainly the undergraduate level. In graduate education the Black public institutions have not received a fair share of graduate and professional programs, except in the traditional field of education. Florida A&M, the only Black public university in the state, only a few minutes' ride from the flagship Florida State in Tallahassee, has held and gained some graduate programs, but it is an exception to the general rule.

Overall, in the South, North Carolina has probably come closest, relatively, to fulfilling the dual mandate of *Adams,* simultaneously advancing structural racial integration in the statewide general system and significantly enhancing the status of the Black institutions. Of the five Black schools, North Carolina A&T and North Carolina Central have made particular progress toward regional area status combined with traditional status as an HBCU. Even there, however, much more modification of the dual structure is required. The Deep South trails far behind.

The future of the HBCU system is reasonably secure, but given the considerations just discussed—and there are many more—it is difficult to see how the "enhancement mandate" can be fully implemented, especially in the areas of quality of education and faculty excellence. For a small number of both public and private institutions the future is very promising. On the other side, a small number of the private Black colleges will be closed, unable to survive financially. Some distinguished Black scholars, young and old, will be "lost" to the HBCUs as these men and women choose, rightly, the mainstream structure with its superior working conditions, rewards, and recognition. There will be some erosion of general white support for the HBCU system in the wake of a conservative public mood, in particular the contention that changes in public policy over the past three decades have more than made up for earlier discrimination against racial-ethnic minorities. Yet, in general, improvement in quality of education and in faculty strength will continue for a majority of the schools in the HBCU system. That is roughly the balance sheet for the 1990s.

For my part, after years of writing about and being part of the historically Black college system, I prefer to end as I began, on a personal note. I see not "the problem of race," but particular colleagues and friends, Black and white, at Hampton, Fisk, North Carolina Central, and other places. I remember what these schools, all their deficiencies notwithstanding, meant to the young men and women who were graduated from them. If I recall our authoritarian president at Hampton, I remember as well Lawrence Green, our most militant student civil rights advocate, who, son of a Baptist minister, always wore suit and tie. And I take memory back all the way home to Brooklyn, to reading so many years ago in Brooklyn that chapter in *The Souls of Black Folk* where Du Bois, contesting Booker T. Washington's acceptance of segregation and primary emphasis on vocational education, called for no less than "the higher training and ambition of our brightest minds." However crippling the racial discrimination from outside, however serious the shortcomings within, that mission the HBCUs sought to carry out. That mission they are still seeking to accomplish.

Finding the Connection:
Personal Passage and Race Relations Research

Looking back over nearly half a century of research in racial-ethnic relations by sociologists of my generation, and reflecting on the impact of that research on social change and public policy, we might be inclined to a deep pessimism when, in terms framed by Gunnar Myrdal, we measure the distance between the democratic ethos of equality of opportunity and the reality of racism and racial-ethnic conflict. In the United States, despite very significant changes in law and in racial-ethnic mobility, many problems remain intractable, such as the over-representation of minorities in the poverty category and underclass and the tragic situation of Native Americans on some reservations. Abroad, resurgent nationalism in Europe has too often been based on ethnic hatred, threatening, even destroying (as in Yugoslavia) the possibility of a sociologically and economically sounder alternative, ethnonational pluralism. National "fronts," like the Le Pen movement in France, revive a virulent racism. And in the Third World, where, as many of us warned, the liberation of colonies from European "white imperialism" would be accompanied by new forms of racial-ethnic conflict, this has proved to be the case in Asia and Africa. (This in no way validates Western racial imperialism after the fact, but what has happened in India, Uganda, Indonesia, Nigeria, and countless other Third World countries has certainly been a sobering lesson for those neo-Marxist and radical sociologists of the 1960s and 1970s who argued that racism had to be solely the product of Western "white" capitalism.)[14]

I do not share the conviction that our work in racial-ethnic relations has been largely in vain, given the dismaying picture I have just drawn. Indeed, I would argue for a tempered optimism, based not only on the prospect of further progress in modifying racial conflict but also on an increasing relevance and centrality of race relations research in bringing about this outcome. This assertion is anchored to three dimensions of change. With respect to each I would emphasize what I have learned along the way and where my research has profited as well from my mistakes and my insufficient grasp of ideas and concepts.

First, race relations sociologists and anthropologists have played a pivotal role in the eventual demolition of the myth of biological determinism of cultural phenomena that gained such ascendancy from the nineteenth century all the way through the first half of the twentieth. True, this is a commonplace by now; Ruth Benedict's succinct one-sentence summary has everywhere won the day: *Race and culture vary independently*. It is equally true that the critically important rejection of the biological-genetic paradigm was largely the work of the preceding generation of social scientists, battling an entrenched doctrine still widely accepted in both scientific and public community. There is a permanent honor roll to be called here. Franz Boas, Ralph Bunche, Alfred Kroeber, Ruth Benedict, Margaret Mead, Melville Herskovits (my teacher), Otto Klineberg, M. F. Ashley Montagu, Kelly Miller, E. Franklin Frazier, and many more are in that number. But it fell to our generation to emphasize the extent to which pseudobiological theories of race were still deeply implanted in law and public policy and ought to be taken out. We wrote on the scientific absurdity of "the fraction Negro" in the texts of the 32 state miscegenation laws; on the "racial" thesis employed to rationalize the totally unjustified Japanese American deportation to concentration camps ("America's worst wartime mistake"); on the biological fallacy written into the "national origins formula" in immigration law, that is, that certain groups were "unassimilable." On this last point, in the depositions that we submitted to the congressional committees considering the McCarran-Walter Immigration Act of 1952 we argued that the national origins formula was as unscientific as it was unjust. This may have helped eliminate the racist Asian exclusion provision, but it was not until 1965 that the national origins formula itself was discarded and the racial-ethnic "quotas" set aside (Robbins, 1965).

Second, I would cite the significance of racial-ethnic research in moving the field from an emphasis on psychosocial values and attitudes to an emphasis on social structure and such components as class, power, and conflict. To oversimplify, attention was redirected from prejudice to discrimination, from tracing the source of racial hatred in the individual's socialization through the life cycle to charting the social action resulting from the interplay of dominant and subordinated groups. When I first entered the field, in graduate school, specializing in international migrations, race relations in the South, and European ethnonationalism, we read extensively in social psychology—on the roots of prejudice, on stereotypes, on projection and displacement, on social distance scaling, on the place of the unconscious in race hatred. Gordon Allport's *The Nature of Prejudice* (1954), justly acclaimed for its insight and incisiveness, concentrated on these matters, though Allport devoted some attention to economic discrimination and the place of law in changing racial attitudes. *An American Dilemma,* the magisterial, encyclopedic work on "the Negro problem" by Gunnar Myrdal (1944), did indeed contain long, detailed discussions on the legacy of slavery and the forms of economic and political discrimination against Blacks. But this vast and valuable volume framed the detailed discussion in a somewhat limiting values-and-attitudes context. When white middle-class liberal Americans would come to see how deeply racism conflicted with the "American creed" (the values of freedom and equality), they would resolve the dilemma by initiating real changes, enduring changes in race relations in American society. Once the moral contradictions were shaken, the structural changes would follow.

Speaking for myself, and perhaps for the few colleagues in race relations research I knew personally then, I never thought there was a fundamental conflict, an either/or, between the values-and-attitudes approach focused on prejudice and the structural approach focused on discrimination and group conflict. Allport and Myrdal were invaluable supports for research; however, my personal passage through the economic and political worlds at home and abroad persuaded me that group conflict would challenge me more than values analysis and attitude formation research. Certain sociologists and certain books reinforced that direction.

At Columbia I studied with Robert Lynd and Bernhard Stern. Lynd was too often polemical, a crusader against the social ills of a predatory capitalism. But in the study of both class and race he introduced a tough-minded sociological realism, American populist as much as Marxist, in treating our major institutions. With Stern I worked specifically on racial and ethnic relations, and under his supervision wrote my first article in 1949 for *Phylon,* a study of the Black press in Harlem. Stern was impossible politically. A committed Stalinist with a profound astigmatism toward the Soviet Union, he contended that the USSR had eliminated anti-Semitism and every other kind of racial-ethnic hostility. As a young democratic socialist I could not help but argue vehemently against this incredible fantasy, and then I gave up. Yet once beyond the Soviet paradise Stern offered an extraordinary sociological voyage, from South Africa to the American South, a survey of countless "ethnic frontiers" where racism was inextricably woven into the fabric of class exploitation and class conflict and where access to power constituted the key strategy for minority groups seeking freedom from oppression.[15] Consequently, I was already headed in this direction when, a little later, Lewis Coser, Ralf Dahrendorf, and others moved the functional study of conflict to the very center of sociology. It remained, however, for one strategic essay, by Robert Merton (1949), to demonstrate for me not the division but the connection between attitude and

action, between prejudice and discrimination. In his celebrated paradigm, framed around Myrdal's American creed, he showed with remarkable precision how underlying values and attitudes about race-ethnicity
can be translated into different forms of action. More, in observing how
strategies of change (including the law of courts and Congress) could
cut into even the deepest values and attitudes, he called into serious
question the Sumnerian thesis that stateways could not truly alter
bedrock social mores. He provided an intellectual foundation for the
great surge in civil rights legislation that was to come.

Today, we continue to explore the mechanisms by which racial-ethnic
prejudice becomes embedded in psychosocial development. In particular, the schools and (surprisingly) the military have introduced a wide
variety of programs that succeed in preparing individuals to accept
cultural diversity and loosen their stereotypes. That application of
social psychological research remains an important, still not completed,
task. All the same, the structural theme has now rightly prevailed in race
relations research—and less parochially as well, in the form of comparative, cross-cultural analysis.

Third, and most broadly, I think we have come to understand over the
years, in the field of racial-ethnic relations, that in theoretical terms we
do not need to search for one comprehensive, overall theory that will
integrate all facets of our subject. Rather, an eclectic approach, where
role theory illuminates this aspect, social structural and conflict theory
that aspect, can serve us best now and in the future. There are reasons,
peculiar to our subdiscipline, that this is so. In the first place, given the
great debate in American society over not simply studying racial-ethnic
prejudice and discrimination but attempting to solve or at least reduce
the problem, we have had to place a very high priority on applied
sociology, on making use of our research to recommend urgent changes
in public policy. Thus very often even the broadest and deepest studies
have been long on description, conceptual analysis, and strategies for
change, and short on theoretical framework. The same is true in the case
of the lamentable neglect of social historical perspective at the expense
of an ahistorical emphasis on present conditions and future policy
applications. In my own work I deeply regret having followed the
familiar practice of including a prefatory chapter or two of "historical
background" before moving on as soon as possible to the research study
itself. That is why the striking increase in the number of important works
in which the reexamination of social history *is* the study is so welcome.
The new, historical understanding of slavery, of the contradictory strands

of idealism and racism in the Progressive movement, of nineteenth-century white paternalistic philanthropy, of an earlier nativism and countervailing immigration reform, of neglected but important figures in Black history and women's history—all these and more have contributed to changing and enlarging a too-tempocentric sociology of racial and ethnic relations.

But these very defects, if that is what they are, involving theory and history are in part balanced out by a number of virtues. We have frequently made effective use of middle-range theory where "grand theory" could not wholly explain the many complexities and contradictions of American democratic society. (I think, for example, of the modification of Marxist theory in studies of working-class anti-Semitism and racism.) We have become more open to the new scholarship of historical revisionism, and we are able to suggest why this reworking of material can itself be subjected to critical analysis from our perspective of the sociology of knowledge. (I think, for example, of the reexamination of the Negro family of a century ago in light of the current debate about Black family structure.) And although the avalanche of studies in our field may have often lacked theoretical and historical depth—certainly the case in my own work—there is something to be said for the sheer documentation, the sheer weight of the description and analysis of all the manifestations of racial and ethnic relations in the United States (and many other countries). If the studies sometimes resulted in different conclusions from the same situations, those charged with changing values and norms, with redirecting public policy, had at least a solid body of sociological knowledge as point of departure. I study; therefore I act.

In racial and ethnic relations the interplay of knowledge and action goes on. In *An American Dilemma,* Myrdal was mistaken in placing so much emphasis on the moral values of white Americans and their capacity to close the distance between the ideal of equality of opportunity and the reality of racial discrimination. (This was reflected in the massive research project itself, in the underuse of distinguished and knowledgeable Black social scientists.) But he was right to assert, in the famous appendix, that social scientists could be committed to democratic values and the reduction of racial inequality without compromising their objective research, their comprehensive description and analysis of "the Negro problem" or any other. The studies stand; research earns approval and criticism from one's sociological peers. That is all. I would like to think, however, in modest terms, that our work, in its cumulative strength, might have had a little something to do with the Civil Rights Act of 1964 and the Immigration Reform Act of 1965. Research, in contributing to an informed activism, advances activism's cause.

Notes

1. See Kaufman (1988) and my commentary on Kaufman's book (Robbins, 1988). In 1967, James Baldwin wrote an eloquent essay on anti-Semitism in Harlem—reprinted in his collected essays, *The Price of the Ticket* (1985)—provoking a critical response from Robert Gordis and other Jewish leaders that he was justifying Black anti-Semitism. Not so. He was simply articulating a bitter truth: As Blacks were unable to strike back at "the Man" (white power in general), they struck back at "the Little Man," "Goldberg" (the Jewish store owner in Harlem). See my essay on this controversy (Robbins, 1967b).

2. But I underestimated the strength and persistence of ethnonationalities' dream of achieving, or returning to, their own nation-statehood. In lectures at Leicester University, England, in 1991, on the eve of the splintering of Yugoslavia, I was still citing that country as a prime example of the viability of ethnonational pluralism.

3. The Association of Social and Behavioral Scientists (ASBS) was founded in 1936 as the Negro social science association by T. E. McKinney of Johnson C. Smith University, in response to exclusion from the "white" social science professional societies. Desegregation did not end the need for such a forum; ASBS continues today. I was vice president for the period 1972-1974, and my first published work on Charles S. Johnson appeared in the ASBS's *Journal of Social and Behavioral Sciences* (Robbins, 1972).

4. One significant measure of change between 1966 and 1988 was the striking increase in the proportion of faculty with the doctorate in the leading Black schools.

5. For a recent profile of the HBCU system, see Jaynes and Williams (1989, pp. 176-179, 437-438). If we count just the 19 states and the District of Columbia that have HBCUs, then the proportion of Black students attending them compared with total Black enrollment in colleges in these states rises to about 35%.

6. Two other novels that are highly insightful on this theme in the era of segregation are J. Saunders Redding's *Stranger and Alone* (1950/1957) and Chester Himes's *The Third Generation* (1954/1989).

7. There are a number of standard histories of Black higher education covering the first to third periods. For all levels, see Bullock (1967); on higher education, see McGrath (1965), Bond (1934/1960), Carnegie Commission on Higher Education (1971), and Wilkinson (1987).

8. See the moving memoir by Anne Moody, *Coming of Age in Mississippi* (1968).

9. This and other episodes from those heady days are described in Robbins (1967a). Frustrated by the lack of progress toward racial justice, Stokely Carmichael abandoned interracial coalition strategy for Black power ideology and the exclusion of whites. (A long evening's discussion in my home ended with, "Sorry, nothing personal, it's not a friendship problem—but all the whites on this Black campus and all the others have got to go.") Understandably, rage ultimately overcame a previous steady existential view of the world. In books he went from Camus's *The Stranger* to Franz Fanon's *The Wretched of the Earth*.

10. There are many grave questions concerning Black faculty in mainstream institutions—their mobility, their vulnerability, their tenure status—but this problem is beyond the scope of my essay (see, e.g., Exum, 1983).

11. Hacker's *Two Nations* (1992) is the most recent of many similar assessments holding that racial equality is still a long way off.

12. *Adams,* the foundation case for numerous lawsuits right up to the present, was first filed in 1970 by the Legal Defense Fund of the NAACP. The U.S. District Court found that the segregated system of higher education continued to be in violation of Title VI of the Civil Rights Act of 1964 (*Adams v. Richardson,* 351 F Supp 636, 637, 1972). The Education Department's Office of Civil Rights would henceforth be required to monitor progress in both two-way integration and intensive "enhancement" of the public Black colleges. Compliance monitoring went on for years. In 1987, the department's secretary, William Bennett, declared 4 southern states in compliance and ordered 6 to take further steps. Civil rights groups argue that none of the 10 had achieved full compliance, and they are pressing forward in litigation, as in the Mississippi case summarized in this essay. Of special interest is the case of the University of North Carolina system, whose lawyers signed a consent decree with the government in 1981. The decree terminated in 1989, with the University Board of Governors and president satisfied compliance had been achieved, and critics insisting it had not been. My own view is that North Carolina's record is probably the best in the South, though in some respects short of full compliance with the intent of Title VI and the consent decree. Raymond Dawson, vice president for academic affairs of UNC, strongly defends the university's effort, in terms of concrete actions, and he makes an impressive case. For criticism of UNC for lack of progress in an earlier time, see Dentler, Baltzell, and Sullivan (1983).

13. Among Black critics, see, for example, Frazier (1957), Harleston (1965), and Sowell (1972). Howard Zinn (1966), the gifted historian and political scientist, who is white and has taught at Spelman, took a different view from that of Jencks and Riesman. He argued that the Black colleges should deemphasize the elusive goal of "catching up" quality of education in favor of showing the world the value of social community that is integrated, multiracial, and international in character. This was an important ideal, but it was based upon a significant increase of whites and foreign students in the Black colleges, which did not materialize.

14. This refusal to recognize the comparability of racism and ethnic persecution in the West and in the newly independent Third World states was only one aspect of the ideological bias of the radical sociology movement (see Robbins, 1969).

15. See, for example, Locke and Stern (1946). Writing from a Marxist perspective, Stern bitterly criticized Myrdal's conception of the American race problem in terms of moral values.

References

Allport, G. W. (1954). *The nature of prejudice.* Reading, MA: Addison-Wesley.

Anderson, J. (1983). *This was Harlem: A cultural portrait, 1900-1950.* New York: Farrar, Straus, Giroux.

Baldwin, J. (1955). *Notes of a native son.* Boston: Beacon.

Baldwin, J. (1985). *The price of the ticket.* New York: St. Martin's.

Bond, H. M. (1960). *Education of the Negro in the American social order.* New York: Octagon. (Original work published 1934)

Bullock, H. A. (1967). *A history of Negro education in the South.* New York: Praeger.

Carnegie Commission on Higher Education. (1971). *From isolation to mainstream: Problems of the colleges founded for Negroes.* New York: McGraw-Hill.

Dentler, R. F., Baltzell, D. C., & Sullivan, D. J. (1983). *University on trial: The case of the University of North Carolina.* Cambridge, MA: Abt Associates.

Du Bois, W. E. B. (1961). *The souls of Black folk.* Greenwich, CT: Fawcett. (Original work published 1903)

Exum, W. (1983). Climbing the crystal stair. *Social Problems, 30*(4).

Frazier, E. F. (1957). *Black bourgeoisie.* Glencoe, IL: Free Press.

Hacker, D. (1992). *Two nations: Black and white, separate, hostile, unequal.* New York: Scribner.

Harleston, B. (1965, November). The Negro in higher education. *Atlantic Monthly.*

Himes, C. (1989). *The third generation.* New York: Thunder's Mouth. (Original work published 1954)

Jaynes, G. D., & Williams, R. M., Jr. (Eds.). (1989). *A common destiny: Blacks and American society.* Washington, DC: National Research Council, National Academy Press.

Jencks C., & Riesman, D. (1969). *The academic revolution.* Garden City, NY: Doubleday.

Kaufman, J. (1988). *Broken alliance: The turbulent times between Blacks and Jews in America.* New York: Scribner.

Locke, A., & Stern, B. J. (1946). *When peoples meet.* New York: Hinds, Hayden, Eldridge.

McGrath, E. C. (1965). *The predominantly Negro college in transition.* New York: Teachers College Press.

Merton, R. K. (1949). Discrimination and the American creed. In R. M. MacIver (Ed.), *Discrimination and national welfare.* New York: Harper.

Moody, A. (1968). *Coming of age in Mississippi.* New York: Dell.

Myrdal, G., with Sterner, R., & Rose, A. (1944). *An American dilemma: The Negro problem and modern democracy.* New York: Harper & Row.

Osofsky, G. (1968). *Harlem: The making of a ghetto, 1890-1930.* New York: Harper & Row.

Redding, J. S. (1989). *Stranger and alone.* Boston: Northeastern University Press. (Original work published 1950)

Robbins, R. (1949, Fall). Counter-assertion in the New York Negro press. *Phylon.*

Robbins, R. (1965). Sociology and congressional law making. In A. Shostak (Ed.), *Sociology in action.* Homewood, IL: Dorsey.

Robbins, R. (1966). *Desegregation and the Negro college in the South.* Washington, DC: U.S. Department of Health, Education and Welfare.

Robbins, R. (1967a, October 8). The Negro college: A long, long, way to go. *Boston Globe Magazine.*

Robbins, R. (1967b, November). Native sons. *Catholic World.*

Robbins, R. (1969, May). Who will liberate the sociology liberation movement? *American Sociologist.*

Robbins, R. (1972, Fall-Winter). Shadow of Macon County. *Journal of Social and Behavioral Sciences.*

Robbins, R. (1988, September 16). Blacks and Jews in conflict. *Boston Globe.*

Sowell, T. (1972). *Black education: Myths and tragedies.* New York: McKay.

Wilkinson, D. Y. (1987). *A profile of the nation's resources.* Washington, DC: National Research Council.

Zinn, H. (1966, May). New directions for the Negro colleges. *Harper's.*

10

White Liberal

Some Reflections on
Personal and Professional Socialization
and the Field of Race Relations

PETER I. ROSE

This essay begins with a caveat. While trying faithfully to write an essay about my personal and professional background and its influence on the research process, I have taken the liberty of broadening that part of the mandate that calls for a focus on a single major race-related project in which I have been engaged. Instead, I write about a number of linked projects, some basic research (as on "the exemption mechanism" and the study of "the sociology of exile"), and other research that is more applied (including a study of the making and implementing of U.S. refugee resettlement policy, an examination of the ongoing conflict between Black and Jewish Americans, and an investigation of the teaching of race relations itself). The rationale for this departure should become clear as I describe my own goals of trying to influence others as a writer, editor, consultant, and teacher, four roles that have led me

AUTHOR'S NOTE: This chapter is an updated and much-expanded version of the introduction to a previously published selection of essays titled *Mainstream and Margins: Jews, Blacks and Other Americans*, copyright 1983 by Transaction Books. Reprinted by permission.

to see myself as much as a catalyst as an analyst in the study of racial inequality and ethnic relations.

Roots and Branches

Although it is difficult to say when my involvement in the sociology of racial and ethnic relations began, I think I can explain how I happened to be drawn into the field. Looking backward, it now seems that such interests were almost ascribed for, as textbook writers used to explain about the socialization process, as my twig was bent, so grew the person I became.

My parents, Aaron and Lillian Rose, were both children of immigrants. Both were engaged personally and professionally in issues of intergroup relations, in the settlement house/community center movement and as directors of a series of summer camps where intergroup understanding was a major aspect of programming.

From as long ago as I can remember, the camps were not the only centers of all sorts of human rights activities; our homes in upstate New York were, too. The people who came there to visit or to organize or to debate the issues of the day were a true "rainbow coalition" long before such an expression ever entered the popular vernacular. They were black and white and brown (and some were "red," Onondagans and Mohawks). They were Catholic, Protestant, and Jewish, young and old. Some were very rich (many of them board members of my father's agency); some were very poor. But mostly they were like my folks: well educated but not terribly well-off; thirty- and fortysomething teachers, preachers, and fellow social workers. (The main difference between the whites and Blacks, as I remember them, was that the latter were always more "properly" dressed, with shirts and ties and jackets, even in the summertime!)

My father died in 1975; my mother in 1986. While my wife and I were sorting through their memorabilia and breaking up their home in Tucson, Arizona, I came upon a 50-year-old citation presented to my father. Dated December 31, 1936, it began, "The officers of the 1936 Campaign of the American Jewish Joint Distribution Committee extend their heartfelt appreciation to Aaron Rose for cooperation and leadership in the Campaign for Aid to the Distressed Jews of Germany and of Eastern Europe." Finding the framed certificate—which once hung in my grandmother's house and is now on my office wall—brought back another flood of memories, for, in addition to those who passed through our home on a nearly daily basis was a small group of people who came there and stayed, for anywhere from a few months to a few years. They were mostly Jewish refugees from Germany and Austria, a small number of the many my father had helped to "place."

I was an only child, but Walter from Leipzig, and Alma and Max from Hanover, and, later, Michael from London became my foster siblings. (Michael, who was nearest to my age and looked more like my mother than I did, was often taken to be her son and I was seen as the refugee. I would be fussed over and clucked at by those who were uninformed of the truth. Some would ask me how *I* liked it in America.)

Sometime in the late 1930s or early 1940s, my parents traveled to Chicago and returned with a present. For an avid reader of (or, at least, looker at) the *National Geographic* it was a special treat, a poster from an exhibition of Malvina Hoffman's sculpture exhibition called "The Races of Man." On the poster were photographs of many of Hoffman's figures scattered about a big map of the world indicating their places of origin. I was fascinated by the differences in the physiognomy of those labeled "Sioux" and "Ubangi," "Mediterranean" and "Malay." We hung the poster in my room. Day after day I stared at it. I decided that someday, I wanted to travel to see where these people lived. I wanted to learn about the racial differences portrayed by Hoffman in her sculpture and the human resemblances of those who visited us—and lived with us. At the age of 9 or 10 I was determined to become a *National Geographic*-type anthropologist and imagined myself going to fascinating places armed with camera, pad, and pencil.

Two years later I changed my mind. I abandoned thoughts of exotic environs for nearby snowy slopes. I was going to become a professional skier.

When we moved from Syracuse, New York, to a tiny rural town in the northern Adirondacks in the mid-1940s, I was in heaven. I skied every day and dreamed of bigger mountains. I also developed an interest in the folklore of the area and the people I met as I would take off, most often alone, along the snow-covered roads along the Canadian border.

In the high school I attended there were three distinct ethnic groups—Yankees, Irish Catholics, and French Canadians. (Actually there were four if one includes the dyad of me and the only other Jew in Chateaugay High School.) It was an interesting experience, and one that was also to shape my future work. But at the time, what was most troubling to me was not the matter of coping with diversity—and being the Jewish ambassador to all who asked why "you Jews" do this or that. My biggest problem was that nobody in Chateaugay wanted to go skiing. "It's too damn cold," they would say, as they headed back to the basketball court. And so I continued to be the odd man out in more ways than one.

By the time I was a senior I was beginning to realize that although I was a good skier, I wasn't great and would never be the hotshot I'd hoped to become. Still, truth to speak, I narrowed my applications to universities on the basis of the size of their ski programs—Syracuse, Dartmouth, and Middlebury—and after considerable anguish, decided on Syracuse, where I was to spend four years as a part-time ski instructor and where I renewed my fascination with the peoples of the world—and, in some ways, rediscovered my social conscience.

During my undergraduate days I spent a good deal of time shuttling back and forth among the ski slopes; the Zoology Department, where I took courses in natural history, evolution, and physical anthropology; and the Maxwell School of Citizenship, where I studied cultural anthropology, sociology, and contemporary politics. I was especially influenced by three teachers: the anthropologist Douglas Haring, author of *Order and Possibility in Social Life*; the political scientist and, later, university vice chancellor, Michael O. Sawyer; and Nathan Goldman, a clinical psychologist with a Ph.D. in sociology from Chicago. Haring introduced me to the rich literature of anthropology; Sawyer showed me the dilemmas of democracy, including the Sacco-Vanzetti Case, the Peekskill riots (against Paul Robeson), and the relocation of the Japanese in 1942; and Goldman led me to the works of Robert Park and the "Chicago school" and two other Chicago social scientists, Robert Redfield and David Riesman, and many others. Interestingly, none of the courses I took was on "racial and ethnic relations." Such courses were simply not available.

Throughout my last year in college I worked part-time with a multiracial group of very poor teenage boys at the Huntington Club Family Agency. The direct and highly intense contact with them and their world, which was very different from my own, led me to consider the possibility of a career in social work. But the consideration was short-lived.

That same year I met the Dutch woman who was to become my wife. Hedy Cohen's experiences as a young girl in occupied Amsterdam, where, quite literally, she lived the life of Anne Frank, hidden in the basement of the cellar of a family friend—experiences she gradually shared with me—doubtless added to my subsequent interest in and later research on the politics of rescue and the psychology of altruism.

Nearing graduation, and having abandoned all hopes of becoming another Hannes Schneider (then the premier ski instructor in the country), I was still in a quandary about which direction to go within the general realm of social science and its application. I applied to and was accepted for several doctoral programs in both anthropology and sociology. In the end I opted to do my graduate work in the combined Department of Sociology and Anthropology at Cornell, I hoped under the guidance of Alexander Leighton, the psychiatrist/anthropologist whose early work, *The Governing of Men,* a study of the incarceration of Japanese Americans and the character of their lives in one internment camp in Arizona, I had read in a Maxwell School course.

Leighton was away for most of my Cornell years. Instead, I studied with a number of sociologists and anthropologists, including Robin M. Williams, Jr., Edward A. Suchman, and Allan Holmberg. They taught me to appreciate the connections among theory (mainly Parsonian), research (decidedly Lazarsfeldian), and practice (uniquely Holmbergian). That combination was to have a decided impact on some of my subsequent work, even as I came to challenge many aspects of the institutional approach, survey research, and interventionist anthropology.

Although members of my graduate school "cohort" read those who were to become known as "conflict theorists"—including Marx and Veblen, Simmel, and Mills, most of us began our careers functionalist in thought (especially interested in the study of value consensus), applied in research orientation (hoping to expose those places where the order seemed to break down), and reformist in action (determined to bring conduct in line with creed). Not surprisingly, we hailed the 1954 *Brown* decision of the Supreme Court as a triumph of our position.

From my early days at Cornell I decided I wanted to zero in on issues of race and ethnicity. Perhaps because of my childhood acquaintance with so many middle-class Blacks and with a number of uprooted asylees, and my own later experience as a Jew in a decidedly Gentile community, I was especially interested in exploring the problems faced by isolated minorities. My master's thesis dealt with "the exemption mechanism" and the significance of such statements as "Why, some of my best friends are . . . ." My doctoral dissertation was based on a year-long study of small-town Jews and their neighbors, the data having been obtained through lengthy interviews (which included considerable life-history information) with members of some 40 families and mail questionnaires returned by more than 100 Jews and nearly 400 non-Jewish "opinion leaders" who lived in rural communities of less than 10,000 population in nonmetropolitan counties of New York, western Vermont, and the northern tier of Pennsylvania. (Eighteen years later, a student of mine, Liv Olson Pertzoff, and I restudied the Jews and interviewed their children. The original and follow-up studies are both reported on in *Strangers in Their Midst,* Rose, 1977.)

The findings of the original studies may be summarized, somewhat cryptically, as follows. With regard to the Jews:

1. Those who had left the confines of the urban ghetto or ethnic neighborhood were not apostates. Rather, they were seekers of economic and social betterment who hoped to find acceptance in the new setting without the loss of ethnic identity.

2. Once they entered the new and "alien" territory, they frequently found themselves in the position of representing "their people" to the community at large. As strangers, they found that their ethnic identity became even more significant in the community and more salient to themselves. More often than not, consciousness of minority membership seemed to increase for those who had become "isolates."

3. The minority group members who lived in the milieu of the majority had an infinitely greater opportunity to adapt themselves to the folkways of the dominant group than did those who lived in the middle of the ethnic enclaves from which many had come. As they were far more apt to interact at a close, personal level with members of the dominant group, they were wont to agree with one who said to me, "You see, we feel we have the best of both. . . . Judaism, with all its traditions, its stress on culture, on learning, on freedom . . . and the fact that we live in a small town, with nice people and good clean air. . . . We wouldn't trade either for the world." Their children were another story, however. Almost to a person, they reported that although they worried that their children would not grow up with a clear enough sense of their ethnic identity, they seemed well adjusted to small-town living and might very well want to stay.

With regard to the non-Jews in the small towns:

1. In the small community the minority group members were constantly in direct contact with the majority. As they got to know the ways of the members of the dominant group, its members could not help but get to know the Jews, if there were Jews in their towns. The isolated minority group members did indeed stand on the threshold of influencing deep-seated images. They could reinforce such images or aid in the recasting of them by those with whom they interacted.

2. The isolated minority group members rarely constituted a threat to the established order, and community members were often willing to accept individual outsiders despite clearly articulated expressions of prejudice (as measured by a variety of scales).

3. Repeated and intensive contact and personal association often appeared to change the mental pictures of the isolate from being "different from" to being "typical of" the group he or she represented. Exemption was viewed as an important possible waystation on the road to reducing prejudice.

For the record, I should report that the follow-up conducted nearly two decades later indicated that the children of the small-town Jews had felt far less secure than their parents had led me to believe. The vast majority told us they had left the small towns for college and never returned. Although not all became religious, more were married to Jewish spouses than were their urban-raised counterparts at the time they were contacted. Exemption may have been useful for their city-born parents' acceptance in the small town, but their own marginality seemed to encourage their "reverse migration."

Starting Out

When I was finishing graduate work, instead of taking a profered temporary job at Dartmouth College (where I might have skied to my heart's content), I accepted a position at a college in Baltimore, a border city undergoing the early pains of desegregation. It proved to be the right choice.

The years in Baltimore were both productive and educational. At Goucher College I was part of a two-person team, expected to teach everything from introductory sociology to anthropological theory. It was quite an initiation. But what was even more challenging was the moonlighting I did as a very junior consultant to the Council of Social Agencies' Research Department. There I became involved in two studies of "unreached youth": a general study of white delinquents (a colleague was doing a parallel study of Black delinquents) and, a year later, a series of interviews, cosponsored by the Anti-Defamation League, with those engaged in the epidemic of swastika smearing that occurred in 1959. (To my chagrin, in several instances my subjects in the second study turned out to be some of the same young men I had interviewed in the first.)

In 1960 we moved to Northampton, Massachusetts, where I had accepted a position in the Department of Sociology and Anthropology at Smith College. It was not until I left the metropolitan area and the near South that I began to write about Black and white relations, a subject that had occupied so much of my thought and activity for so many years. For the first time, I began teaching a course called "Ethnic Minorities in America," a course that is still being offered. (Recently I had occasion to look back at more than 30 years of syllabi for Soc 213. I found it interesting to see what was emphasized in the early 1960s, the late years of that decade, in the 1970s, in the 1980s, and today. A very quick summary would note that a principal theme in the first years was "intergroup relations and the campaigns for civil rights," then "Black power, Black consciousness, and the resurgence of ethnicity," then—actually, now—debates over "immigration policy," "affirmative action," "English only," and, once again, "what it means to be an American.")

The early 1960s were, for many young white liberal social scientists, a time of turmoil and of reawakening. With our students, we were beginning to learn and see more of "the other America" and to recognize the depth of the chasms that divided our society. We read Paul Goodman and laughed at his lampooning of sociologists while finding his analysis profoundly sociological in its own right—and deeply disturbing. Americans did seem to be growing up absurd, and many "consensus-oriented" sociologists began to feel they had failed to recognize fundamental differences between those who had made it and were trying to get out of the closed rooms and the others who peered in and sought entry. I was especially impressed by the growing paradox within what was still called "the Negro community." On the one hand, many of its members were precisely the outsiders who wanted in. "What do you want?" we asked in one questionnaire and interview after another. And they answered, quite directly, "What you have." On the other hand, it was clearly apparent that Blacks could not forever remain supplicants waiting to be admitted to the Big White House.

Long involved in the civil rights movement, I became increasingly convinced that Blacks would have to play a much larger role in determining their own destinies. Ironically, my first real break with liberal integrationists was when I went back to Baltimore and gave a talk on the need for whites to step aside, for Blacks to move into middle- as well as upper-level (and not just titular) leadership positions, and for all to recognize the necessity for what, in a rather Durkheimian presentation, I called "the coalescence of community." I even said that some separatism on the part of Blacks might be required to allow them time to regroup, organize, and then confront the system with a more unified front so that people on all sides could deal with one another from a posture more akin to political parity than the lopsided asymmetry of the traditional relationship. That, I argued, could lead to real negotiations and more meaningful integration. But the message got lost and I, who in 1962 was advocating some sort of "Black power," although I did not call it that, was viewed as a supporter of apartheid! (Ten years later, *not* to advocate separatism [or "pluralism"]—or at least indicate an understanding of the desire for it—meant being labeled an insensitive and narrow-minded racist. Twenty years later, eschewing an even more group-oriented stance was, in some places, grounds for a challenge to a person's right to speak on the issue at all.)

My first contribution to the broader study of racial inequality and race relations was not so much the result of original research but a series of reflections and commentaries on the field itself. It was published in the form of a textbook, *They and We: Racial and Ethnic Relations in the U.S.* (1964). Unlike most texts of the time, it was written as a series of interlocking essays. Although considering the general topics of prejudice and discrimination, the book focused on the relationships between those in dominant groups and minorities, emphasizing the responses of the latter to their place and placement in society. *They and We* became a classroom standard and, I am told, remains a useful introduction to the field. It has been updated, revised, and expanded three times. The most recent edition (1990) includes an assessment of "the Reagan years and beyond," a very difficult period in the history of racial and ethnic relations in this country.

Partly as a response to the first edition of *They and We,* Charles D. Lieber, then editor in chief of the College Books Division at Random House, and Jesse Stein, vice president, invited me to join my friend and first editor Charles H. Page as the second consulting editor in sociology. I accepted the offer. I was made responsible for several subfields, including general social science texts, but racial and ethnic relations remained my central concern. Among the books on race relations I brought in and for which I was more of less responsible were Inge Powell Bell's *Core and the Strategy of Non-Violence* (1968), Lewis A. Killian's *The Impossible Revolution? Black Power and the American Dream* (1968), William Moore, Jr.'s *The Vertical Ghetto: Everyday Life in an Urban Project* (1969), Minako Kurokawa's anthology, *Minority*

Responses: Comparative Views of Reactions to Subordination (1970), Richard A. Schermerhorn's *Comparative Ethnic Relations* (1970), Sethard Fisher's reader, *Power and the Black Community* (1970), Richard Frucht's edited volume, *Black Society in the New World* (1971), and Michael Lewis's *The Culture of Inequality* (1978).

In the late 1960s my editorial responsibilities were expanded somewhat when I became general editor of a series of Random House books on the topic of "ethnic relations in comparative perspective." Over the next few years nine volumes were "commissioned," each to follow a somewhat similar outline describing the history of a particular group, relationships with others, the character of ethnic organization, and patterns of interaction, acculturation, and so on. Eight were completed, accepted, and published, seven of them by Random House. The Random House books, several of which are still in print, some in second and third editions, are Lewis M. Killian's *White Southerners* (1970), Joseph Lopreato's *Italian Americans* (1970), Marshall Sklare's *American Jews* (1971), William Petersen's *Japanese Americans* (1971)—in which he elaborated on his now-controversial sobriquet "model minority"—Sheila Allen's *New Minorities, Old Conflicts: West Indians and East Asians in Britain* (1972), Ellwyn Stoddard's *Mexican Americans* (1973), and Stanford M. Lyman's *Chinese Americans* (1974).

I had also invited my colleague at the University of Massachusetts, William Julius Wilson, to write a book on the African American experience for the series. He did so. However, the end product was, according to the managing editor at Random House, more treatise than text, as it had a definite thesis that sought to explain why the gap between poor and other Blacks was widening. In one way, the point was well taken, for the author had not followed the rough outline mapped out for each volume in the series. Yet, to me, this "failure" was more than offset by the fact that the manuscript was, in many ways, the most imaginative and the most controversial of the lot. I fought to keep it as it was, but the in-house editors stood fast. They said they would only publish it if it were changed to conform more closely to the other books in the series. Wilson was reluctant to make the changes, and, in the end, with my full support, he decided to send the manuscript to the University of Chicago Press, where it was published as *The Declining Significance of Race* (1978). (The episode with Random House had a considerable impact on my thinking about the role of the consulting editor and, though I stayed on for a few more years and edited a number of other books, including several in racial and ethnic relations, things were never quite the same again. Since 1980 I have eschewed editing for Random House and turned to book reviewing not only for scholarly journals—which I had done all along—but also for magazines and newspapers, including the *Christian Science Monitor,* for which I reviewed regularly from 1983 to 1987, and, more recently, *Newsday.*)

During the mid-1960s my students and I conducted a nationwide study of "traditional ideologies and the teaching of race relations." The findings were published in a small volume, *The Subject Is Race* (1968). The research summarized a broad-based survey of the history of the then-present efforts to prepare and teach courses on the topic. The analysis was based on responses from colleagues at more than 1,700 colleges and universities in the United States and a selected study of students on a number of campuses.

Perhaps the most surprising finding of the second part of the project was that there was a marked difference in the attitudes of those who were not interested in taking such courses and those who had either done so or hoped to. The former group scored much higher on measures of ethnocentrism and what we would later label "racism" than those in either of the other cohorts. (For those who teach the subject, there was some satisfaction in knowing that those who took the courses were far better informed than all the others. At least we could say, "They did learn something!")

Professional Involvement

In addition to editorial duties and research of my own during my first 10 years at Smith, I became increasingly involved in the affairs of the profession, mainly, though not exclusively, in the Society for the Study of Social Problems, the Society for Applied Anthropology, the Eastern Sociological Society, and the American Sociological Association. Most of that involvement was with committees on intergroup relations and minority affairs, but in time I worked on other matters.

As I got to know sociologists throughout the country, I also found myself concerned about the narrow paths on which so many seemed set. They were becoming more and more concerned with "professionalism," I with the problem of reconciling what was to me a humanistic discipline with the scientism that others stressed. (This was not long after the time the American Sociological *Society* changed its name to the American Sociological *Association.*) With a few others, I began speaking up at annual SSSP, ESS, and ASA meetings about civil rights and the war in Vietnam, urging fellow members to take collective stands in opposition to policies that seemed to be violations of democratic principles and matters especially relevant to those professionally concerned with human relations. Our remarks were not always greeted with equanimity. Many stood up to challenge us, saying that meetings of learned societies might be arenas for discussion of some of these matters, but taking public positions, especially in an official way, was most inappropriate. Others did not think they should be discussed at all.

As we moved further into the 1960s, others, far more radical than I, voiced stronger sentiments in those ubiquitous Hilton ballrooms, often couching their critiques in revolutionary rhetoric. Splinter groups and caucuses formed to effectively mobilize for action inside the organization and in the world beyond. The targets were many besides Lyndon Johnson, Richard Nixon, and the members of Congress. Among them were social scientists who consulted for government agencies and, it was said, helped solidify the "welfare-warfare state"; social researchers who "manipulated" people, especially those described as "culturally deprived"; and social theorists who wrote uncritically of this society where ethnocentrism was fostered and prejudice instilled, where individuals learned about achievement by being taught to accept the principles of meritocracy in a manner that urged them to blame themselves and not the system for their failure to achieve. Much of what these critics said made sense, but what was troubling was that few of them—and equally few of us—had a viable plan to reorganize society to make it both free and fair.

I remained active in the civil rights and antiwar movements inside the sociological associations, on campus, and, to some extent, in the streets. But I frequently found myself in the awkward position of agreeing with what many around me were saying while strongly objecting to some of the techniques used, especially what seemed to be a growing "left-wing McCarthyism" that sought to stifle any who might disagree with the blanket condemnation of "Amerikkka." (We are seeing a variation on this theme in recent attempts to foster "politically correct" expression on college campuses today.)

At the height of the upheaval of the late 1960s and early 1970s, old friends found themselves ideological enemies, old socialists were attacked as fascists, integrationists were called racists, and liberals were labeled reactionaries. Tensions outside the campuses (and the Hiltons) flowed through the gates and into the classrooms, where a new band of young sociologists, instructors and students, often served in the vanguard of the frontal attack on the system. Still, the general message did get across and at least some segments of society (and the ASA) responded to charges of elitism, racism, and sexism and even began to look "through different eyes" themselves. By the mid-1970s it seemed that everyone was regrouping, including the sociologists.

During a stint on the ASA Council in 1974-1977, I observed some significant changes in official policy, self-examination (as evidenced in the very thorough reports on the status of minorities and women), and the composition of that ruling body itself. One result (which some critics saw as co-optation) was a growing respect for differing viewpoints, a return to civil discourse even in consideration of potentially explosive issues.

As I tried to address myself to some of the issues that were so pressing in those days, I felt a gnawing sense of inadequacy in terms of my education and that of many sociologists. I felt we were limited in our understanding of history and poorly informed about literature that was not *the* literature (of the field) and began to do more comparative work with both European and American historians. I began to read more widely, most particularly in those many ethnocentric ethnographies, the first novels of immigrants and minority writers. I also found a new outlet, writing essays through which I could combine *my* varied interests and concerns in the spirit of Robert Frost's wonderful line, "My object in living is to unite my vocation with my avocation as my two eyes make one in sight." Among the early essays were pieces titled "The Black Experience: Issues and Images," "The Ghetto and Beyond: Jewish Life in America," and " 'Nobody Knows the Trouble *I've* Seen': Some Reflections on the Insider-Outsider Debate."

By the end of the decade there were further fissures in society and further fragmentation within the ranks of those who studied it. There were not just good guys and bad guys, but various types of protesters, all proclaiming universal truths to very partisan cohorts. (Many engaged in what Michael Lerner once aptly called "respectable bigotry": expressing categorical affection for Black and other poor people while finding members of the white working class, well ensconced in their "ticky-tacky houses," ideal scapegoats.) Society was reeling. It seemed an appropriate time to try to assess how people saw each other within and between communities. This led to five new projects—and to six edited volumes.

The first was a book of essays on Jews, *The Ghetto and Beyond* (1969). The second was a two-volume series published under the overall title of *Americans From Africa* (1970a, 1970b). The first volume, *Slavery and Its Aftermath,* included chapters on four controversies: Africa and the new Americans, the legacy of slavery, similarities and differences in southern and northern experiences, and community, class, and family life. The second volume, *Old Memories, New Moods,* contained chapters on four more controversies: A chapter titled "Who Was Nat Turner?" explored the significance of his and others' revolts; another chapter discussed the quest for "freedom now"; another sought answers to the question "whither Black power?" and ended with a consideration of African American identity and the acceptance of being Black. The last section was headed "Negroes Nevermore."

The third project was a text/reader titled *Nation of Nations,* which contained excerpts from 10 classic "literary ethnographies," all novels about the meaning of being a minority in America, and a series of articles, adapted as chapters, titled "The Ethnic Experience and the Racial Crisis" (1971/1982).

The fourth book was, in many ways, the most challenging and, I now think, most interesting of the lot. It came about as a result of my trying to get some handles on the growing polarization in the nation—especially between Blacks and whites at many levels in this society—and as a result of seeing the remarkable Japanese film *Rashomon.* I invited two colleagues, Stanley Rothman, a political scientist also at Smith College, and Bill Wilson, who was still at the University of Massachusetts, to join me in a preparing "a Rashomon approach to race relations." They agreed and we then persuaded 10 Black and 10 white writers to offer their views on various aspects of the situation, circa 1970. Each of us also added our own views to those who offered what we called "A Spectrum of Black Views," including the voices of the urban poor, the Black bourgeoisie, Black immigrants, integrationists, and nationalists; to "White Perspectives," which tried to reflect the sentiments of various white southerners, members of "the silent majority," and representatives of Irish, Jewish, and other "white ethnic" communities; to the stances of those we called "Politicians, Public Servants, and the People," especially Black politicians, white politicians, welfare workers, policemen, teachers, and prison personnel; and to the views of those we included in a section titled "On the Campus," white professors, white students, Black professors, and Black students. We called our book

Through Different Eyes: Black and White Perspectives on American Race Relations (Rose, Rothman, & Wilson, 1973).

That same year, I published *Many Peoples, One Nation* (1973), a volume of stories, essays, and songs about the United States that was to supplement the basic ninth-grade course in American history and to provide a corrective to what I wholeheartedly agreed was a white-washed interpretation of nearly 200 years of nationhood. The book proved to be a forerunner in an area that was to become known as "multiculturalism."

Moving On

Something rather unrelated to the activities outlined above occurred in my life in the mid-1960s that was to have a profound effect on my later work and interests. I spent 1964-1965 in England (as a Fulbright Professor at the University of Leicester). For the first time I was not only exposed to another kind of sociology, but to life in a somewhat different society. One of my first lessons was that, in some places, *everybody* talks about social class, not just sociologists! I also discovered that my interest in intercultural relations extended far beyond U.S. borders.

It was extremely stimulating (and very depressing) to observe race relations in the United Kingdom and to try to get a sense of how commonwealth immigrants and other minorities were reacting to their treatment there. (My reflections became the subject of one of the first of the essays just mentioned.)

While in the United Kingdom, I conducted some research and made many contacts, especially with members of the Indian Workers Council and the newly established organization, CARD, the Committee Against Racial Discrimination. I also participated in one of the first sit-ins in the Midlands, a protest against the refusal of the landlord of a pub called the Lord Nelson to serve an African American colleague from the university. The latter incident, and participation in a conference titled "Race Relations in Britain," led to further involvement in issues there. (I remain interested in the subject and have become particularly interested in modest attempts to introduce the idea of "multiculturalism" in certain sectors of British society.)

The year abroad not only opened my eyes, it also whetted my appetite for more foreign experiences. Three years later I was back in Europe and have been abroad every year since, usually for a total of two months. My work as a consultant, lecturer, and researcher has included extended teaching stints in Japan and Australia and shorter visits to more than 50 other countries, some in Africa but most in Europe, Asia, and the South Pacific.

As I became peripatetic, new interests in comparative higher education and intercultural exchanges were added to my "fields of specialization." A two-year study of the Senior Fulbright Program in East Asia and the Pacific gave me an opportunity not only to evaluate a program that I had known as a former Fulbrighter, but required conducting interviews with more than 100 top-level academicians in 11 countries in the area. While on three field trips back to the area, I made additional contacts with a number of scholars who were conducting research that was of continuing interest to me. Among the most prominent topics were studies of interethnic conflict in Southeast Asia; examinations of the political rhetoric used by those seeking to complete the emancipation of "Japan's invisible race," the *Buraku-min*; surveys of ambivalent attitudes toward American society and culture in places with close contact with the United States, especially Korea, Taiwan, Thailand, and the Philippines; and suggestions for research on those whose hostility to the United States was not at all ambivalent. One of my great regrets is that I never carried out a planned study on anti-Americanism that I had hoped eventually to publish under the title "Yank Is a Four-Letter Word." (In 1975, the matter that had exacerbated if not initiated such sentiments, the war in Vietnam, was ending, and floods of refugees were beginning to stream out of that country. Those "first-wave" refugees—and others who followed, not only from Vietnam but from Laos and Cambodia—became a topic of concern for a small number of social scientists. I was to become one of them, as I shall indicate below.)

Often the academics I would meet would invite me to speak to their colleagues or students about American society in general and racial and ethnic relations in particular. Such activities led to increasing interaction with faculty members and students in foreign universities and growing involvement with those often known abroad as "Americanists." They also complemented a new assignment I had taken on at Smith, directing a unique diploma program in American studies for foreign graduate students—a program that I was given the chance to reshape (and one in which I am still involved).

Shortly after I assumed the directorship, the program was reorganized and expanded. Each year 12-15 candidates were to be accepted. They were—and they are. Those in each "class" spend two semesters and are required to take a year-long seminar titled "American Society and Culture," the second part of which focuses heavily on race, ethnicity, class, and gender; to take four courses in their own fields of specialization (ranging from art, history, and literature, including American ethnic literature, to issues of foreign affairs and domestic social policy); and to write a thesis. Over the past 20 years a number of students have written insightful analyses of various aspects of American society, some targeted on problems of racial and ethnic relations, often based on data gathered firsthand. Recent studies include an examination of the concept of "success" among Polish Americans in the Connecticut Valley by a student from Warsaw; problems of Soviet-Jewish acculturation by a student from Krakow; women's roles in Chicopee's Luso-American community by a student from Lisbon; code switching in the learning of English among elderly Italian immigrants by a student from Rome; Indian shopkeepers in New York City by a student from Calcutta; the initiation of bilingualism by a student from Cordoba in Argentina; and the African identity of African American students by a woman from Nairobi. (This year's cohort includes candidates from Argentina, China, Czechoslovakia, France, Germany, India, Italy, Japan, Norway, Russia, Serbia, and Vietnam.)

Midcourse Meanders

In the early 1980s I began pulling together many of my disparate interests and personal commitments—in international and intergroup relations, problems of marginality and loss, issues relating to forced migration and the search for asylum, and adaptation and acculturation in new environs—in a series of studies of the rescue, relief, and resettlement of refugees. This meant looking at the limited (but now growing) sociological literature on the subject and attempting to develop my own sociology of exile.

The new turn in my research activities, or, perhaps better stated, expansion—for many who are forced to flee are ethnic minorities as well as political dissidents (and often they are both)—has meant conducting fieldwork in a variety of settings. During the past decade I have spent a considerable amount of time observing and interviewing refugee workers and their "clients" in Europe, Southeast Asia, and throughout the United States. My objective was to develop a clearer understanding of how American refugee policy is made and implemented.

As part of the research venture, and in keeping with a continuing commitment to assure that any social science project in which I am engaged has an "outreach" component to stimulate interest in examining pressing if often neglected issues, I sought funding from a variety of foundations. I eventually obtained small grants from the Weatherhead Foundation and the Exxon Educational Foundation that provided sufficient support for me to host five conferences and one lecture series at Smith College in Northampton.

The first conference was called "A Cry for Commitment: The Crisis in Cambodia." It brought together political activists, Khmer refugees, several professional refugee workers and a number of volunteers.

The second, and largest, was titled "Working With Refugees." More than 40 refugee workers attended that meeting, including the highest-ranking international civil servant in the United Nations High Commission for Refugees, a number of U.S. government officials from the Departments of State and Justice, the heads of most of the voluntary agencies that actually resettle refugees as well as a number of their field supervisors and frontline workers, and a cross-section of recently arrived refugees. The conference and its recommendations were the subject of a new book, *Working With Refugees* (1986).

The third meeting, "Toward a Sociology of Exile," focused on theoretical issues and research on refugees. Social scientists, including Lewis Coser, Aristide Zolberg, Barry Stein, Norman and Naomi Zucker, Gil Loescher, and John Scanlan, and a small number of practitioners were the principal participants.

The fourth gathering was cosponsored by the Carnegie Council for Ethics and International Affairs. It was oriented to curriculum building using the issue of refugees as a focal point for courses not only in the social sciences but in the fields of religion and philosophy. To this end, in addition to several specialists who delivered papers prepared expressly for the meeting, attendees were academics who had an interest in but little knowledge of the problems of forced migration.

The last conference in the series, held in conjunction with the Massachusetts Office for Refugees and Immigrants, was geared to examining resettlement in Massachusetts and problems of adaptation and integration and intergroup relations. More than half of the 100 participants in the two-day conference were former refugees; others included key figures in the government, the voluntary agencies, the school system, industry and labor, and representatives of African American, Hispanic, and other minority communities. The conference concluded with a series of recommendations for a new effort to facilitate the integration of newcomers. This was institutionalized as the Medina Project and is still active.

The 10-week lecture series, "Breaking Waves: U.S. Immigration and Refugee Policy," brought leading experts on the issue to the Smith campus as part of a newly instituted course in the Program in Public Policy. Here, as in the conferences, there was a double objective: to inform and to encourage further involvement.

Some of my own early ideas on the subject were expressed in several articles published in the United States and in the United Kingdom and in four invited lectures delivered at the University of Tilburg in the Netherlands in 1982 and published, along with four other papers, in a 1983 book I coedited with Hans Adriaansens, *Over Vreemdeling en Vluchteling* (On Strangers and Refugees).

The personal rewards of the recent work have been considerable in that a number of Smith and other "Five College" students (from Amherst, Hampshire, Mt. Holyoke, and the University of Massachusetts) and six from Harvard (where I taught a course called "The Dependency of the Dispossessed" in 1983-1984) who studied with me and/or participated in various conferences or attended the lecture series have gone on to become professional refugee workers, immigration lawyers, and, in five cases, academic specialists in the field. I now see many of them at meetings on refugee policy and discover their work in a variety of places. I also find myself frequently calling upon one or another of these experts for advice on a variety of problems that continue to plague me, not least the continuing tensions between newcomers and older American minorities.

Continuing interest in these matters led me to choose "Natives, Newcomers and the Sociology of Immigration" as the theme for the 62nd Annual Meeting of the Eastern Sociological Society, held in Arlington, Virginia, in April 1992. For a long time before the actual meeting I debated about how most effectively to use the rare opportunity (provided by the presidential address session) to have a bully pulpit from which to speak to a large number of colleagues on any matter whatsoever.

Because of growing concern about debates about the meaning of *E Pluribus Unum* in an age of particularism, a subject that involves a panoply of issues relating to the character of American culture, immigration policies, demographic shifts, patterns of intergroup relations, resurgent nativism, and the strident assertion of ethnic bloc power, I first thought of presenting a speech titled "The House *We* Live In: Personal Reflections and Professional Concerns." In the end, however, I decided to keep my remarks more focused, zeroing in on the matter— referred to above—that has occupied so much of my own thinking and research in recent years, the sociology of exile and the politics of rescue.

The intent of my address, titled *The Tempest-Tost,* was, at least in part, to urge fellow sociologists to consider more serious involvement— not just academic involvement—in the plight of those forced to flee their homes and homelands and in trying to understand the role of others in the processes of rescue, relief, and, especially, resettlement. In remarks delivered in Arlington I spoke of a sociopolitical phenomenon in which "the normative order has broken down, old rules no longer obtain, social groups have been torn asunder, and [where] there is often nowhere to turn." I pointed out that "for many refugees anomie is the pervasive social reality" and noted that "while it is often assumed that alienation is a result of anomie, here is a situation in which anomie is born of alienation, alienation in its most literal sense" (Rose, 1992).

While consciously trying to stick to the narrower subject of refugees and refugee policy, I ended by commenting on many of the things that would have been more fully developed had I stayed with the original topic, not least retreaded ideas about in-groups and out-groups, further thoughts about marginality, concerns about the relationship between international relations and domestic pressures, and consideration of the particular—and sometimes peculiar—character of American responses to those who suffer. They are all of a piece.

Redux: Toward a Humanistic Sociology

If there is a leitmotif running through all of the things I have reported on here, and touched on or alluded to in many of my writings and in my remarks in Arlington, it is the sentiment expressed by a little voice only I can hear (my internal Jiminy Cricket) that reminds me over and over that sociology belongs as much in the humanities as in the social sciences. The voice is one I have been listening to for years. It has long told me to work toward a more humanistic sociology, a sociology that seeks to examine, comprehend, analyze, and, wherever possible, convey to others a concern about the fragility of the fabric of modern society.

In the introduction to my book of essays titled *Mainstream and Margins: Jews, Blacks and Other Americans* (1983), I reiterate what I alluded to earlier in this essay, specifically the fact that, like many of my generation, I have been concerned not only with the direction our society has been taking and what has recently been described as the rising "meanness mania," but with the direction many of those in our discipline have chosen.

There was a time when C. Wright Mills lambasted his colleagues for doing either "abstract empiricism" or "grand theory." This dichotomy, I note, still exists. It exists today in some ways even more sharply, especially in those circles where, almost in counterreaction to the politicization of the field in the 1960s (and the deep involvement of sociologists in political action), there has been a retrenchment, a turn back to "scientism." With others, I have grown to realize that sophisticated quantitative methods are important. But they are not the be-all and surely not the end-all. "Not all things that count can be counted." The proclivity to try to assure our students and each other that we are true scientists reveals a continuing uncertainty (some would say a paranoia) about who we are and what we are about.

At bottom, I think we are (or ought to see ourselves as) humanists, and our field as a double bridge: between C. P. Snow's "two cultures" and between the social asepsis of the laboratory and library and the ordered chaos of the world beyond. Allowing ourselves to range more widely, to be more speculative, to include in our "data base" much more of that soft material that is not so easily measured, to become less concerned with statistical significance and more so with social importance does not mean abandoning the sociological perspective but enhancing it. That orientation still offers the framework within which to understand what is being explored, observed, summarized, and analyzed—the larger picture of the systems in which people live, work, play, and suffer.

Elaborating this point a few years earlier, in a paper originally presented as a lecture titled "Nobody Knows the Trouble I've Seen," I suggested that, after all, all groups—Blacks, whites, Jews, Gentiles, Chicanos, Anglos, Irish Protestants, Irish Catholics—institutionalize their behavior patterns, set criteria for the conferring or denying of status, indicate the tolerance limits of accepted and expected behavior, and maintain social systems of great intricacy even when they, themselves, have difficulty articulating their character. Explaining these things should remain the primary role of the sociologist.

I believe that what I said in the conclusion of that paper still obtains: I now feel very strongly that much of our work is like that of the

Japanese judge in *Rashomon,* the one who asks various witnesses and participants to describe a particular event as seen through their own eyes. Like the judge, neither teachers of sociology nor our students can be allowed to get off the hook. We must analyze the disparate pieces of evidence and then try to figure out how they fit together. If we use the suggested approach, then, perhaps, we will be better able to know the troubles others have seen and be better able to understand them.

Note

From the time I learned that the editor intended to use it, I objected to the misleading subtitle of this volume. I still do. The phrase states that the authors represent America's *first* generation of race relations scholars—which, of course, we are not.

My colleagues and I are, in the main, members of a postwar generation who built upon many concepts, theories, and studies of a diverse pantheon of true pioneers: William Graham Sumner, W. E. B. Dubois, Albion Small, W. I. Thomas, Florian Znaniecki, Zora Neale Hurston, Robert E. Park, Louis Wirth, E. Franklin Frazier, Everett Hughes, St. Clair Drake, Horace Cayton, Robert MacIver, Oliver Cox, John Dollard, Allison Davis, Gunnar Myrdal, Arnold Rose, and a host of others to whom we are profoundly indebted.

References

Allen, S. (1972). *New minorities, old conflicts: West Indians and East Asians in Britain.* New York: Random House.

Bell, I. P. (1968). *CORE and the strategy of non-violence.* New York: Random House.

Fisher, S. (Ed.). (1970). *Power and the Black community.* New York: Random House.

Frucht, R. (Ed.). (1971). *Black society in the New World.* New York: Random House.

Killian, L. A. (1968). *The impossible revolution? Black power and the American dream.* New York: Random House.

Killian, L. M. (1970). *White southerners.* New York: Random House.

Kurokawa, M. (Ed.). (1970). *Minority responses: Comparative views of reactions to subordination.* New York: Random House.

Lewis, M. (1978). *The culture of inequality.* New York: Random House.

Lopreato, J. (1970). *Italian Americans.* New York: Random House.

Lyman, S. M. (1974). *Chinese Americans.* New York: Random House.

Moore, W., Jr. (1969). *The vertical ghetto: Everyday life in an urban project.* New York: Random House.

Petersen, W. (1971). *Japanese Americans.* New York: Random House.

Rose, P. I. (1964). *They and we: Racial and ethnic relations in the U.S.* New York: Random House.

Rose, P. I. (1968). *The subject is race.* New York: Oxford University Press.

Rose, P. I. (Ed.). (1969). *The ghetto and beyond.* New York: Random House.

Rose, P. I. (Ed.). (1970a). *Americans from Africa: Vol. 1. Slavery and its aftermath.* New York: Atherton.

Rose, P. I. (Ed.). (1970b). *Americans from Africa: Vol. 2. Old memories, new moods.* New York: Atherton.

Rose, P. I. (Ed.). (1973). *Many peoples, one nation.* New York: Random House.

Rose, P. I. (1977). *Strangers in their midst: Small-town Jews and their neighbors.* Scarsdale, NY: Richwood.

Rose, P. I. (Ed.). (1982). *Nation of nations.* New York: University Press of America. (Original work published by Random House, 1971)

Rose, P. I. (1983). *Mainstream and margins: Jews, Blacks and other Americans.* New Brunswick, NJ: Transaction.

Rose, P. I. (1986). *Working with refugees.* Staten Island, NY: Center for Migration Studies.

Rose, P. I. (1990). *They and we: Racial and ethnic relations in the U.S.* (4th ed.). New York: McGraw-Hill.

Rose, P. I. (1992, April). *Tempest-tost.* Address delivered at the 62nd Annual Meeting of the Eastern Sociological Society, Arlington, VA. Published as Tempest-tost: Exile, ethnicity and the politics of rescue. *Sociological Forum, 8* (1), 5-23 (March, 1993).

Rose, P. I., & Adriaansens, H. (Eds.). (1983). *Over Vreemdeling en Vluchteling* [On strangers and refugees]. Gianotten, Netherlands.

Rose, P. I., Rothman, S., & Wilson, W. (Eds.). (1973). *Through different eyes: Black and white perspectives on American race relations.* New York: Oxford University Press.

Schermerhorn, R. A. (1970). *Comparative ethnic relations.* New York: Random House.

Sklare, M. (1971). *American Jews.* New York: Random House.

Stoddard, E. (1973). *Mexican Americans.* New York: Random House.

Wilson, W. J. (1978). *The declining significance of race: Blacks and changing American institutions.* Chicago: University of Chicago Press.

11

A Francophone African Encounters the Theory and Practice of American Race Relations

PIERRE L. VAN DEN BERGHE

Whether consciously or not, all social science is autobiography. Some of my more positivistically inclined colleagues make it a virtue to conceal that fact. I, on the contrary, have always believed that the quality of social science is enhanced by a self-conscious awareness of the intimate relationship between one's life and one's thoughts, and I have repeatedly tried to make these connections explicit, most recently in my autobiography (van den Berghe, 1989), but also in at least a dozen other works on race relations (e.g., van den Berghe, 1965, 1967a, 1967b, 1970, 1975, 1981). Inevitably, the present account will entail some repetition.

As the title implies, I am looking at American race relations as an outsider, even though I carry a U.S. passport and have spent most of the last 41 of my 58 years in the United States. I first came to the United States in 1950, as a 17-year-old freshman at Stanford. At 17, one has already lived most of one's formative experiences and one bears the indelible stamp of one's native language and culture. The rest of one's life is largely protracted postscript. At best, it only makes the latent manifest.

From the very start, I have felt not only alien to American society, but actively irritated by it. Far from gradually becoming assimilated to it, as the Chicago School model of ethnic relations would have me, I reacted against American society, and much of my intellectual and

233

academic life is a product of that alienation. As the heir to a family from the intellectual bourgeoisie, the recipient of a demanding Jesuit education, and a member of a language group imbued with a sense of self-confident cultural superiority, I have always looked *down* on my host society as anti-intellectual, racist, crassly capitalist and consumerist, educationally backward, politically naive, and culturally philistine. Such ethnocentrism continues to be well received in American academia, in part because anti-Americanism is the anti-Semitism of intellectuals, in part because such values are the ones through which academics seek to dissociate themselves from their ambient society.

In any case, it was clear to me at the outset that the ivory tower was the only tolerable North American habitat for me. Academia has been almost a caste occupation on both sides of my family. As to why I became a social scientist specializing in race and ethnic relations, the reasons are not far to seek: my birth as a colonial in the then Belgian Congo, my mixed Belgian and French parentage, my upbringing in a bilingual country constantly racked by ethnic conflicts, four years of German occupation in Brussels during World War II, and a return to the Congo in late adolescence.

My Congo years (1948-50) were especially formative for me as a participant observer in a colonial system. I might easily have become a run-of-the-mill racist colonial were it not for the fact that my father directed a research institute (IRSAC; Institut pour la Recherche Scientifique en Afrique Centrale) that played host to social and natural scientists of many countries, including many anthropologists, such as Mary Douglas, Jan Vansina, and Jacques Maquet. The last of these, in particular, was my first professional "role model" (a term I detest) when I saw him work among the Tuzi of Rwanda. He helped me see the complexity and richness of an African civilization, different from but not inferior to my own. The fact that my father was a friend of the king of Rwanda also helped, for in them I saw two tall aristocrats associating as equals, in total contempt of racial barriers. Both my parents rejected racism as a vulgar attempt by their social inferiors to justify their undeserved dominance in colonial society. Paradoxically, their disdain for racism as something characteristic of *petits blancs* was a reflection of their elitism, and I clearly recognize the same pedigree in my own antiracism. I basically feel sorry for people who have to resort to racism to prop up their self-image. My social egalitarianism is based on intellectual elitism. Social snobbery of any kind, I have always felt, is the refuge of the mediocre and untalented.

That climate of racial liberalism was, of course, reinforced in IRSAC circles, which were a very atypical intellectual enclave in colonial society. The Jesuits, my teachers, were also racial liberals on the whole (even though they ran race-segregated schools). Parenthetically, my small high school graduating class of nine produced, besides myself, another future American social scientist: the historical demographer Etienne van de Walle. The combination of a colonial setting and a good education was, I think, more than averagely productive of good social science. Indeed, I would argue that rotten societies frequently produce first-rate social science, South Africa being one of the best cases in point.

Coming to Stanford in 1950, it did not take me long to realize that the United States, too, was a profoundly racist society, and exhibited a form of racism that struck me as peculiarly ridiculous: These ignorant, provincial colonists of a barely conquered frontier who could not even place Africa on a map were looking down at their cultural betters, the Chinese and the Japanese! I breezed through to a B.A. in two years. Stanford courses were undemanding after my Belgian Jesuit high school, although I have fond memories of a handful of teachers, notably Richard T. La Piere in sociology and George Spindler in anthropology. I followed up a double major in political science and sociology with an equally undemanding M.A. in sociology in 1953. By then, it had become clear to me that I wanted to be a sociologist-cum-anthropologist, and that race and ethnic relations were going to be a long-lasting interest of mine.

What had not become clear to me was whether the distinction between sociology and anthropology made sense, and which I would label myself. It seemed to me that sociologists tended to study whites in their own societies, whereas anthropologists studied Blacks in their colonies. Thus the racial and colonial nature of the societies that spawned both disciplines created and perpetuated a distinction that did not seem to make much scientific sense. More by luck than by design, I picked the Social Relations Department at Harvard, which made a virtue of overcoming disciplinary boundaries among sociology, anthropology, and psychology, to complete my graduate education. At last, I was at a real university, in the sense that faculty and students formed an intellectual community, as distinguished from a loose congeries of teachers, athletes, socialites, playboys, and GPA busters, as Stanford had seemed to me.

My serious professional education can be said to have begun at Harvard, under the influence principally of Homans, Parsons, Barrington Moore, Stouffer, Mosteller, and, in the field of race relations,

Gordon Allport and Tom Pettigrew. Tom and I began graduate school together, but he got his Ph.D. a couple of years before me because Uncle Sam rudely interrupted my studies and sent me for two years to defend the frontiers of American imperialism on the Rhine. This, it turned out, was where I met my German wife. I also used the opportunity to spend a year at the Sorbonne before returning to Harvard and completing my Ph.D. in 1960. In Paris, I concentrated principally on becoming an Africanist (with Georges Balandier as a major influence), but Roger Bastide and Claude Lévi-Strauss also introduced me to Brazil. By then (1956-1957), it had become clear that the focus of my scholarly career would be an effort to make sense of the entire spectrum of race and ethnic relations, and that I must of necessity be a comparativist with primary concentration in sub-Saharan Africa and Latin America.

The rest of my career was largely a succession of field trips to South Africa (1960-1961, 1989), Mexico (1959, 1977, 1990), Peru (1972-1973), Kenya (1967-1968), Nigeria (1968-1969), and Guatemala (1966, 1987), interspersed with spells of teaching, mostly in Seattle, my port of call for more than a quarter century now. My research program was a succession of anthropological-style case studies of regional race and ethnic relations, alternating between African settings, where race and ethnicity tend to have greater salience than class, and Latin American ones, where the reverse is generally true. The key to understanding the structure of complex, heterogeneous societies, it was becoming clear to me, consisted in untangling the dynamic relationships among class, ethnicity, and race.

After this brief overview of my formative experiences (much more extensive versions of which can be found in my 1989 autobiography), let me now focus on how the U.S. literature on the subject affected the development of my own intellectual trajectory. Perhaps the first and most obvious question to be answered is why so little of my research has been *on* the United States. The answer is quite simple, and twofold. First, I have pursued every opportunity to leave the United States for breaths of intellectual fresh air, and also to broaden my scope as a comparativist. I can think of no overseas stint of any duration (say, three months or more) that did not significantly modify or refine my outlook on some aspect of race or ethnic relations or deepen my contextual understanding of important relationships among key structural variables. Second, I am so irritated by the American obsession with race and exasperated by the self-defeating clumsiness of attempts to overcome race by further institutionalizing it that I would quickly "lose my cool" studying American race relations.

Perhaps one of my deepest resentments about American society is that it does not give me the personal option of ignoring race, that it imposes on me and everyone else a racial label that I regard as irrelevant, that it forces me to be race conscious, and, therefore, that it makes normal, uninhibited relations between "whites" and "Blacks" nearly impossible. Nearly all Americans, whites and Blacks alike, are so steeped in their racial perceptions of themselves and each other that they simply cannot *conceive* of a society without racial consciousness or identity. Paradoxically, they frequently define true *indifference* to race as racism and "insensitivity." Racial consciousness, racial guilt, and racial discrimination are built into the very definition of political liberalism, and true color-blindness is defined as Utopian at best, an insensitive mask for privilege at worst.

The psychopathology of American racial guilt has devastating consequences for intellectual discourse, as well as for social intercourse in general. The fact, for instance, that the interpretation of what one says is always contaminated by the pigmentation of the speaker impedes open discourse, that is, affects the very foundation of what a university is about. The subject of race at an American university is so smothered in intellectual and social taboos, and subject to such an orthodoxy of politically correct thinking sustained by the threat of being labeled a "racist" if white, an "Oreo" if Black, that one can approach it only at the peril of one's integrity, tranquility, or even safety.

However well intentioned this "liberal" discourse of racial guilt and victimology is, it is profoundly demeaning and incapacitating for all concerned. For whites it is paternalistic and ultimately based on the unstated premise that Blacks are categorically inferior and therefore in need of special treatment. For Blacks, it invites the game of manipulating white guilt with the threat of moral blackmail in order to obtain *differential* (not equal) treatment. In essence, this is a modern version of playing Sambo in a system of neopaternalism that hides the old dogma of Black inferiority under a facade of liberalism.

My almost complete lack of research on American race relations was thus driven by both "push" and "pull" factors. On the one hand, I have found American race relations irritating to live with and I have been ideologically alienated by what I see as misguided and self-defeating attempts at changing them. On the other hand, I have been attracted by other societies for a variety of reasons. In the cases of Latin America and West Africa, I found them refreshingly free or nearly free of racism. In the case of South Africa, the attraction was a kind of perverse intellectual curiosity about where extreme, consistent, institutionalized racism would lead. Although I found South Africa even more aversive than the United States as a society (van den Berghe, 1967b), the prospect of leaving the country after the research was over made the discomfort tolerable.

Although I did little research on U.S. race relations, I obviously read a good deal about them, and, what is more, I had to endure them. Thus there is no question that they affected the development of my ideas on the subject. Yet the influence has been overwhelmingly *reactive*. I have looked at the United States from the perspective of an outsider looking in. I have deepened what I fancy to be my understanding of American race relations not by studying them, but by becoming sensitized to them through my extensive exposure to, and study of other societies. Understanding can be achieved only by comparison, and, in the case of a complex, contextualized subject such as race relations, by comparison achieved through successive depth immersion in a variety of as diverse societies as one can find. Knowledge of other societies helped me see the provincialism of much U.S. literature on race and ethnicity, understand the reasons for both the similarities and differences between the United States and other countries, and foresee the futility of certain U.S. social policies.

When I first arrived in the United States, I was struck by the fact that it was a racist society; yet, its racism was quite different from the one I had just experienced in the then Belgian Congo (now Zaire). To my surprise, I discovered in the antebellum South a system of race relations that seemed to have more in common with my African colonial experience than with the contemporary United States. By the time I reached Harvard as a graduate student (1953-1954), my readings had extended to Brazil, the Caribbean, and South Africa, and I also had experienced a summer in Mexico. Among influential early readings on race and ethnicity were Myrdal (1944), Park (1950), Tannenbaum (1947), Cox (1948), Dollard (1937), Herskovits (1928), Drake and Cayton (1945), Davis, Gardner, and Gardner (1941), Doyle (1937), De Kiewiet (1941), Williams (1947), Redfield (1941), and Pierson (1942). From that short list two things are evident: the overwhelming North American dominance of the field and the importance, first, of the "Chicago School" and later of the *American Dilemma* team in shaping the field.

A few tentative conclusions seemed to emerge slowly from these readings and experiences, although in retrospect I may exaggerate the clarity of my thinking at that stage. The American literature on race and ethnicity appeared provincially circumscribed by the twofold American experience of African slavery and European immigration, each dominated by a rather limiting paradigm: the "caste-and-class" scheme in the first case, and Park's four-stage cycle of ethnic relations in the second. The latter was really little more than a refinement of the popular notion of the melting pot. As to the former, coming as it did from an ahistorical, idealist tradition that trivialized class and used a misleading analogy with India, it obscured the relations of power and production at the core of the American "race problem" and put the burden of explanation and resolution on the ideological contradictions of the "American dilemma."

There was yet a third strain of writing on race that was even more clearly off the mark. Dominated by Dollard et al.'s (1939) "frustration and aggression" theory and Adorno, Frenkel-Brunswick, Levinson, and Sanford's (1950) study on the "authoritarian personality," it was built on the quicksand of psychoanalysis and the expediency of wartime ideology. The questions were, What makes fascists tick? How can you find them? How can you cure them of their deep-seated wrongheadedness? Richard La Piere at Stanford, and then Gordon Allport at Harvard, soon convinced me that Freud was a brilliant crackpot with some flashes of insight but no scientific standing. Certainly, the reduction of race relations to individual psychopathology and the therapeutic approach to egalitarianism struck me as being both intellectually ludicrous and politically naive in the extreme. Yet, the tradition of psychologizing race relations is still very much alive in such notions as that people need same-gender, same-race role models, must develop positive racial self-images (as distinguished from being indifferent to race), and can and must be taught to be nice to others through racial sensitivity classes. The key to good race relations, in short, is to maintain racial awareness and sensitivity at fever pitch at all times!

An alternative approach to race and ethnic relations was slowly taking shape in my mind. It contained, albeit in a still relatively inchoate manner, the following elements:

1. Race and ethnic relations are, first and foremost, a form of inequality between social defined groups that occupy different and unequal positions in systems of power and production. To understand race and ethnic relations

one must, therefore, focus the analysis on political and economic inequalities that include, but are not limited to, class.

2. Race and ethnicity are special and different from class, because they are defined through common history and background rather than through mere commonality of economic or political interests, as is class. Therefore, race and ethnicity cannot be reduced to class, as many Marxists would have it. Even though race and ethnicity frequently overlap and interact with class, they are both analytically and empirically distinct.

3. Even though race and ethnicity share analytic components, both being rooted in real or putative common ancestry, and thus more primordial than class, it remains nonetheless useful to distinguish between them for two reasons. Ethnicity is based on cultural markers of membership, such as language, religion, and countless symbols such as clothing, holidays, music, literature, tattooing, and so on, whereas race is marked by heritable phenotypes. Systems of racial stratification are thus intrinsically more *rigid* and more *invidious* than systems of ethnic stratification.

4. Although there can be, and often is, considerable overlap of cultural and phenotypical criteria of group membership, the degree of overlap varies greatly, with a good many "pure" or nearly pure cases at both ends of the continuum. That is, one *can* find cases where racial criteria of membership overwhelm cultural criteria and vice versa. My Mexican experience was especially important in making me realize that, even in societies with a wide spectrum of skin color, there could be a wide degree of social indifference to phenotype, and a total absence of racially defined group boundaries. This was true even though Mexico is highly stratified on the basis of both class and ethnicity. Being "Indian" in Mexico is clearly a cultural category, not a racial one, and there is no social category of Afro-Mexican, although African ancestry is about as common in Mexico as in the United States (Aguirre Beltrán, 1946).

5. Types of race and ethnic relations seemed to polarize into two radically different syndromes that corresponded roughly to predominantly rural, agrarian societies and urban, industrial ones. Although each of these two types, which I labeled "paternalistic" and "competitive," recurred repeatedly in societies different in culture and separated in time and space, the same society could and frequently did evolve from one type to the other as its socioeconomic structure was transformed.

That typology of race relations was probably the most distinctive feature of my early contribution to the field. It first appeared as an identification item on a test in Gordon Allport's graduate course on prejudice and discrimination, to which I had given a presentation in 1958, and it was to become the topic of my dissertation, completed in

1960 under the codirectorship of Parsons and Allport. The dissertation was immediately followed by a two-year stint in South Africa (1960 and 1961), that culminated in the publication of my first two books (1964, 1965), the first a community study of company paternalism in a Natal sugar town, the second a general analysis of apartheid at its Verwoerdian apogee.

My stay in South Africa had an enormous impact on the development of my ideas on race. I deliberately picked South Africa because it represented an extreme case of making race an entrenched principle of group membership and social organization, and I certainly was not disappointed. Apart from satisfying my fascination for studying the mania of racism driven to its ultimate logical consequences, South Africa became for me a useful comparison case for the United States. Clearly both societies shared the facts of being deeply racist and of classifying people into rigid, endogamous categories based on their physical appearance and irrespective of class and cultural characteristics. South Africa pushed the logic of racism further and longer than the United States, but the similarities between, say, the South Africa of the mid-twentieth century and the American South of a few decades earlier were strikingly obvious (Fredrickson, 1981).

The only unshakable convictions South Africa left me with were that *race* as a criterion of social differentiation is always invidious, demeaning, and stigmatizing, and that it is always imposed by a dominant group on other groups it considers categorically inferior. Ethnicity, on the other hand, can be stigmatized also, but not *necessarily* so; furthermore, ethnic affiliation tends to grow from inside the group, as distinguished from being imposed from the outside. At the very least, one can think of numerous examples of noninvidious ethnic distinctions, whereas cases of noninvidious racial distinctions seem to be rare or nonexistent.

If race is intrinsically demeaning, it follows that *any* recognition one gives it both reinforces the category and is harmful to members of subordinate groups. This is especially true of official recognition of racial categories by government agencies, even in such seemingly innocuous exercises as census taking, and even when the stated intent of the policy is benevolent. After all, even apartheid in South Africa was always couched in a benevolent-sounding paternalistic ideology of respect for diversity, encouragement of autonomy, and prevention of intergroup conflict. Any recognition given by the state to racial categories has the effect of reifying, legitimating, and perpetuating these distinctions, and therefore of consolidating the underlying structure of inequality. This is no less true when the stated goal of race-based policies is the elimination of racial discrimination and inequality. There is an irreducible contradiction in seeking to eliminate a distinction one deplores by entrenching its existence in the first place. This later became my principal (as well as principled) objection to race-based affirmative action in the United States. The recognition of race as socially significant is always noxious, even with the best of good intentions.

The other main influence of my South African stay on my perspective on race relations was largely derived from my close association with Leo and Hilda Kuper, and, through them, with the "British School of Anthropology" (which was in fact peopled mostly by foreigners such as Malinowski and colonials such as Max Gluckman, Isaac Schapera, Michael G. Smith, and Meyer Fortes). I was a visiting lecturer in Leo Kuper's sociology department at the University of Natal, but my research among South Africans of Indian descent also put me in close touch with Hilda Kuper. Incidentally, Edna Bonacich (then Miller) was my research assistant and probably owes both her sociological vocation and interest in middleman minorities to her early field experience in my Caneville study (van den Berghe, 1964). I convinced her to get a doctorate in sociology at Harvard, instead of a B.Litt. in English at Oxford, where she was headed.

In South Africa, the colonial situation had given rise to an analytic literature attempting to deal with the conflicts of what came to be labeled "plural societies." It included the works of Hilda and Leo Kuper, Clyde Mitchell, Max Gluckman, and others, and paralleled the Asian research of Furnivall (1948) and Boeke (1953) in Asia. I also recognized that Georges Balandier's (1955) notion of the "colonial situation" and the Mexican anthropologist Gonzalo Aguirre Beltrán's (1957) "region of refuge" had independently arrived at very similar formulations. Soon, the Jamaican anthropologist and Hausa specialist Michael G. Smith was also to become a leading theorist in what became known as the "plural society" or the "conflict pluralist" school, whose "manifesto" was the important edited volume by Leo Kuper and M. G. Smith (1969). During the 1970s, that approach became quite influential in comparative race and ethnic relations, as evidenced by the work of Leo Despres (1967) on Guayana, Philip Mason (1971) on India, Sammy Smooha (1978) on Israel, John Rex (1970) on the United Kingdom, William Wilson (1973, 1978) and Richard Schermerhorn (1970) on the United States, and many others.

My own little 1967 text, *Race and Racism,* a comparative analysis of the United States, South Africa, Mexico, and Brazil, was also clearly in that tradition, and was to become the best-selling and most cited of my 22 books to date (van den Berghe, 1967a). The undergraduate textbook market was obviously ready for a short treatment of comparative race relations, and the ideological climate was ripe to accept my thesis that the United States was a deeply racist society, a "Herrenvolk democracy" as I call it, along with South Africa. However, the book did more than sell well. It became widely influential in a number of important analyses of comparative race and ethnic relations (e.g., Francis, 1976; Mason, 1971; Rex, 1970; Schermerhorn, 1970; Wilson, 1973), and, in a second wave, it became enshrined, excerpted, garbled, and bowdlerized in a spate of that most dismal of literary genres—introductory sociology textbooks. I was also given an opportunity to put my stamp on the field by being invited to contribute entries in various dictionaries and encyclopedias, including the *Britannica* (van den Berghe, 1974).

During the 1960s, my views on race were clearly in the ideological mainstream of liberalism, perhaps even with a dash of radical chic, and this ideological conformity with the academic liberal establishment undoubtedly contributed greatly to the acceptance of my scholarship. All the social sciences are rampant with ideology, and the field of race more than most, to the extent that the scope of rational discourse is quickly approaching the vanishing point.

In 1967-1969, I was on one of my periodic overseas trips, establishing a Sociology Department at the University of Nairobi, Kenya, and developing graduate studies in sociology at the University of Ibadan, Nigeria, as part of the Rockefeller Foundation's African Universities Development Program. The rudest culture shock that U.S. society ever dealt me hit me on my return to Seattle in 1969. In the brief space of my two-year absence, the ideological climate of American race relations and the civil rights movement had abruptly changed from one of slow but steady integration and deracialization to one of Black separatism and emphasis on racial distinctions. The irony was that, although the Black Power movement probably never reflected the views of more than a fourth of Black opinion, it was reacted to with alacrity by the white establishment, partly out of panic at the prospect of massive urban unrest, partly out of expediency.

Suddenly, a new set of policies, generally labeled "affirmative action," were implemented that now made it mandatory to classify people by race and apply different sets of race-based criteria for the distribution of scarce resources (such as schooling and jobs). The federal government suddenly shifted its enormous weight from a policy of stamping out racial discrimination to one of mandating it. Perhaps one of the most glaring examples of this was in the field of school integration. The famous 1954 U.S. Supreme Court decision in *Brown v. Board of Education* was a decision *against* racial school busing. It stated that children must be assigned to their neighborhood schools irrespective of race, and could not be bused away from their neighborhoods on the basis of race. Though initially resisted in the South, the implementation of the decision was fairly successful in the long run, and the South today has a better-integrated school system than the non-South. Starting in the 1970s, however, *Brown* was quite literally turned on its head: It now became mandatory to classify students by race and to bus them *away* from their neighborhood schools, irrespective of parents' wishes. The outcome is well known: massive opposition, mostly but not exclusively by whites; massive exodus of the middle-class, both white and Black, to suburban school districts and private schools; massive academic deterioration of public schools; and a nearly total failure to achieve the stated goal of "racial balance" in schools. The net outcome was an increased polarization of educational opportunities by class: the poor, Black or white, ended up with even worse schools than they started out with because the property tax base of central cities collapsed; the middle and upper classes bought themselves better facilities, either in private schools or through local property taxes in the suburbs.

The tale of woe and failures of race-based affirmative action is a sad one, and, curiously, it has not yet been told with the scholarly care it deserves. It resulted in little more than cosmetic window dressing through co-optation of the Black middle class in a highly visible but token sprinkle of positions in government, business, and the universities, and it left the Black underclass (both northern urban and southern rural) in a worse position than ever. It demeaned Blacks and cast a categorical doubt on their qualifications and achievements because of the presumption that they were the recipients of preferential treatment. It polarized Blacks by class, favoring the few, ignoring the many. It created an angry white backlash of heightened racial prejudice and conflict, as well as reactive white ethnic revival. It divided minority groups against one another, with rising levels of hostility among Blacks, Hispanics, and Asians. It detracted attention from more fundamental class inequalities and from class-based policies. Worst of all, it forced everyone to be race conscious and race biased, on a daily basis. American society was being massively reracialized. Ironically, the few islands of Black success are in fields where Blacks have not been demeaned by affirmative action: sports, entertainment, and the military.

In short, a more dismal failure is hard to conceive of. Sadly, the failure was highly predictable, and I was among the first to sound warnings (van den Berghe, 1972a, 1972b). Equally sadly, the better alternatives were glaringly obvious, either through universalistic welfare-state policies (such as social security and medicare) or through *class*-based affirmative action. School integration, for instance, could have been approached through race-blind parental choice of any school in large metropolitan districts, backed up by college admission policies that would discriminate against private and suburban high school graduates and in favor of central district and rural schools, irrespective of race. If the goal is to achieve greater equality of opportunity, a class-based approach is both broader in scope and more equitable than one based on race or ethnicity. My opposition to race-based affirmative action has always been from the left, not from the right, although I have generally been misinterpreted as being a neoconservative à la Nathan Glazer (1975) or Thomas Sowell (1981a, 1981b, 1984). My actual position is closest to that of William Wilson (1978, 1987), though generally to the left of him. I think his diagnosis of the predicament of the Black underclass is quite accurate, realistic, and free of ideological cant, based as it is on an analysis of fundamental changes in the economic structure. It also has the merit of interpreting individual behavior as rational responses to ambient conditions rather than as sociopathology or the consequence of racism. John Ogbu's (1978) analysis of the educational system has the same strengths.

Perhaps the most glaring failure of social policy on race in the United States (if one assumes that its intent is benevolent—a dangerous but common assumption that must always be critically examined) is a failure of diagnosis. Predicated on a logic of collective guilt, atonement for past wrongdoings, and psychopathology of racism and prejudice, the policy adopts remedies that are certain to aggravate the ailment. It ascribes persistent inequalities to racism and seeks to redress racism through race-specific measures that can only exacerbate racial consciousness. Race-based policies, for all their pseudoliberal appearance, are in fact conservative, if not downright retrogressive, because they detract from a sound structural analysis of relations of power and relations of production that account for the different positions of various class, racial, and ethnic groups in American society.

Such an analysis is further impeded by lumping all "minority groups" together, despite enormous heterogeneity between and within each of them. The fundamental differences between race and ethnicity; between slavery and conquest; between indigenous, territorialized groups and immigrant, dispersed ones; between types of migration; and between occupational niches in the ethnic division of labor are all hopelessly obfuscated in a vague grand design of uniform proportionality of representation of all groups in all places, at all times, in all positions. We are told that we cannot rest until the grand mixer of race and ethnicity produces an undifferentiated blend of 80% vanilla, 20% chocolate. Finally, to obfuscate the issue further, we throw gender into the affirmative action Cuisinart, for a touch of strawberry.

Meanwhile, the fundamental class-based inequalities are not only left untouched, they are accentuated. It is, I think, difficult not to conclude that the conscious *intent* of many proponents of affirmative action is the preservation of the status quo. Indeed, it is difficult to conceive of a policy better designed to produce that effect. The prescription for "change" is, Don't change the system; change the skin pigmentation of a few incumbents (especially of no-win jobs, such as mayoralties of bankrupt, decaying cities).

Needless to say, my position in American society has not been a comfortable one for the past 20 years. My academic specialty in race and ethnic relations, and the content of my courses, made it impossible for me to ignore racial and ethnic issues, especially as they threatened the intellectual integrity of the academic enterprise itself. With a mounting sense of frustration and futility, I have tried to sound warnings, to contribute constructive alternatives, to preserve some semblance of universalism in university life, and to keep myself and my colleagues honest. I think I can say that I failed in every respect, except in my own continued adherence to a principled indifference to race. In order to keep honest, I have had to resign from numerous committees and associations over issues of racial discrimination, and I felt both morally and intellectually obligated to take public stands, with the certainty of being misunderstood at best, vituperatively abused and even physically threatened at worst.

Accusations of racism have never had any power of moral blackmail against me, because I learned long ago to be indifferent to the opinions of those I deem to be dishonest, self-interested, or ignorant—that is, the vast majority of the members of my species. Nevertheless, I continue to be disappointed by the cowardice, dishonesty, and stupidity (frequently in a mixture in which it is hard to assess the proportion of each) of the vast majority of my American colleagues in dealing with issues of race. Race is simply an area where Americans, even professors, have suspended any pretense of rationality. I suppose the most deep-seated reason for this cravenness and irrationality is that ingrained American need for approval and popularity, one of the U.S. cultural values that I have always felt contemptible, and, indeed, incompatible with intellectual honesty.

My position has always been simple and clear: I will not be a party to racial or ethnic discrimination, but almost everything else is negotiable. I never, for instance, made a fetish of "keeping up the standards." I would be quite prepared to live with open university admissions, the elimination of grades, or almost any other radical educational reform to democratize access, provided it does so across the board and irrespective of race. I would even favor a race-blind, universalistic method of favoring the admission of students from disadvantaged high schools by some kind of formula that would rank schools by performance on a standardized test such as the SAT, or by giving greater weight to class standing within school rather than to absolute scores. As to financial aid, it should be strictly a function of economic need. What I find unacceptable and iniquitous are policies based an race or ethnic preference and entitlement. Racial double standards are not only unjust and legitimately resented, they are also demeaning to all concerned because they are based on a racist assumption of categorical inferiority. Of all the "minority" groups, African Americans bear the brunt of that stigma, and affirmative action has been especially disastrous to them, as a few Black intellectuals are belatedly recognizing in public, but as many have long privately admitted.

Not only are racial double standards grounded on a *postulate* of racial inferiority, they ensure, in fact, continued differential *performance* by race, and, therefore, reinforce the prejudice on which they are based. The university where I teach, for instance, accepts roughly the top quartile of high school classes (in terms of GPA and SAT scores) if one is white. Only a small minority of the Black students who are admitted meet these criteria. Supposedly, the double standard applies to four racial minorities ("people of color" in current phraseology), but most Asians meet or exceed the "white" standards, and Hispanics and Native Americans are too few to be visible and are much less actively recruited. In fact, the university ends up with two student populations: a visibly noncompetitive Black one and a highly competitive Euro-American and

Asian American one. The assumption of Black inferiority is constantly reinforced. The same phenomenon would occur if the same principle were applied to other fields. Imagine, for instance, the performance of a basketball team that deliberately recruited five white players against a universalistically selected team. I could think of no better formula to demonstrate the athletic inferiority of whites.

One of the best starting points in a move toward a nonracial society would be for the U.S. Census to stop asking racial questions, because the very asking of the question inevitably reifies the answer. In the last (1990) census, 9.8 million Americans checked the "other" category on race, in effect rejecting the U.S. Census Bureau's taxonomy (*New York Times,* March 11, 1991, p. A12). Among Hispanics and Hawaiians, especially, many individuals resent having racial labels ascribed to them. Yet, the Census Bureau remains adamant about reclassifying the "others," on the assumption that its categories are valid and that the "others" were mistaken or confused. But any attempt to inject some kind of objective and consistent meaning to the Census's racial categories immediately reveals the inanity of the exercise.

The census requires individuals to classify themselves, but then doctors their answers according to pseudoobjective criteria (*New York Times,* March 11, 1991, p. A12). "Blacks" are defined primarily by skin pigmentation, but the very label is glaringly inaccurate, as some "Blacks" are no darker than some "whites." "Whites" are defined primarily by geographical location of their ancestry (provided Africa was not in the picture). "Hispanics" can be of any "race" and are defined by "Spanish surname," even though millions of Latin Americans who speak Spanish have non-Spanish names. And what of Brazilians? Are they "white, non-Hispanic," a category oftentimes classified as "Anglo"? "Anglo," incidentally, excludes Black speakers of English, so, notwithstanding appearances, it is a racial term. "Asian" might seem straightforward enough, until one realizes that it excludes the population of most of the land mass of Asia: Siberia, the Middle East, and Soviet Central Asia. Arabs are supposedly "whites," although many obviously are not, by the common American definition. Had Anwar Sadat, for example, been governor of Virginia rather than president of Egypt, he would clearly have been Black. As for "Native Americans," the term excludes some 98% of those who would seem to qualify. What matters is not place of birth but fractions of "blood," cultural tradition, and/or membership in "tribal" councils. Time to quit? Not if you are a racially obsessed census taker who literally cannot conceive of *not* asking the question.

My alienation from American society and academia, and from sociology as a discipline, has continued to grow since the early 1970s, not only because of the racial issues just discussed, but also because I became increasingly dissatisfied with the cultural relativist and dogmatically environmentalist view of human behavior. It became increasingly obvious to me over the years that behavior, too, evolved by natural selection. Therefore, an understanding of human behavior and culture must, of necessity, incorporate modern evolutionary biology, that is, an interactive view of ourselves as organisms adapting to a complex biotic, physical, and social environment. To ignore our genome is, I feel, a form of intellectual obscurantism that social scientists can no longer afford. As I have expressed my views on the subject repeatedly elsewhere, I need not repeat myself here, except to say that sociobiology helped me realize that my two main substantive areas—kinship and marriage, and race and ethnic relations—were much more closely related than I had ever suspected. My 1979 book, *Human Family Systems,* was an attempt to integrate the anthropology of kinship and marriage to the biology of mating and kin selection. My 1981 book, *The Ethnic Phenomenon,* sought to show that ethnic and race relations shared with family relations the element of common descent, and thus that the primordial basis of ethnocentrism and racism lay in the biology of nepotism. I also tried to demonstrate that the supposedly antithetical theories of primordialism and instrumentalism in ethnic relations were but two sides of the same interactive model: an organism adapting to an environment.

Needless to say, the mere mention of biology elicits ideological knee jerks from the great majority of social scientists. In conjunction with various policy stances I have taken on race, my views on sociobiology helped convince many of my colleagues I was indeed the racist and reactionary they always suspected I was, and spared them the intellectual effort of understanding what I was saying.

Most recently, a new ethnic issue has found me at variance with "politically correct" thinking, namely, that of ethnic studies requirements, and more broadly of "diversity." As one who spent his entire teaching and research career exploring the whole range of human cultural diversity, exposing his students to a variety of non-Western cultures, stressing the educational enrichment of multilingualism and multiculturalism, and pushing most of his graduate students toward doing research outside the United States, I need not be convinced of the desirability of intellectual and cultural diversity. I even agree with the deconstructionists, poststructuralists, semioticians, and sundry varieties of radical subjectivists who state that a text is meaningless without context, and that much of the ideological superstructure of "high culture" is a "hegemonist" legitimation of the status quo. In fact, stripped of their esoteric catchphrases, their pretentious stylistic turgidities, and their nihilistic, solipsistic narcissism, the radical neosubjectivists do nothing but reinvent arguments that are at least a century old.

What is new, however, is the political convergence of campus-based affirmative action with this intellectual "deconstruction" to assail the fundamental structure of the American university (D'Souza, 1991). My reaction is the same as I had toward the "New Left" of the 1960s: I agree with much of the indictment of the university as subservient to conservative political and economic interests, corrupted by commercialized athletics, and run by spineless, opportunistic administrators, but the remedies proposed are far worse than the disease. For all its failings, the American university remains an oasis of relative freedom compared with the rest of the society. Now that freedom is being massively assaulted by anti-intellectuals of the self-styled Left in the name of good race, ethnic, and gender relations. Not only are there numerous attempts to curtail free expression on such issues as race, gender, and the role of biology in human behavior, but the new politically correct orthodoxy constitutes nothing less than a frontal attack on the central value of the university, namely, *universalism.*

This supposed drive for "diversity" is, in fact, the epitome of provincialism, particularism, psychologistic subjectivism, and anti-intellectualism. It is conducted in a climate of moral blackmail and manipulation of liberal academics' vague gropings for atonement of alleged collective guilt. In the characteristically American politics of compromise, nonsense is seldom rejected but merely watered down. Of course, once nonsense is institutionalized, it becomes self-perpetuating, because a constituency instantly develops in its defense.

The assault against universalism was conducted on two main fronts: gender and race/ethnicity. Let me emphasize here the latter, which I like to call Operation Academic Apartheid. It began with the academic ghettoization of ethnic and women's studies into separate (and automatically stigmatized) nondepartmental units, instead of "mainstreaming" these topics and perspectives into the half dozen or more existing departments that already addressed them (although often inadequately). Once these stigmatized units were established and staffed through particularistic race- and gender-based appointments of often dubious competence, the next phase of the operation was to legitimate and entrench these units through the creation of tenured positions and the granting of departmental status. We are now entering the third wave of Operation Academic Apartheid: the imposition of ethnic studies requirements on all students. Left to themselves, most students of all "racial" groups had the good sense to stay away in droves from courses of dubious intellectual value and near-zero marketability. So compulsion has to be resorted to, in the name of fostering "sensitivity" and "diversity."

It can be safely predicted that, for a variety of reasons, the move toward ethnic studies requirements will not only fail in its stated objectives, but even boomerang:

1. The premise that better race relations can be achieved in the classroom is naive at best, especially when the curriculum aims at heightening racial consciousness and stressing racial differences.

2. The parochialism of American ethnic studies is the very antithesis of broadening, liberating diversity, and the epitome of paralyzing fragmentation. The field is narrowly focused on the United States; it is internally balkanized by race and ethnicity; it wallows in the uniqueness of each group's experience; it has failed to develop any kind of intellectual paradigm beyond reiterated accusations of "institutional racism" and a hagiography of victimization; it is manipulated by student and community activists for narrow political ends totally divorced from intellectual issues; its pedagogical philosophy stresses "role modeling" based on gender, race, and ethnicity and the nontransferability of experiences across ethnic, racial or gender lines.

3. Being forced to take courses, many of dubious quality and blatant ideology, is more likely to make students resentful of what they might perceive as an irrelevant waste of time or an obnoxious attempt at indoctrination than to make them aware and tolerant of diversity.

Will the United States ever overcome its obsession with race? When I started my career, I hoped it would, certainly by the turn of the millennium. I knew then that it was not only possible for societies to become deracialized, but that it could happen quite fast, in the course of a few years. Latin American countries underwent a secular decline in the significance of race that started in the eighteenth century. In the postcolonial Africa of the 1960s and 1970s, the same happened even more rapidly, as political realities changed. Even South Africa now stands a better chance of deracializing itself faster than the United States, I believe. The American racial virus is so potent that it even infected the colonial dependencies to which the American empire extended: Hawaii, Puerto Rico, and Panama are good examples. America is the kind of society where one is simply not *allowed* to think in nonracial terms. Try as one may to escape, one's nose is always rubbed into race. The supreme irony is that nonracialism is now defined as racism, whereas, conversely, racism is restyled as liberalism. It is, therefore, with a feeling of deep frustration and pessimism that I come near the end of a career devoted in large part to an attempt to illustrate and demonstrate the folly of paying attention to race.

I have also lost any faith in the power of reason to sway human behavior. I long clung to a residual belief that perhaps my colleagues at the university were a little less irrational than the hoi polloi beyond the ivy walls. That too was a delusion. In fact, if anything, the untrained mind probably does better than the professionally deformed one. For example, my fellow sociologists daily invoke the race- or gender-based role-model theory of learning. Blacks are best taught by Blacks, women by women, and so on. When I tested the theory on my 15-year-old son, he immediately asked the rhetorical question: "Oh, this means first graders should be taught by midgets?" Good for him! I may despair as a sociologist, but not yet as a parent.

References

Adorno, T. W., Frenkel-Brunswick, E., Levinson, D. J., & Sanford, R. N. (1950). *The authoritarian personality*. New York: Harper Brothers.

Aguirre BeltrÁn, G. (1946). *La Población Negra de México, 1519-1810*. Mexico City: D. F. Ediciones Fuente Cultural.

Aguirre BeltrÁn, G. (1957). *El Proceso de Aculturacion*. Mexico City: D. F. Universidad Nacional Autonoma de México.

Balandier, G. (1955). *Sociologie Actuelle de l'Afrique Noire*. Paris: Presses Universitaires de France.

Boeke, J. H. (1953). *Economics and economic policy of dual societies*. New York: Institute of Pacific Relations.

Cox, O. C. (1948). *Caste, class and race*. Garden City, NY: Doubleday.

Davis, A. W., Gardner, B. B., & Gardner, M. R. (1941). *Deep South: A social anthropological study of caste and class*. Chicago: University of Chicago Press.

De Kiewiet, C. W. (1941). *A history of South Africa, social and economic*. Oxford: Clarendon.

Despres, L. (1967). *Cultural pluralism and nationalist politics in British Guiana*. Chicago: Rand McNally.

Dollard, J. (1937). *Caste and class in a southern town.* New Haven, CT: Yale University Press.

Dollard, J., et al. (1939). *Frustration and aggression.* New Haven, CT: Yale University Press.

Doyle, B. W. (1937). *The etiquette of race relations in the South.* Chicago: University of Chicago Press.

Drake, S. C., & Cayton, H. (1945). *Black metropolis; A study of Negro life in a northern city.* New York: Harcourt, Brace.

D'Souza, D. (1991, March). Illiberal education. *Atlantic Monthly,* pp. 52-79.

Francis, E. K. (1976). *Interethnic relations.* New York: Elsevier.

Fredrickson, G. M. (1981). *White supremacy.* Oxford: Oxford University Press.

Furnivall, J. S. (1948). *Colonial policy and practice.* London: Cambridge University Press.

Glazer, N. (1975). *Affirmative discrimination.* New York: Basic Books.

Herskovits, M. J. (1928). *The American Negro.* New York: Alfred A. Knopf.

Kuper, L., & Smith, M. G. (Eds.). (1965). *Pluralism in Africa.* Berkeley: University of California Press.

Mason, P. (1971). *Patterns of dominance.* London: Oxford University Press.

Myrdal, G., with Sterner, R., & Rose, A. (1944). *An American dilemma: The Negro problem and modern democracy.* New York: Harper & Row.

Ogbu, J. (1978). *Minority education and caste.* New York: Academic Press.

Park, R. E. (1950). *Race and culture.* Glencoe, IL: Free Press.

Pierson, D. (1942). *Negroes in Brazil.* Chicago: University of Chicago Press.

Redfield, R. (1941). *Tepoztlán: A Mexican village.* Chicago: University of Chicago Press.

Rex, J. (1970). *Race relations in sociological theory.* New York: Schocken.

Schermerhorn, R. A. (1970). *Comparative ethnic relations.* New York: Random House.

Smooha, S. (1978). *Israel: Pluralism and conflict.* London: Routledge & Kegan Paul.

Sowell, T. (1981a). *Ethnic America: A history.* New York: Basic Books.

Sowell, T. (1981b). *Markets and minorities.* New York: Basic Books.

Sowell, T. (1984). *Civil rights: Rhetoric or reality?* New York: William Morrow.

Tannenbaum, F. (1947). *Slave and citizen: The Negro in the Americas.* New York: Alfred A. Knopf.

van den Berghe, P. L. (1964). *Caneville: The social structure of a South African town.* Middletown, CT: Wesleyan University Press.

van den Berghe, P. L. (1965). *South Africa: A study in conflict.* Middletown, CT: Wesleyan University Press.

van den Berghe, P. L. (1967a). *Race and racism: A comparative perspective.* New York: John Wiley.

van den Berghe, P. L. (1967b). Research in South Africa. In G. Sjoberg (Ed.), *Politics, ethics and social research.* Cambridge, MA: Schenkman.

van den Berghe, P. L. (1970). *Race and ethnicity: Essays in comparative sociology.* New York: Basic Books.

van den Berghe, P. L. (1972a, October). Academic apartheid. *Worldview,* pp. 25-29.

van den Berghe, P. L. (1972b). Neo-racism in America. *Transition, 41,* 15-18.

van den Berghe, P. L. (1974). Racism. In *Encyclopaedia Britannica* (Vol. 15, pp. 360-366). Chicago: Encyclopaedia Britannica, Inc.

van den Berghe, P. L. (Ed.). (1975). *Race and ethnicity in Africa*. Nairobi: East African Publishing House.

van den Berghe, P. L. (1979). *Human family systems: An evolutionary view*. Prospect Heights, IL: Waveland.

van den Berghe, P. L. (1981). *The ethnic phenomenon*. New York: Elsevier.

van den Berghe, P. L. (1989). *Stranger in their midst*. Niwot: University Press of Colorado.

Williams, R. M. (1947). *The reduction of intergroup tension*. New York: Social Science Research Council.

Wilson, W. J. (1973). *Power, racism and privilege*. New York: Macmillan.

Wilson, W. J. (1978). *The declining significance of race: Blacks and changing American institutions*. Chicago: University of Chicago Press.

Wilson, W. J. (1987). *The truly disadvantaged: The inner city, the underclass and public policy*. Chicago: University of Chicago Press.

12

Race Stratification and the Culture of Legitimation

FRANK R. WESTIE

We become what we do, and we are, at any point as we live our biographies, the sum total of what we've done. If in your formative years you worked as a carnival shill, you'll find it easy to adjust to a related field—say, selling junk bonds to widows in California. If, on the other hand, you're the son or daughter of a college professor and you enjoyed a peaceful academic journey, sailing smoothly from freshman to Ph.D., your voyage interrupted only by summers in Vermont, you'll hardly notice the difference when you assume your first duties as an assistant professor at some lucky university. You'll see long summer idylls as your due, and you won't have the vaguest idea about how to go about changing your oil. You may even take pride in your "learned disabilities," as Veblen called them, as you enjoy the leisure of the theory class. You will have become what you do almost before you started. This, I suppose, describes the careers of some of our colleagues, but for most of us it is but a dream that might have been had we chosen the right parents.

But there's always the phenomenon of reaction-formation. Many sociologists chose their field because it seemed at the time to be the opposite of what their parents hoped for them: The issue of the loins of the Methodist minister becomes a sociologist, and if that weren't enough, perhaps a Unitarian, and maybe even an atheist. And the reverend to his dying day wonders, "Where did I go wrong?"

When I decided to become a sociologist it wasn't because it was the opposite of what my parents hoped for me, but it was indeed the opposite of what I had been doing. Before I became a sociologist I was in the business of killing people. As a B-17 bomber pilot in Europe in World War II, I helped destroy a country and its population. I say this with great sadness and a burden of guilt that will remain with me until the day I die. After the war I was sick over what I'd done, and yet I knew then, even as I know now, that I'd have again volunteered to do it if I knew there was abroad a racist society bent on foisting its model on the rest of the world. Moral choices are rarely easy, or clean.

I came from a family of pacifists, albeit pragmatic pacifists. My father, as both he and my mother stated publicly—quietly and without apology—"dodged the draft" (their words) in World War I by joining the Michigan National Guard. And then, after the war, when their offspring appeared, they taught them that war, all war, was the most stupid and grossly immoral of all human activities. They came from a line of aberrant Christians who took seriously the Sermon on the Mount. They sent their children to Sunday school and even went to church themselves, but when the members of our local congregation, in Dearborn, Michigan, began going for one another's jugulars over minor organizational matters, they said to hell with all that and quit the whole business, as indeed their pacifism required.

At the outbreak of World War II in Europe, before America's involvement, my brother and I, true to our parents' teaching, swore to each other that we'd go to jail before we'd bear arms. (I was an apprentice toolmaker at the time, going to Wayne University on the side, or maybe it was the other way around.) I was 18 at the time, my brother 20. By the time the United States entered the war, two years later, I had learned what Hitler and the Nazis were about. To me the destruction of whole populations in the name of race was the ultimate horror, to be stopped at any cost. And yet I had deeply internalized the precept that war was the greatest immorality. I wrestled with my dilemma day and night for several months. I finally decided that the greater good lay with stopping the Nazis. In putting my dilemma to rest once and for all, I volunteered to become a military pilot. In the same spirit, my brother joined the army. Incidentally, as a toolmaker at the Lincoln Motor Company in Detroit (which was producing army trucks), I had a permanent deferment from the draft. In looking back, I see my motives in enlisting as having been purely ideological, yet I wonder if I wasn't more than a little influenced by a popular song of the time that began, "Off we go, into the wild blue yonder."

I came very close to perishing before I ever published. I flew 35 missions—a full tour—as a B-17 bomber pilot in the American Eighth Air Force in Europe. There were two certainties that influenced my life at the time and ever after: I was certain, like almost all my bomber-flying colleagues in the Eighth Air Force, that I was going to die, and soon. We were told upon arrival at our airbase in England, "You're dead. Get used to the idea and do your job." I got used to the idea quickly: I came back from my first mission with more than 300 holes in my plane. This acceptance of the very temporariness of life affected my worldview permanently, most importantly engendering the view that, should I by some miracle survive, I should do something socially useful with my life.

The other certainty: I knew people were dying with each load of bombs I dropped on German cities. Even though I knew then, or thought I knew, that all of our targets were military targets, I also knew you couldn't bomb, say, the Tempelhof Airdrome or the Reichstag in the middle of Berlin—which I in fact did—without hitting surrounding neighborhoods. I was constantly aware of the consequences of what I was doing, but I retained a semblance of sanity by continually remind-ing myself of what Hitler was doing. But there are limits to rationaliza-tion and dissonance reduction.

The final dissonance came when I learned later, after the war, that I had in fact participated in the worst atrocity in American military history. On February 15, 1945, I flew a B-17 to Dresden, ancient Dresden in the far eastern reaches of Germany, Dresden teeming with tens of thousands of civilian refugees fleeing from the Russian armies to the east. We dropped our bombs on radar through a solid undercast, without seeing the holocaust we were fueling with incendiary bombs. (We'd been told in briefing we were bombing a railroad marshaling yard.) I learned later, after the war, that the American Eighth Air Force, along with the British Royal Air Force, had in fact decimated Dresden's civilian population along with its massed refugees, not once but several times over, creating a firestorm that resulted in casualties that exceeded even Hiroshima. When I learned this, after the war, I wanted to die. For more than 40 years I never told anyone I was one of the Dresden pilots. Perhaps it's about time now.

As regards my pacifist brother, Charles Westie: He landed on Omaha beach in the invasion of the continent. Some weeks later he lost one of his legs to a strafing Messerschmidt somewhere along a hedgerow on the road to St. Lo in France. After a while, both of us became sociologists. Sociology seemed the opposite of what we had been doing.

It seemed to me that sociology offered the greatest hope for reconciliation of disparate societies with one another and of antagonistic racial and cultural peoples within those societies. Strangely, I saw in sociology, of all places, the possibility of reconciliation with myself. I hoped, like Tennyson, "that mind and soul according well, may make one music as before."

Writers, by which I mean gifted writers such as Flaubert, Bellow, and Vonnegut, see ordinary events in extraordinary ways.[1] And so it is also with sociologists, by which I mean gifted, unusually literate (and literary) sociologists such as Robert Merton, David Riesman, Peter Berger, Andrew Greeley, and Kurt Wolff. I had the rare privilege of studying with Kurt Wolff, America's premier sociologist of knowledge. (I had been accepted for graduate school at Chicago and Harvard, but finally opted for Ohio State because Kurt Wolff was there.)

After the war, during my first semester as a graduate student at Ohio State University, Kurt Wolff invited me to join his seminar in the sociology of knowledge. The seminar was perpetual, a floating crap game of sorts, meeting regularly throughout my graduate career in a variety of places, including Hennick's, a campus bar where a permanent sign on a huge round table proclaimed, "Reserved for Sociology Seminar."

It is fair to say that no one who was invited to participate in Kurt Wolff's perpetual seminar ever shed its influence. Among the participants were Donald T. Campbell, the psychologist who eventually became president of the American Psychological Association; John Hemphill, distinguished psychologist at Princeton; David Bakan, the philosopher; Jeanne Chall, well-known educator at Harvard; John Bennett, the anthropologist; and, among other sociologists, Melvin Seeman and his late, brilliant colleague at UCLA, Richard T. Morris.

Kurt Wolff had come to the United States from Germany by way of Florence, Italy, where he had been a student after escaping Hitler's Germany. He had studied with Karl Mannheim at Frankfurt. Mannheim's *Ideology and Utopia* (1955) and *Man and Society in an Age of Reconstruction* (1967) remain two of the most influential books I ever read in sociology, and Mannheim himself, as interpreted by Kurt Wolff, remains an even stronger influence for me. In my more grandiose moments I consider myself an intellectual son of Kurt Wolff, and a grandson of Karl Mannheim.

The sociology of knowledge may be conceived in a variety of ways, but in retrospect I see it, in one of its aspects, as controlled, cognitive cynicism. I say *controlled* and *cognitive* to contrast it with outraged ideological sociology, and *cynicism* because to the sociologist of knowledge the sacred and the profane, the ethereal and the mundane, and the murderous and the humane are alike social constructions of reality, agreements entered into by social entities, now or in the distant, often indiscernible, past.

And so it was that I came to see every aspect of race relations as socially agreed-upon constructions of reality, including stereotypes, prejudices, normative orders prescribing appropriate relations, laws, definitions of who fits into which race, structured interaction patterns as we perceive them, and one group's "knowledge" of another. There's nothing new in this to any modestly sophisticated student of sociology today, but it was new to me then, and once I internalized this perspective I came to see that whatever humans construct in the way of definitions of race and race relations, whether in their minds or in their actions, they are neither carved in stone nor printed in the DNA, and are thus susceptible to deconstruction and reconstruction. Of course this is what sociology, more generally conceived, is all about.

Something else happened in that seminar: Because we spent so much time analyzing intellectual products as social constructions, we developed a healthy skepticism about our own intellectual products. I remain very skeptical about my own work. May I add, gratuitously perhaps, that 20 years later this skepticism led me to do an empirical study of the illusions of sociologists, demonstrating that we sociologists have a capacity for self-deception worthy of, say, actors who confuse their stage personas with reality (Westie, 1972).

If it's true that before the emergence of mass society the masses held the elites in awe, then we graduate students in sociology immediately after World War II were a pre-mass society lot. We held the elites in our field in unabashed awe. I have in mind such giants as Sorokin, Parsons, Merton, and Lundberg. When I was in the military service I was once within 20 or 30 feet of the *Presence* of General George C. Marshall, the commander in chief of all of the armed forces at the time. No parish priest who suddenly found himself in the presence of the pope could have been more awestruck than I was at the time. A couple of years later, when I was a graduate student, I don't think I would have been any less awestruck to have found myself in the presence of Sorokin. All of which has something to do with my initial faculty appointment at Indiana University.

In 1949, my mentor, Kurt Wolff, invited me and a couple of other graduate students to accompany him to the meetings of the Central States Anthropological Association at Indiana University in Bloomington. During a break in the meetings I sat on a limestone bench with Kurt Wolff in front of the Student Union building where the meetings were held. It was a beautiful April day. The redbuds and dogwood were in bloom in the heavily forested central campus of Indiana University. Gothic limestone buildings, ivy covered, most of them well over 100 years old, circled the forest and were themselves encircled. I had never seen a more beautiful campus. I remarked to Wolff that this was exactly the sort of setting I had imagined myself teaching in—in my wildest dreams, of course. (I was never fully convinced I would achieve the Ph.D. Most graduate students in those days never did.) Wolff said, "Why don't you call on Edwin Sutherland and tell him you'd like to teach here?" My reaction was something like, "What? *The* Edwin Sutherland, the famous criminologist, the recent president of the American Sociological Association?"

Kurt Wolff talked me into it. I found a map of the campus and walked through the woods along a moss-covered brick lane to the social science building at the far edge of the forest. When I knocked at Professor Sutherland's door I hoped he wasn't in. He was. In fact, he was in conference with Professor John Henry Mueller, a professor of sociology and a musicologist of some note. I told them of my interest in teaching at Indiana. Quite coincidentally, I had recently read Sutherland's book on criminology and, in retrospect incredibly, I had only weeks before read Mueller's esoteric, recently released monograph on the history of changing tastes in classical music in America. (I had an undergraduate degree in music and, strangely, physics.) We had a good discussion of musical tastes in changing social systems—essentially an issue in the sociology of knowledge, which, as I've indicated, was one of my primary interests. After a time, Sutherland called in Professor Alfred Lindesmith, who happened to be in his office. Again, by coincidence, I had recently read Lindesmith's book on opiate addiction. We had a good discussion on "analytical induction," a methodological approach introduced in Lindesmith's book. The upshot: I couldn't have been better prepared for the meeting had I planned it. After a rather animated, highly enjoyable discussion of the issues raised in the books I just happened to have read, Professor Sutherland asked me if I would step out into the hall while he and his colleagues conferred. Some 15 or 20 minutes later, Sutherland came out and offered me an instructorship, subject to approval of his faculty. In those days everyone started out as an instructor. In fact, I was an instructor for four or five years before I was promoted to the exalted rank of assistant professor.

This was the first and only job interview I ever had in my career, and it really wasn't a job interview, but an academic discussion. I never filled out a job application, ever. I never, as a candidate anywhere, made a supplicant's presentation to a gathered faculty. I never suffered the indignity of those serial, candidate-grilling interviews with individual faculty members of varying competence and incompetence, nor did I ever, as a candidate, meet with adversarial deans of varying degrees of incompetence.

I loved Indiana University, and there I remained, despite many job inquiries and concrete offers, some from very distinguished universities. I never played a job offer. I couldn't bring myself to pretend I was genuinely interested in joining another university's faculty when I knew there was no way I was going to leave Indiana University. What other university could offer opera every Friday and Saturday night, with Metropolitan Opera stars and their students, performing in a grand opera house with massive moving stages and tiers of balconies that rivaled the finest opera theaters in Europe? And six symphony orchestras, every one of them good. And free recitals and concerts by such faculty luminaries as Janos Starker, William Primrose, Eileen Farrell, Charles Kullman, the Berkshire Quartet, and countless other world-famous musicians on the faculty. It goes without saying that my sociological career was greatly compromised by the Indiana University School of Music, by far the largest school of music in the world. But I have no regrets, even though it sometimes seemed I was paid in music more than money.

I retired from Indiana in 1983, some nine years before I would have been forced out, and moved to Tempe, Arizona, where, as an adjunct professor, albeit sporadically, I've enjoyed the colleagueship of a friendly group of fine sociologists at Arizona State University. I say sporadically because my wife and I spend all except the winter months at our summer home on a lake in northern Michigan, where I write fiction—and an occasional sociological piece. I recently finished a huge novel—1,200 pages—which has been received well by a distinguished literary agency in New York. The first agent who read the novel wrote back, "Tolstoi you are not. Cut, cut, cut!" And so I cut, mourning each paragraph as it fell into the wastebasket. I'm now collaborating on a screenplay with a highly successful Hollywood screenwriter (who invited me to join him on this project after reading the novel). The chances that something will come out of all of this may or may not be significantly different from zero.

Back to sociology: Not too long after arriving at Indiana University as a neophyte instructor, I made the mistake of asking two of my new colleagues, Alfred Lindesmith and Anselm Strauss, to read and comment on a paper I'd written from my dissertation on status differentials and race attitudes. I couldn't have picked two people more unfriendly to the ideas expressed in my paper. Attitudes! Lindesmith and Strauss, distinguished symbolic interactionists and both of them former students and colleagues of Herbert Blumer at Chicago, were just as unfriendly toward attitude research as Blumer. (Years later, I heard Blumer talk on the subject. He seemed to take the very idea of attitude research as a personal affront.) After I got Lindesmith's and Strauss's reactions to my paper I wanted to burn both the article and the dissertation and go back to work in one of Henry Ford's factories, where I started out in my working life.

But then my wife, Margaret, fellow sufferer in graduate school as well as psychological counselor to her uncertain husband, pointed out that even though the paper—and, by implication, the dissertation—was something of a disaster, it did in fact introduce a new method for the measurement of attitudes. Why not try it out on one of my statistically minded colleagues who might appreciate the methodological contribution? And so, with much trepidation, I gave the paper to Karl Schuessler, Complete Statistician and Methodologist, for his comments. Another disastrous choice. Karl, like Lindesmith, a gentle soul, tried to soft-pedal his criticisms, but I could see that, clearly, I had violated every methodological canon in the methodological bible of the time, to wit, Lundberg's *Social Research*. I wanted to die. Not in the figure of speech sense—I mean really.

Finally, Margaret, my erstwhile fellow graduate student, now my counselor and copopulator of the planet, insisted the time had come to lay it on the line, to find out once and for all if I'd chosen the right occupation. Send "the thing"—we'd both learned to hate the article by now—off to the *American Sociological Review*. Let the chips fall where they may. And so, after rewriting the apologetic cover letter countless times, I took the thing to the post office. After I dropped it into the slot

I wanted to get it back. Margaret was with me. She wouldn't let me appeal to the post office people.

As luck would have it—bad luck, I thought at the time—the editor of the *American Sociological Review* was one George Lundberg, *the* George Lundberg, the distinguished leader and champion of scientific sociology. (Graduate students at the time, I among them, argued endlessly the merits of Lundbergian versus Parsonian sociology.) *The* George Lundberg, the prophet who satteth, rightfully, I thought, on the right hand of Auguste Comte. I *really* wanted to take that article back from the post office.

Lundberg must have been a well-organized deity. He turned the article around, by my calculation, in nine days and four and a half hours. I remember it well because I didn't eat or sleep during that time. At last the fearfully awaited envelope arrived, the envelope with the terrifying return address: George Lundberg, Editor, *The American Sociological Review*. I brought it home unopened.

Margaret opened the letter while I contemplated the merits of carbon monoxide versus a one-way swim up the length of Lake Michigan. The gist of Lundberg's response: He and his colleagues at the University of Washington thought the article a major substantive contribution and a model of scientific procedure. They regarded the "summated differentials method" I had developed for measuring attitudes as a significant invention. Finally, he and his colleagues at Washington were prepared to offer me an associate professorship in their department.

Me, a $3,200-a-year instructor, now an Associate Professor at one of the best departments in the country! I've always believed that life holds wonderful surprises for us, and as I look back this surprise ranks on the wonder scale with landing my B-17 safely on the runway after my last required mission over Germany; with the first kiss of the woman who was to become my wife; with my first hearing, as an adolescent, of the *Liebestod* from *Tristan und Isolde*. There was dancing in the street in front of our flat-roofed, two-bedroom home. We borrowed $3 from the rich professor across the street and went out and had two drinks apiece.

Although I finally decided not to accept George Lundberg's offer, I'll always be thankful for his vote of confidence, and the subsequent offers of a position by Robert E. L. Faris, Lundberg's distinguished successor in title at Washington. Graduate school was in those days, like now, a trial by ordeal in which the first casualty was, typically, the student's confidence. My instructorship at Indiana was a mere continuation of graduate school. As I look back I find astounding the indignities we suffered, and at such miserable salaries. Even correcting our salaries for inflation, most of us instructors with children would have qualified for food stamps today.

The moral of this story: Never, never let your department colleagues have the final say on the quality of anything you create. Just as Immanuel Kant observed that there is that about the worst tragedy that may befall your dearest friend that is not totally displeasing, so also there is that about your greatest success that is less than fully pleasing to your most beloved colleagues.

The Culture of Legitimation

In most of my studies of race relations I have not been concerned with structural phenomena but rather with what I've chosen to call *the culture of legitimation,* that is, the socially shared *norms* (prescriptions for discrimination), shared *attitudes* (prejudices), and shared *cognitions* (myths and stereotypes) that together form a cultural system that serves to justify race stratification. Given this emphasis, I've decided to resurrect for reinterpretation here selected findings from three research projects I pursued early in my career and that speak more or less directly to these issues. The findings haven't changed, but with all that has happened in the field and in the world of race relations since these studies were done, my perceptions of what the findings mean have changed considerably. The first two studies demonstrate the normative nature of prejudice and discrimination. The last one deals with the ways in which the prejudiced society "explains itself."

A Study of the
Development of Prejudice in Children

Table 12.1 presents findings—never published before—from a study I did (with Marcia Segal) in Indianapolis in the 1960s. We asked children, from first grade through college, "If you could choose which group you'd like to be from, which would be your first choice, your second choice . . . ?" We asked the youngest children the same question, but with variations and repetitions, and of course in simpler form, such as, "Which would you most like to be?"

Table 12.1 demonstrates how children, as they get older, come to think like adults in their racial and ethnic preferences. We assumed that college juniors and seniors qualify as adults, and that their rankings would pretty much match the way adults in general would rank the groups. Therefore, we ran a rank-order correlation between the rankings of each grade level and the rankings of college juniors and seniors as we attempted to establish the pattern whereby children came to think like adults. As is readily apparent, the correlations between the hierarchies of grade school children and adults are modest, but by high school the correlations approach unity, with the biggest jump toward adulthood occurring between junior high school and high school.

By way of interpretation, Table 12.1 speaks to the degree to which racial and ethnic preferences, and of course race prejudice, are cultural-normative phenomena—as opposed to purely psychological or economic—transmitted from one generation to another through socialization. For example, the youngest children had not yet learned how to rank Mexicans in an adult fashion, which is to say they hadn't yet been socialized to adult expectations, or, if you like, adult prejudices. Grade school children thought it would be pretty nice to be Mexican. In their open-ended oral responses they spoke of the colorful costumes of Mexicans, Mexican foods, and adventurous Mexicans in cowboy movies, all of which they liked. They hadn't yet been exposed to adult stereotypes and preferences. Their open minds hadn't quite achieved adult closure.

But: Although the youngest children hadn't been socialized to adult preferences regarding most groups, they already ranked "Negroes" much as the adult population ranked this group. It would seem that socialization to adult preferences regarding America's most significant minority, Blacks, comes early indeed. Note please that the term *Negro* was used originally in all of the studies discussed herein, this in keeping with accepted usage in sociology as well as in polite company at the time. In the present essay I've changed all earlier references to *Negroes* to *Blacks* wherever I could do so without doing violence to the findings or the historical context. I must say, however, that as a one-time teacher of cultural anthropology I am most pleased with the recent emergence, in the scientific literature as well as the mass media, of the appellation *African American.*

This study was done in the 1960s. It would be interesting to see how children would order their preferences in the 1990s. Much has happened in the way of structural and cultural change in the past 25 years. My guess is that majority children who have been exposed to Blacks in higher-ranking business or professional positions, either personally or

Table 12.1 Rank Ordering by 451 In-School Respondents of Racial and Ethnic Groupings, by Grade, mid-1960s

Rank Order	Grade						College Students	
	1-2	3-4	5-6	7-8	9-10	11-12	13-14	15-16
1	Mexican	English	English	English	English	English	English	English
2	English	Mexican	Mexican	Mexican	Irish	Irish	Irish	Irish
3	Italian	Irish	Irish	Mexican	Italian	Italian	Italian	Italian
4	Irish	Italian	Italian	Italian	Mexican	Polish	Polish	Polish
5	Jewish	Jewish	Jewish	Jewish	Polish	Japanese	Jewish	Jewish
6	Japanese	Polish	Japanese	Polish	Japanese	Mexican	Russian	Japanese
7	Polish	Japanese	Polish	Negro	Jewish	Jewish	Japanese	Russian
8	Russian	Russian	Negro	Japanese	Russian	Russian	Mexican	Mexican
9	Negro	Negro	Russian	Russian	Negro	Negro	Negro	Negro
Rho[a]	.47	.63	.57	.65	.82	.92	.98	—

a. Rank-order correlations between the ordering by each grade level and the ordering by college juniors and seniors.

through the mass media, would rank Blacks higher than heretofore. One would expect also that those majority children who have come to know, through television, the likes of Bill Cosby, Michael Jackson, Diahann Carroll, Michael Jordan, Isiah Thomas, and General Colin Powell, among a host of other Black celebrities, would rank Blacks higher than their age peers did 20 or 30 years ago. I herewith invite any budding sociologist seeking a useful dissertation project to repeat this study.[2]

Categorical Thinking
and Social Distance Differentials

I pursued two studies of social distance that further demonstrate (a) the normative nature of prejudice and discrimination, and (b) the fact that prejudice toward racial out-groups varies with the socioeconomic status of both the respondent and the status of the out-group person to whom he or she responds. The first of these studies examined the degrees of social distance preferred by whites in relation to Blacks (Westie, 1952). The second study examined the degrees of distance preferred by Blacks in relation to whites (Westie & Howard, 1954). Figure 12.1 summarizes the findings of the two studies in the form of a "social distance pyramid" I developed in an analysis published with Margaret Westie (Westie & Westie, 1957).[3] This diagram is reminiscent of the famous diagrams constructed earlier by W. L. Warner and Gunnar Myrdal (among others), but it differs from theirs in one important respect: It is derived empirically rather than hypothetically.

In the first study, persons from three randomly drawn samples of three socioeconomic levels in Indianapolis were interviewed to assess the degree of social distance they would prefer to maintain between themselves and Blacks of various socioeconomic levels. In the second study, Blacks from three socioeconomic levels were interviewed regarding the distance they would prefer to maintain between themselves and whites of various socioeconomic levels.

The dark, horizontal arrows on the left side of the social distance pyramid depict the degree of social distance preferred by whites on three socioeconomic levels in relations with Blacks—the longer the arrow, the greater the distance preferred. The equivalent arrows on the right side of pyramid depict the social distance preferred by Blacks in relation to whites.

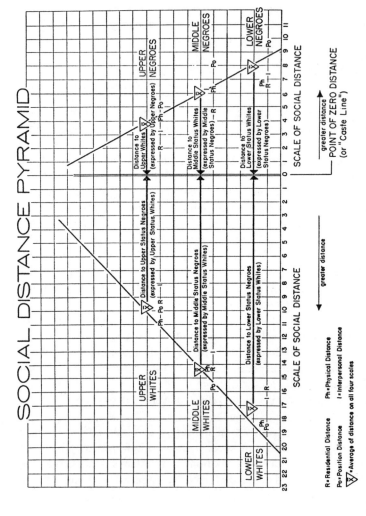

Figure 12.1. Social-Distance Measures Derived Through Analysis of Scale Responses of Whites to Negroes (left-hand side) and Negroes to Whites (right-hand side)

NOTE: Respondents are classified according to occupational rank.

268

Four scales were used to assess four dimensions of social distance:

1. Residential Distance
2. Physical Distance (the limits of physical proximity preferred in interpersonal relations)
3. Position Distance (distance preferred between ego and "racial others" in varying status positions)
4. Interpersonal Distance (types of social relationship one would feel comfortable or uncomfortable with)

The length of the arrows in the diagram represent the average scores for all four scales, and the symbols (R, Ph, Po, I) beneath each inverted triangle indicate the approximate distance preferred by each stratum of each race on each of the four dimensions of social distance.

The relationships represented in Figure 12.1 may be summarized as follows:

1. Upper-status whites would maintain least distance between themselves and high-status Blacks, whereas, reciprocally, high-status Blacks would maintain least distance between themselves and whites of similar position.
2. Lower-status whites would maintain greatest distance between themselves and Blacks of low status, whereas Blacks of lower status would maintain greatest distance between themselves and whites of low status.
3. In all three of the relationships between "equivalent" classes, there is a "social distance differential"; that is, at any given level the distance preferred by whites from Blacks is greater than that preferred by Blacks between themselves and whites.

Space does not permit presentation of the responses of each stratum to persons of varying status in the out-group, but I would like to mention one substantive finding and comment on its methodological importance: *The responses of whites to Blacks varied considerably depending on the occupational status of the Black person and the situations in which hypothetical interactions might occur. The same goes for the responses of Blacks to whites.* This means that people aren't nearly as categorical as we had supposed in their thinking about racial outgroups. We do violence to reality when, for example, in our research projects on anti-Black prejudice, we ask people to respond to "Blacks" categorically, without specifying any attributes of the particular Black persons we are asking about or the situations in which interactions might occur. Given the great increase in occupational and economic differentiation in the Black population, such specification is much more important now than it was when I did this study some 40 years ago. Respondents today are even more likely to ask, Which Black? or Which Blacks? Do you mean people like the family in the Bill Cosby show, or someone pushing crack in a ghetto? Fair enough questions, yet researchers persist in forcing people to be more categorical than they already are.

Was Gunnar Myrdal Right?

In the late 1950s and early 1960s I conducted a study designed to test empirically Gunnar Myrdal's (1944) famous dilemma theory. Has the Myrdal theory stood the test of time? By the same token, would the findings of my research be viable today? And would I interpret those findings differently than I did some 30 years ago? It seems to me a reexamination of the dilemma theory would have been in order about now, quite apart from the opportunity presented by this essay.

From the standpoint of its impact on American social thought, Myrdal's *An American Dilemma* may well be without peer among sociological studies. Myrdal was eventually awarded the Nobel Prize in economics, probably because there wasn't a Nobel Prize for sociology. He wasn't that great an economist, but he was a truly great social scientist, and his stature as a social scientist rested largely on his classic, *An American Dilemma.*

In the conclusions to my published report, I said Myrdal's theory was partly right and partly wrong (Westie, 1965). I should have said, quite simply, that the theory was wrong. Maybe I waffled because Myrdal was still alive, and I admired him very much. I knew then, as now, that any theory is wrong if certain of its essential premises are wrong, and some of Myrdal's primary premises were indeed wrong. Had major elements of Kelvin's theory of heat transfer been wrong, than the whole theory would have been wrong, and it wouldn't have predicted actual thermodynamic outcomes, as in fact it does. Although Myrdal's theory did in fact describe *certain aspects* of race relations as experienced by *some* Americans, it did not predict empirical outcomes with any degree of accuracy.

The fact that *An American Dilemma* helped awaken America to its long-repressed social dis-ease, racism, adds no more to the validity of

the theory than, say, the revolutionary impact of Alfred Kinsey's original report on human sexuality adds to the reliability of its highly flawed
samples—a point that, incidentally, I argued personally (and naively)
with Kinsey when both of us were faculty members at Indiana. However, Kinsey knew, and in a sense hypothesized, that Americans were,
sexually, a highly active people—and indeed imaginative—*and he
demonstrated it,* however picky we may choose to be about his sam-
pling. And once the secret was out, America was never the same again.
Similarly, Myrdal "knew," and in a sense hypothesized, that Americans
suffered from a monstrous dilemma, believing in democracy as they did
and simultaneously practicing a system of totally undemocratic race
relations. In calling the nation's attention to the issue, he influenced
American social thought as no other social scientist before him, but he
neither tested nor demonstrated the validity of his theory.

In enunciating Myrdal's theory, most people get it wrong. If I am to
claim Myrdal was wrong, as indeed I do here, then I had better get his
theory right: Myrdal's two basic concepts in the theory are *valuations,*
defined as conceptions of "what ought to be," and *beliefs,* conceptions
of "what is" or "what was." Beliefs may be empirically valid or bizarre
myths. The valuations embraced by any individual range from the very
general, including the tenets of the "American creed" ("Everyone in
America should have equal opportunities to get ahead"), to very specific
("My kids ought to go to school with their own kind"). The dilemma
exists, the theory avers, in the minds and consciences of individuals as
a result of the contradictions between their specific valuations and their
general valuations.

The theory further assumes that Americans value rationality highly
and that they perceive, or at least sense, the irrationality inherent in their
holding to highly contradictory valuations, and thus find it necessary to
restore an element of rationality by invoking beliefs to bridge the gap
between their specific valuations and their general valuations. Thus, by
implication, the dilemma is assumed to be cognitive as well as emotional. In this sense the Myrdal theory is a theory of collective cognitive
dissonance.

I developed and pretested any number of techniques for getting at the
dilemma before finally arriving at three forms that ultimately guided
the interviews. Form I contained 10 items designed to assess the degree
to which the respondent endorsed the *general valuations* subsumed
under the rubric of the "American creed." Form II was made up of 10
social distance-type items describing hypothetical but quite plausible

situations that permitted the respondents to indicate the degree of social distance they preferred to maintain between themselves and Blacks. Each item in Form II was matched with an item in Form I in such a way as to maximize the possibility of conflict as well as to enhance the likelihood that the respondent would recognize his or her conflicts where they existed. Form III was designed to record the respondents' open-ended "explanations" of the value conflicts elicited by the items on Forms I and II, and to record and classify the degree of probing required to get the respondent to recognize his or her moral conflicts.

We had people respond *first*—before they knew the study had anything to do with race relations—to each of the 10 general "Christian-democratic" (Myrdal's term) articles of faith. Almost all subjects agreed with the most general of these tenets quite readily, often seizing eagerly the opportunity to declare their commitment to America's highest ideals. Then, after their commitment, so to speak, we asked them to respond to the social distance items, which included questions such as, How would you feel about a Black family moving in next door? Or having a Black man as your supervisor at work? Or having a Black family spend the night in your home under emergency circumstances?

Not surprisingly, the social atmosphere changed abruptly when the first race-relations items were introduced, as though I had inadvertently touched upon a dark family secret. Quite often, what had been a friendly exchange between reasonable persons of goodwill became suddenly strained. Many respondents clearly couldn't wait for the interview to end. In this project, as in other projects, I was on occasion invited to leave in no uncertain terms. (May I add that sex research would have been much easier. In fact, numerous respondents in Indianapolis, knowing I was a professor from Indiana University, home of the Kinsey Institute, were disappointed that I didn't ask them about their sex lives.)

Herewith, then, are some reinterpretations of the empirical test of the dilemma theory. As regards the "logic" of prejudiced persons in an ostensibly democratic society, although I found that roughly half of the responses were more or less logical in the sense Myrdal predicted, much more significant, I think, is the fact that people just as frequently resorted to a childlike illogic, "explaining" their contradiction by simply repeating their prejudicial valuation, saying something like "What contradiction? Negroes shouldn't live with whites. That's all there is to it." No beliefs were invoked as rationalizations.

It is axiomatic that all modern, complex societies are, by their very nature, rife with contradictions. If it's true that for any social system to survive, most people must learn to think and act the way they must for the system to work, then in modern society they must certainly learn to live with contradictions without too much wear and tear on their consciences or logical powers. In this context, it seems to me now that Myrdal made a major error in presuming a certain time sequence wherein people *first* recognized (or felt) their moral contradictions and then found rationalizations (beliefs) to resolve the particular contradiction bothering them. In my investigation I found that that's not quite how it works. Rather, the society that builds normative contradictions into itself *simultaneously socializes its oncoming generations to culturally shared rationalizations of its moral contradictions.* This, it seems to me, should be a primary principle of sociology.

It would seem that the notion that persons in modern society go about burdened with moral conflicts is pretty much an academic abstraction quite remote from reality. The normative conflicts sociologists sometimes talk about are more often conflicts that would exist in the consciences of individuals were it not for the existence of ready-made rationalizations that, in a sense, solve moral dilemmas even before they're experienced. I rather think this applies not only to would-be dilemmas regarding race relations, but also to the vast panoply of would-be moral conflicts faced by any thoughtful person in modern society.

The society that pressures a father to let some guy live out of wedlock with his precious daughter simultaneously provides the father with a repertoire of rationalizations as alternatives to killing the no-good son of a bitch who would violate his daughter. Thirty years ago he would have done it. Now, with a rich repertoire of collective rationalizations available, he might concede that in a society in which one out of every two marriages ends in divorce, maybe trial marriages aren't that bad an idea. Trouble is, the guy sleeping with his daughter might be on his tenth trial marriage. But the system provides rationalizations even for that. The culture even provides sexed-up evangelists with ready-made rationalizations for their forays into the choir. It's only when the good reverend is caught that he breaks into tears and confesses publicly his fall from Grace—or whatever her name. For most predators, whether on Wall Street or in the pulpit, the crime is getting caught, and only then does the moral dilemma emerge, if indeed it rears its ugly head even then. Mark Twain knew this. Recall, if you will, his observation that conscience is the still, small voice in the wee hours of the night that tells you you might get caught. It would seem societies provide rich, anticipatory rationalizations for everything except getting caught.

It's not surprising, then, that it's hard to find many people who are particularly shook up about our society's moral contradictions, whether in the arena of race relations or sex or finance or whatever. As sociologists we need simply look at ourselves, not only in our role as scientists, but also in our more subtle, self-appointed role, however stoutly denied, as guardians of moral rectitude. Do we lose sleep over the fact that our own children (or, in the present instance, our grandchildren) have new Little League uniforms and crisply starched Brownie outfits and all the Big Macs their little tummies can accommodate while, in our land of equal opportunity, millions of homeless Americans, including children, scrounge for scraps of food, sometimes in garbage cans and dumpsters? If we sociologists, with our heavy load of social consciousness, aren't that upset, then what should we expect to find in our business schools, or our medical schools, or in the world of business itself, or wherever else the primary motives are economic?

One finding in the dilemma study sticks in my mind above all others: *People apologized (or were quick to offer explanations) for their democratic feelings and choices as frequently as they did for their undemocratic choices.* This finding declares eloquently the simple fact that prejudice and discrimination were every bit as normative, and thus as "moral," as those general Christian and democratic norms of which Myrdal spoke. Throughout most of American history, nonprejudice and nondiscrimination on the part of majority persons have been as morally repugnant as, say, the sight even today of a white woman on the arm of a Black man. (Please indulge me another gratuitous tangent: I've formally researched the emotional responses—as indicated by autonomic physiological responses—of majority persons to the sight of white women with Black men, and I'm left with the hypothesis that in this situation the moral repugnance of the white observer increases directly with the degree of beauty, youth, and whiteness of the woman, and with the Blackness of the man [Westie, 1959]. I would also hypothesize that the moral repugnance revealed in the facial expression of the white man [it seems to me men are more revolted by all this than women] tends to vary inversely with the size of the Black man: The bigger the Black man, the more pleasant the feces-consuming grin on the face of the outraged white man as the mixed couple passes by.)

I would hypothesize that even today in most small, private social gatherings of majority persons, expressions of race prejudice enjoy a higher degree of normative approval than their opposites. I must repeat the phrase, in most small, private gatherings of majority persons. Please understand I'm not talking about social gatherings among university faculty members or among college students, although even on college campuses we see racism rearing its ugly head anew. Whether or not prejudice is expressed depends on the situation and definitions of the situation as perceived by the prejudiced person. I've often thought that if researchers were to take, for experimental purposes, the role of a bigot, sending bigot cues to their respondents before administering prejudice scales, they'd find far more racial prejudice in American communities than heretofore imagined. In most projects involving personal interviews, respondents tend to assume that the interviewer is unprejudiced and that unprejudiced responses are the order of the day. It strikes me that such a project would make a great dissertation for some thick-skinned graduate student, but then, on further reflection, I realize there are ethical issues involved. Can one in good conscience present oneself to one's respondents as the opposite of what one really is? Anyway, if a researcher were able to successfully rationalize such issues I think such a project would yield results that might be very surprising, indeed dramatic.

For all the ethical issues, I can't shake the idea of such a study because of experiences I've had. Many of you will have had comparable experiences. You live in a white, middle-class neighborhood. You're at a neighborhood dinner party. The guests, men and women, are professional or business people, and all are of white, Northern European, Christian descent (WNECs, as opposed to WASPs, who are often neither Anglo-Saxon nor Protestant). Someone tells an anti-Black, or anti-Mexican, or anti-Semitic joke. Everyone laughs but you. You say, "I don't think that's funny." Who's the deviant? Who'll not be invited back? I've been there. I've not been invited back. It seems to me that even today, wherever middle-class whites gather together in small, private social settings, more often than not *it is the democratic person acting out his or her democratic commitments who is the oddball or the deviant*—this despite the democratic reforms in race relations we've achieved in the past 40 years. I'm talking about the world out there, not the cozy campus or the gown side of a college town.

I've thought of another research design along similar lines, again for any thick-skinned researcher—white or black, male or female—who settles the ethical issues to his or her own satisfaction: Go to a community far from your own, join majority voluntary associations where you're likely to find yourself in close contact with majority persons. Express, categorically and without qualification, your (ostensible) upset

with all affirmative action, "the total criminality of the ghetto populations," and other such issues, and record mentally—and as soon as
possible in writing—the frequency and degree of agreement and disagreement with your implied position. How many people insist on your
qualifying your statements? How many agree? My hypothesis is that
you'll find far more agreement than disagreement. If you, the researcher, happen to be Black, chances are you'll be loved for your
wisdom. You may even be elevated to the status of "an exception" in
the eyes of your newfound majority friends. You will be invited back.
If you're a woman and you find yourself in a group of men, express
your upset with the "hordes" of women abandoning home, hearth, and
husbands in their pursuit of careers. You may find yourself honored,
even loved, by most men and a lot of women, for your wisdom and
refreshing honesty. Not only will you be invited back, you may even be
invited to speak on "family values," whatever that is.

On the Relationship
Between Prejudice and Discrimination

There was a time when sociologists, whether or not they believed it,
gave the impression that they assumed a one-to-one correspondence
between prejudice and discrimination, and that by adequately assessing
patterns of prejudice they could expect to predict patterns of discrimination. Corollary to this assumption, and equally naive, was the implicit
assumption that alteration of attitudes must precede any changes in
patterns of discrimination. A host of sociologists, particularly among
symbolic interactionists, were terribly upset not only by such (perceived) assumptions, but by attitude research in general. As noted
above, the most vociferous of these, Herbert Blumer, regarded attitude
research as terribly misguided and, indeed, worse than useless. Arnold
Rose went so far as to say that "prejudice has little to do with intergroup
relations." This would be less an overstatement had Rose added the
phrase "in most race relations situations."

Whatever the provenance of the anti-attitude writers' position, their
concern provided impetus for some of the most significant research in
race relations since World War II. I have in mind such research projects
as those by Lewis Killian (1952), Joseph Lohman and Dietrich Reitzes
(1954), J. D. Minard (1952), and Bernard Kutner, Carol Wilkins, and P.
R. Yarrow (1952)—these among numerous others in sociology and

psychology. The work of each of these people demonstrated the failure of attitudes to predict overt behavior in specific situations. Southern white workers set aside their deeply ingrained anti-Black prejudices as they worked side by side in the North with northern Blacks; Northern white union members declared their solidarity with their Black union brothers in the union hall, and then went home to participate in their neighborhood improvement associations, the purpose of which was to keep Blacks out of their neighborhoods; southern white coal miners broke bread with their Black brethren deep in the bowels of the earth, but reverted to racist type as they emerged from the pits into the light of day.

Melvin DeFleur and I conducted studies of verbal attitudes and their relationship to overt acts, with much the same sort of findings as cited above (DeFleur & Westie, 1958). In light of findings such as these, we proposed an approach that abandons the "latent process" conception of attitudes in favor of a rather straightforward conception in which measured attitudes are seen simply as probability constructions that assess the likelihood that a person will respond in a given direction and in a given degree to the attitude object on one or all of three dimensions of attitudes: verbal, emotional, and/or overt action (DeFleur & Westie, 1963).

The degree to which one responds on these three dimensions consistently with previously measured attitudes depends on situational contingencies—themselves measurable but rarely measured—including definitions of the situations by others, one's perceptions of the attitudes of others, and one's perceptions of how one's social, economic, and political interests are served by one's expression of one's attitudes or by acting them out overtly.

DeFleur and I spent the better part of two years in the psychology laboratory at Indiana University measuring white research subjects' verbal attitudes toward Blacks on elaborate dimensional inventories, and then wiring our subjects to apparatus to assess their autonomic physiological responses upon instantaneous exposure to colored slides of Blacks in situations with whites—including Black men with white women. Having assessed the verbal and emotional components of the subjects' attitudes, we then presented them with real-life behavioral choices for interactions with Blacks (DeFleur & Westie, 1958; see also DeFleur & Westie, 1959). We found marked differences between and among the verbal, emotional, and overt action responses within individuals. In the present context I would emphasize that situational constraints, which we varied systematically, were clearly the most powerful force contributing to discrepancies between privately held attitudes and overt actions. In short, our laboratory findings were consistent with the findings of the surveys cited immediately above.

If behavioral scientists were willing to expend the time and energy required to measure attitudes in their several dimensions and the contingency circumstances under which they operate, it's very likely that the disparity between measured attitudes and overt behavior would be considerably less. Unfortunately, as the rigor of sociological and psychological research declines along with standards of performance in society at large, we find our colleagues using increasingly elaborate analyses on increasingly crude data. Peruse, if you will, journals from the 1970s and 1980s. You will even find many studies in which the "data" were gathered *by telephone* by graduate students for their professors, the senior authors of the articles, and then the ultimate irrationality: all of it analyzed with elaborate multivariate and path analyses in surrender to the illusion that elaborate formulas have some sort of purifying effect.

Shortly before I retired from full-time teaching in 1983, just for the hell of it I conducted a modest study—heretofore unpublished—in which I compared the attitude studies reported in the *American Sociological Review* in the 1950s with the attitude studies reported in the same journal in the 1970s. The results: The "decline in ambition" or, if you like, the decline in the "urge toward science" across two decades was truly remarkable. By the end of the 1970s, one-item and two-item "scales"—which aren't scales at all—had become quite common. It was clearly apparent that genuine scale construction, always incredibly painstaking and time-consuming, had been replaced by quickie one-item or two-item, arbitrarily selected opinion inquiries masquerading as "attitude measurement." It is enough to make one weep when one recalls the monumental efforts of those pioneers who worked so hard to elevate sociology and psychology to the level of science—Thurstone, Guttman, Likert, and a host of other methodological saints who from their labors rest. How many Guttman scales have you seen lately? I didn't find any in the seventies. Were there any in the eighties?

Despite my interest in the relationship between attitude and overt behavior, it never was my purpose to predict patterns of discrimination in any direct sense from attitudes. Rather, my purpose across the years in studying prejudice was much like that of Adorno, Frenkel-Brunswick, Levinson, and Sanford (1950) in studying authoritarian personalities. Their assumption, and mine in pursuing a study of "the tolerant personality" (Martin & Westie, 1959) was that through understanding of the etiology of bigotry societies might guard against repetition of kind of mass hysteria that in Nazi Germany led ultimately to Dachau and Auschwitz. Implicit in this assumption is the further assumption that widely held attitudes, particularly attitudes shared across the breadth of a nation, will ultimately influence national policy. Throughout history demagogues have tuned their antennae to the attitudes of the masses and exploited those attitudes to their own political purposes. Who would argue that the long history of European anti-Semitism, which is to say widely shared anti-Semitic *attitudes,* was irrelevant to the rise of Hitler? Who would argue that the anti-Semitic *attitudes* of millions of Germans prior to Hitler's emergence were irrelevant to the unspeakable consequences of Hitler's political success?

The "New Racism"

The past few years have seen the emergence of the concept of "the new racism" and its equivalent, "modern racism," as contrasted with "traditional racism" in America. Traditional racism was naive, "innocent," and unself-conscious, based as it was on what may be called presociological constructions of reality, largely myths and stereotypes, that admitted no alternatives. (In a sense—arguably, to be sure—a rudimentary sociological awareness has been diffused in the literate population at large.) The theory of modern racism maintains that (a) it's no longer acceptable, as it was traditionally in the United States, to declare publicly such canards as "Blacks are inherently less intelligent than whites" but that (b) it's quite acceptable socially today to express one's prejudiced attitudes in a manner that one feels is eminently logical and justified given certain social developments of the past 20 years or so, particularly the increase of crime and violence in our urban ghettos and the dissemination of the news of such in the mass media.

Robert H. Entman (1991), a student of modern racism, quotes David Sears (1988), who cogently summarizes some of the perceptions and articles of faith of modern racists: Blacks are seen as "'pushing too hard' and moving too fast. . . . [There is] resentment toward . . . racial quotas on the job or education, excessive access to welfare, [or] special treatment by government, . . . [and there is] denial of continuing discrimination."

Researchers have shown that people who see the world of race relations in such terms will endorse such statements as "Blacks are getting too demanding in their push for equal rights" or "Over the past few years, the government and news media have shown Blacks more respect than they deserve" (quoted by Entman, 1991, from Sears, 1988, who quotes McConahay, 1988, p. 93). I've personally encountered these and other such statements on the part of persons who, I'm certain, on the basis of other evidence, harbor anti-Black prejudices.

There can be no doubt that racist attitudes are expressed today quite differently from the way they were 40 years ago. They are more overt, self-righteous, and confident. This confidence is a consequence of racists' conviction that their attitudes are eminently logical given the events of the day. A modern racist might declare, "I'm not prejudiced. What I'm saying is based on reality. I'm simply looking at the evidence." Once a person makes such a declaration, a resurrection of the old "well-earned reputation" sort of argument is sure to follow: Our ghettos are full of pregnant teenagers, drug addicts, and violent criminals. Am I prejudiced because I happen to be against the kinds of crime and immorality that are shown every day in our newspapers and on local television? The answer to this person is, Yes, you are, if your antagonism encompasses all or virtually all people living in our inner cities, and if your perceptions fail to acknowledge the fact that millions of hardworking, law-abiding Black citizens live in our inner cities and that they more than any other segment of our population are the victims of ghetto crime and lawlessness.

The differences between traditional expressions of prejudice and the newer forms are crucial. Because the attitudes that form the new racism can be assessed by asking respondents to indicate agreement or disagreement with the cognitive supports for their attitudes, we can reasonably expect that *scales* designed to measure the new racism will yield attitudinal data predictive of behavioral choices, particularly political and economic, and most particularly choices made in the privacy of the voting booth.

I don't know if the students of modern racism would argue that there are substantive psychological differences between the attitudes, *qua attitudes,* of modern racists and the traditional racists of the kind I studied in the 1950s and 1960s. Race prejudice, whether modern or traditional, is race prejudice if it (a) focuses on a racial group and it is (b) negative, (c) emotional, (d) categorical in degree, and (e) irreversible in the face of evidence that contradicts it. What we called "race prejudice" in an earlier day met these criteria. It seems to me that what is called "modern racism" or the "new racism" or "modern race prejudice" also meets these criteria. I say this not to minimize the importance of the distinction, but rather to clarify the concepts.

The earlier myths that supported traditional racism have been largely disproved and even disavowed by a large segment of the population of prejudiced whites, but the cognitive supports for the new racism continue to grow as reports of crime and violence in our ghettos proliferate in the mass media. Only a constitutional ignoramus would argue that such stories should be repressed, but one would hope that the media would find as newsworthy, more often than now, the triumphs over adversity of the millions of good citizens in our inner cities. But even as I speak I know that civility is rarely newsworthy, whereas crime and violence always are. We can also hope for fairer coverage of crime in the media. A recent content analysis conducted by Robert Entman indicates that local news presentations of crimes on television remain slanted in an anti-Black direction.

On the face of it, it would seem we have come a long way toward eradicating overt expressions of prejudice and stereotypes in our society. Yet when we acknowledge the emergence of the new racism, with its cognitive supports that are seen as so compelling, one wonders. I would ask, Did we, as students of race relations across the past four decades, make a difference? Still in a wondering mood, What would things be like today if we hadn't made the effort? Perhaps we would have even more vestiges of the old racism than we have.

Notes

1. Bellow and Vonnegut studied sociology and cultural anthropology in graduate school at the University of Chicago before they became writers.

2. Anyone interested in repeating this study should contact Professor Marcia Segal, Department of Sociology, Indiana University Southeast, Jeffersonville, Indiana, for a copy of the questionnaire.

3. The theoretical procedure employed in these studies is presented in Westie (1957).

References

DeFleur, M. L., & Westie, F. R. (1958). Verbal attitudes and overt acts: An experiment on the salience of attitudes. *American Sociological Review, 23,* 667-673.

DeFleur, M. L., & Westie, F. R. (1959). The interpretation of interracial situations: An experiment in social perception. *Social Forces, 38,* 17-23.

DeFleur, M. L., & Westie, F. R. (1963). Attitude as a scientific concept. *Social Forces, 50,* 17-31.

Entman, R. M. (1991, May 23-27). *Blacks in the news: Television, modern racism and cultural change.* Paper presented at the annual meeting of the International Communication Association.

Killian, L. M. (1952). The effect of southern white workers on race relations in northern plants. *American Sociological Review, 17,* 327-331.

Kutner, B., Wilkins, C., & Yarrow, P. R. (1952, July). Verbal attitudes and overt behavior involving racial prejudice. *Journal of Abnormal and Social Psychology,* pp. 649-652.

Lohman, J. D., & Reitzes, D. C. (1954). Deliberately organized groups and racial behavior. *American Sociological Review, 19,* 342-354.

Mannheim, K. (1955). *Ideology and utopia: An introduction to the sociology of knowledge.* New York: Harcourt, Brace.

Mannheim, K. (1967). *Man and society in an age of reconstruction.* New York: Harcourt, Brace.

Martin, J. G., & Westie, F. R. (1959). The tolerant personality. *American Sociological Review, 24,* 521-528.

McConahay, J. (1988). Modern racism, ambivalence, and the modern racism scale. In J. Dovidio & S. Gaertner (Eds.), *Prejudice, discrimination, and racism: Theory and research.* New York: Academic Press.

Minard, J. D. (1952). Race relations in the Pocahontas coal field. *Journal of Social Issues, 8,* 29-44.

Myrdal, G., with Sterner, R., & Rose, A. (1944). *An American dilemma: The Negro problem and modern democracy.* New York: Harper & Row.

Sears, D. (1988). Symbolic racism. In P. Katz & D. Taylor (Eds.), *Eliminating racism.* New York: Plenum.

Westie, F. R. (1952). Negro-white status differentials and social distance. *American Sociological Review, 17,* 550-558.

Westie, F. R. (1957). Toward closer relations between theory and research: A procedure and an example. *American Sociological Review, 22,* 149-154.

Westie, F. R. (1959). Autonomic responses and their relationship to race attitudes. *Journal of Abnormal and Social Psychology, 58,* 340-347.

Westie, F. R. (1965). The American dilemma: An empirical test. *American Sociological Review, 30,* 527-538.

Westie, F. R. (1972, May 18). *Academic expectations for professional immortality: A study of legitimation.* Presidential address delivered at the meeting of the North Central Sociological Association, London, Ontario.

Westie, F. R. (1973). Academic expectations for professional immortality: A study of legitimation. *American Sociologist, 8,* 19-32.

Westie, F. R., & Howard, D. H. (1954). Social status differentials and the race attitudes of Negroes. *American Sociological Review, 19,* 584-591.

Westie, F. R., & Westie, M. L. (1957). The social distance pyramid: Relationships between caste and class. *American Journal of Sociology, 63,* 190-196.

Appendix

A Letter of Acceptance

Frank R. Westie,
P.O. Box 292
Glen Arbor, Michigan 49636

Professor John H. Stanfield II
Department of Sociology
College of William and Mary
Williamsburg, Virginia 23185

Dear Professor Stanfield:

I shall be happy to write a piece for your anthology. I like the concept very much. As soon as I read your letter the wheels began turning, then humming, and finally whirring to a high pitch. I found I had the answers to your explicit and implicit questions in storage, as it were. I had merely to boot them up.

When one reaches the second half of one's sixties one senses the presence of *The Lurk,* scythe in hand, ready to cut one's props out from under. Such an event would of course play havoc with one's intracranial hard disk. Perhaps one day our Successors in Title will develop a Program for Posthumous Retrieval, but I'd rather not rely too heavily on that possibility. I thus welcome this opportunity to participate in your anthology.

Keats in his dotage, relativistically speaking, wrote a poem that began, "When I have fears that I may cease to be/ Before my pen has gleaned my weary brain . . . " Chalk this up to Keatsian prescience, or perhaps a hacking cough he couldn't seem to shake off. Whatever, he died at age 26, having already produced a monumental, immortal literature. No word processor, no printer, no typewriter. Just a quill pen, a penknife, a stack of foolscap, and a candle perhaps. I share

Keats's fears and I must say your suggestions regarding a research-autobiography offer at least passing assuagement.

It occurs to me that a study I did some years ago on "Academic Expectations for Professional Immortality" has relevance for your present enterprise. I found that two-thirds of the sociologists I studied expected to be remembered after their demise for their contributions to the field—this despite the fact that most of them knew nothing about (or even heard of) the people on the list of sociologists I presented to them. Many accused me of making up many of the names on the list. Actually, the list was a list of all the past presidents of the American Sociological Association.

Your project is relevant in that it will reduce the Delusionary Quotient (DQ) for each of us, your contributors, if only a cubit or two. The DQ is the ratio between The Expected and The (posthumous, likely to be) Observed, and as such a Chi Square of sorts. It can be calculated by comparing Ego's expectations for him/herself with others' expectations for Ego, or, more validly, by comparing Ego's expectations with others' controlled observations after Ego's demise. My research indicated that, of our surviving giants, Robert Merton's DQ will be the lowest, regardless of his expectations, because he is the most "remembered" or recognized. I am sorry to say, however, that the research indicates that most of us will have very high DQs indeed, given our high expectations for being remembered and the low probability of same. My original hypothesis in all this: No reality tests, however overwhelming to outside observers, can compromise our constructions of reality where the need for such constructions is strong. And of course the need is always strong.

Given these research findings, I predict you will find that few indeed of us "significant contributors" (as you graciously refer to us) to the study of race relations will decline this opportunity to validate our constructions of professional self and our expectations for our posthumous future. Those few who decline because of health or professional commitments will at least enjoy a small measure of validation by your very letter which declares the recipient to be "a significant contributor." Incidentally, two-thirds of my sociologist-subjects regarded themselves as among the top ten contributors to their primary specialty. Many of these had published no more than one or two articles in their specialty, or any other specialty for that matter. All of this to apprise you of the great contribution you, by your very letter, are making to the psychological health of many of your far-flung colleagues. Many will have framed selected passages by now, and proud wives will have hung the document in a place of honor. Eventually a choice passage may even be carved in stone, perhaps the phrase "a scientist widely regarded as having made significant contributions to the understanding of race relations." And who among us will begrudge our fallen colleague his wife's modest editing?

I look forward to hearing from you. Please address any correspondence to the letterhead address above. I am an Adjunct Professor at Arizona State University, where I enjoy the colleagueship of some fine sociologists, but I spend all except the winter months in northern Michigan. I've written my piece for you in my mind. All I have to do now is write it down. I remain

Yours truly,

Frank R. Westie

P.S. I still do sociology, but I spend considerable time these days at what is called creative writing. I just finished yet another version of a weighty (sizewise, as they say) novel and I'm now working as a collaborator with a much-produced Hollywood screenwriter on a screenplay. He read my novel in manuscript and went for it big and invited me to collaborate with him on a project closely related to the novel. The chances that nothing will come of it are reasonably good. On the other hand I know, deep in my heart of hearts, that I may well be on my way to achieving yet another measure of professional immortality.

About the Editor

John H. Stanfield II is the Frances and Edwin Cumming Professor of American Studies and Sociology, Scholar in Residence, Commonwealth Center for the Study of American History and Culture, at the College of William and Mary. His research interests include sociology of knowledge approaches to the study of race and sciences. His current research focus is on the comparative sociological history of race and colonialism in the formation of nineteenth- and early twentieth-century sciences.